Fannie's
LAST SUPPER

Library of Congress Cataloging-in-Publication Data

Kimball, Christopher.
   Fannie's last supper / Christopher Kimball.—1st ed.
       p. cm.
   ISBN 978-1-4013-2322-6
  1. Dinners and dining—United States—History—19th century.   2. Cookery, American—History—19th century.   3. United States—Social life and customs—19th century.   4. Farmer, Fannie Merritt, 1857–1915. Boston cooking school cook book.   5. Victoriana—United States—Miscellanea.   I. Title.
   TX737.K52 2010
   641.3097309'034—dc22

2010007877

Hyperion books are available for special promotions and premiums. For details contact the HarperCollins Special Markets Department in the New York office at 212-207-7528, fax 212-207-7222, or e-mail spsales@harpercollins.com.

FIRST EDITION

10   9   8   7   6   5   4   3   2   1

SUSTAINABLE FORESTRY INITIATIVE — Certified Fiber Sourcing — www.sfiprogram.org

THIS LABEL APPLIES TO TEXT STOCK

We try to produce the most beautiful books possible, and we are also extremely concerned about the impact of our manufacturing process on the forests of world and the environment as a whole. Accordingly, we've made sure th paper we use has been certified as coming from forests that are ma the protection of the people and wildlife dependent upon them.

Fannie's

LAST SUPPER

Re-creating One Amazing Meal from
Fannie Farmer's 1896 Cookbook

 Christopher Kimball

HYPERION
•••••
NEW YORK

For Kate

ACKNOWLEDGMENTS

FIRST OFF, THANKS TO MY WIFE, ADRIENNE, FOR MANAGING the restoration of our 1859 bowfront in Boston, including sleuthing about for the silver, crystal, and china required to set a properly Victorian table. Working with my researcher, Meg Ragland, is like having one's own historical drive-thru: facts, figures, and photos were instantly produced, no matter how offbeat the request. Mike Ehlenfeldt is an inspired man-of-all-trades, assembling and training the service staff as well as researching and procuring the wines, liqueurs, and cheeses, plus supervising the creation of our beloved ice mermaid, the woman José Andrés fell in love with. Thanks, Mike. David Erickson lovingly restored the large Number 7 cookstove that was the heart and soul of our enterprise. He is an artist of cast iron. My long-term test cook, Jeanne Maguire, also contributed mightily, especially with many of the daily Victorian recipes that appear in this book.

I owe a huge debt to all those who actually cooked the dinner, including sous-chef Keith Dresser, Andrea Geary, Dan Souza, Yvonne Ruperti, and Andrew Janjigian, with Marie Eleana and her son Ryan handling cleanup. Big thanks also to the waitstaff, including Mike's wife, Cindy, along with Jake McDowell, Debbie McDowell, Emile Arktinsal, and Melissa Klein. A special thanks to Yvonne for reverse engineering the spectacular Mandarin Cake and to Andrea for spending weeks playing with jellies and homemade calves' foot gelatin. And when goose was no longer available, the folks at D'Artagnan saved the day.

Thanks to all of the folks at DGA Productions for filming the evening and putting together the public television special, with special thanks to Michael Rothenberg, Jan, Elena, and the entire crew. Their wit and goodwill, not to mention their expertise, were deeply appreciated.

David Black, my agent, gets the credit for initiating this project and bringing it to life. He is one of the few people to whom I actually listen when he says, "Rewrite, rewrite, rewrite." Leslie Wells, my editor at Hyperion, proved that great editors still exist at New York publishing houses—she transformed a mediocre manuscript into something vastly better but you, the reader, can be the judge. And more than a small thanks goes to Deborah Broide, my longtime publicity director and good friend.

Last, but by no means least, I owe a rich debt of gratitude to my culinary partner on this project, Erin McMurrer. Each day in the kitchen, Erin brought her sense of culinary adventure, her goodwill, and her rigorous approach to test cooking married to a buoyant playfulness that made this project both possible and the most fun I have had in years. Thanks, Fannie!

CONTENTS

A Culinary Time Machine
A Seat at the Victorian Table 1

The Punch Bowl
In Which We Move to the Wrong Side of the Tracks 7

Oysters
Fannie Farmer Is Born, Survives Polio, Takes Over
the Boston Cooking School, and Sells Over 360,000
Copies of *The Boston Cooking-School Cook Book*. 23

Mock Turtle Soup
A Walking Tour of Fannie Farmer's Boston 39

Rissoles
Fannie Farmer Sexes up Her Food:
Was She Really the "Mother of Level Measurements"? 53

Lobster à l'Américaine
Eating out in Boston and Why the Tavern Club Owned a Bear 69

Saddle of Venison
The Old Boston, the New Boston, and Social Nudism 81

Wood-Grilled Salmon
How to Cook on a Short, Hot Coal Cookstove 101

Fried Artichokes
It's 1896: Let's Go Shopping 117

Contents

Canton Punch
Everyday American Food, 1896:
Try the Roast and Beans but Skip the Fish 137

Roast Stuffed Goose
The Transformation of the Victorian Kitchen:
The Lady of the House Rolls Up Her Sleeves 159

Wine Jelly
The Science of Cooking, According to Fannie 179

Cake
Technology Transforms the Victorian Pantry 193

Coffee, Cheese, and Cordials
The Coffee Industry Awakens America 213

The Dinner Party
Amy Shakes Her Jelly and
José Andrés Falls in Love with a Mermaid 225

Requiem for Fannie
Fannie's Last Word 241

NOTES 245

SELECTED BIBLIOGRAPHY 249

INDEX 253

Fannie's
LAST SUPPER

A Culinary Time Machine

A Seat at the Victorian Table

A high Victorian dinner party was a modern re-creation of the ancient ritual of class and culinary artistry, displaying the plumage of high society while underlining the rigid rules of proper social intercourse. It was tails for the gentlemen and full dress costume for the ladies. One was expected to arrive neither early nor more than fifteen minutes late. When dinner was announced, the guests were led in procession from parlor to dining room, the host escorting the honored lady of the evening. The standard twelve courses were to be served briskly, in no more than two hours, yet there were few restraints on the amount of silverware used, with up to 131 separate pieces per setting in myriad styles from neoclassical, Persian, and Elizabethan to Jacobean, Japanese, Etruscan, and even Moorish. The rules of behavior were well known to all diners: one was never to appear greedy, draining the last drop from a wineglass or scraping the final morsel from the plate; one never ate hurriedly, which implied uncontrolled hunger; and since meal preparation was not something to be shown in public, plates were prepared out of view.

Within this rigid construct, food was the creative spark, the manna for imagination, and the kitchen a place where one was at last allowed to express one's wildest desires. Victorian jellies with ribbons of colors and flavors, Bavarian cream fillings, and hundreds of custom molds were a culinary free-for-all, as was the sheer variety of a twelve-course menu, from oysters and champagne to fish, turtle, goose, venison, duck, chicken, beef, vegetables, salads, cakes, bonbons, coffee, and liqueurs, all carefully orchestrated from soup to crackers to provide an eclectic, wide-ranging array of tastes and textures. Among the very wealthy, these dinners occasionally crossed the line from artistic perfection to excess, with menus that included roasted lion, naked cherubs leaping out from live-nightingale pies, chimps in tuxedos feted as guests of honor, and gentlemen in black tie dining on horseback. The Victorian dinner table was a moment in time that encapsulated the dreams of a young country—the radical pace of change from farm to city, from water to steam power, from local to international, from poor to rich—that defined our nineteenth century, and this food, these menus, this dining experience have today remained dormant for over a century, just waiting to be rediscovered: the old cast-iron stove lit once again, the venison roasted, the geese plucked, and the dining table decorated using the furthest reaches of culinary imagination.

And so, in 2007, with Fannie Farmer's original 1896 Boston Cooking School cookbook in hand, using a twelve-course menu printed in the back of the book and an authentic Victorian coal cookstove installed in our 1859 Boston townhouse, I set out on a two-year journey: to test, update, and master the cooking of Fannie Farmer's America, re-creating a high Victorian feast that I hoped to serve in perfect succession to a dozen celebrity guests for a televised public television special.

The project had begun with a book. It was horse chestnut brown, the color of a dark penny roux, mottled through a century of use, and measuring just 5 by 7¾ inches. The cover had separated from the binding, and there was no printing on the front or back—just a simple mustard yellow title on the upper spine: *Mrs. Lincoln's Boston Cook Book*. It was subtitled, on the inside, *What to Do and What Not to Do in Cooking*. The book was published in Boston by Roberts Brothers in 1890, seven years after the first edition; it was 536 pages. In 1896, Fannie Farmer, the new head of the Boston Cooking School, revised, updated, and expanded Mrs. Lincoln's work.

I had found it in 1983 through an act of pure serendipity, in the library of a house I was thinking of purchasing at the top of Mine Hill Road in Fairfield, Connecticut. It was a two-story white clapboard number, more a square than a colonial rectangle, well proportioned and big enough for a small family, but no trophy house by any stretch. The former occupant, well in her eighties, had just died; she had been the German mistress of a long-departed lawyer in town who had willed her the use of the house during her lifetime. Coming up the back steps into the kitchen for our first inspection, my wife-to-be, Adrienne, and I noticed the antique gas stove, the even older four-door General Motors refrigerator, and a screen door between the kitchen and the dining room, as if the occupant had kept live chickens or goats secluded from the rest of the living quarters.

As the Realtor took Adrienne on a tour of the upstairs, I sat on a window seat and read the preface of the small cookbook I'd found abandoned on a shelf. In it, Mrs. Lincoln put forth her premise: to compile a book "which shall also embody enough of physiology, and of the chemistry and philosophy of food." Hmm, that sounded quite modern to me, hardly what I might have expected from a book published in 1890. She went on to define cooking as "the art of preparing food for the nourishment of the human body. [Cooking] must be based upon scientific principles of hygiene and what the French call the minor moralities of the household. The degree of civilization is often measured by its cuisine." Clearly, she was a heck of a lot more enlightened regarding cooking and diet than 99 percent of all cookbook authors today, most of whom were promising meals in minutes.

Who were these Victorian cooks? Years later, while researching this book, I came across an awe-inspiring account of the Boston Food Fair of 1896. This made the contemporary Fancy Food Show look like amateur hour. A series of over-the-top meals was served, including a "Mermaid's Dinner." There was an electric dairy in the convention hall that churned out three thousand pounds of butter each day, a towering replica of a castle to promote flour, and a giant barn with grass, trees, and a Paul Bunyan–sized cow whose only purpose was to promote canned evaporated cream. Women queued up for free samples from two hundred different vendors: shredded wheat, cereals, gelatins, extracts, ice cream, candy, and custards. Other booths promoted shredded fish, preserved fruits, olives, baking powders, and dried meats. And then, just to remind us that we were still in the Victorian age, tucked darkly under the stairs, was the perfect dour touch: a melancholy exhibit of gravestones to remind passersby of their inevitable end. Just as today, food and cooking were at the convergence of popular entertainment and capitalism.

In fact, in the late 1800s, the culinary world was on fire, as technology came to the rescue of the exhausted home cook with modern versions of classic ingredients. Powdered gelatin had recently replaced ungainly thickeners such as isinglass, made from the swim bladders of sturgeon, or Irish moss, made from seaweed, or, God forbid, calf's-foot jelly, a smelly proposition indeed. Jell-O was even marketing an ice-cream powder in vanilla, strawberry, chocolate, and lemon as an alternative to making the real thing. Gas stoves were coming into use, replacing dirty, high-maintenance coal cookstoves. Fruits were being shipped in from California and the Northwest, mushrooms from France, extra-virgin olive oil from Italy, and cheese from all over Europe, including real Parmesan and Emmanthaler. Sugar was now modern and highly refined, no longer consumed in yellow loaves, but pure white and granulated. Contemporary cookbooks, especially *The Epicurean* by Charles Ranhofer, exhibited an advanced knowledge of cooking and the assumption that home cooks were up to the task of creating elaborate masterpieces.

Then a strange and self-indulgent notion struck me. Trying to understand the culinary past through old cookbooks and newspapers is a dodgy enterprise at best. A century or two from now, would historians be able to paint an accurate picture of home cooking in the early twenty-first century by reading the *New York Times* food pages or looking at Amazon best-sellers in the Cooking, Food, and Wine category? Instead, why not just cook my way back through history—investigate the ingredients and the techniques; make the puddings, the soups, the roasts, the jellies, and the cakes; and then give myself a final exam, a twelve-course Victorian blowout dinner party that I would serve to the most interesting group of guests I could cobble together? Oh, and I should do all of this on an authentic coal cookstove from the period and make everything from scratch, including the stocks, the puff pastry, the gelatin, and the food colorings. It would be like building a culinary time machine: I could travel back through history and stand next to Fannie as she cooked, feeling the intense heat of the cast-iron stove and the chill of the thin strips of salt pork as I larded a saddle of venison, and then follow her instructions precisely as I handled a poached calf's brain so gently that it did not dissolve into custard.

This idea was to remain nothing more than a daydream until 1991, when I moved to Boston and purchased an 1859 brick bowfront only a few blocks away from Fannie Farmer's home in 1896, the year that she published *The Boston Cooking-School Cook Book*. I still had to renovate the house and re-create an authentic Victorian kitchen—all of that would take years—but the seed had been planted. My fantasy dinner party, sleuthing the Victorian age through its recipes, was about to be born.

The Punch Bowl

✳

In Which We Move to
the Wrong Side of the Tracks

The house or, more explicitly, the 1859 brick Victorian bowfront, was located in a neighborhood referred to as St. Elsewhere of TV show fame, just one block from Boston City Hospital and on the wrong side of the tracks. The elevated trolley that ran down the center of Washington Street was demolished in 1987, and, sadly, the social demarcation still existed. The neighborhoods east of Washington Street (and therefore farther away from Back Bay and the central shopping district) were still considered to be a no-man's-land in terms of real estate value and personal safety, even though the physical dividing line, the one that had separated our neighborhood from the rest of the South End, was now gone. In fact, the entire South End, the term for the 526 acres of Victorian housing that was the flip side of Back Bay, was a complete train wreck in 1991, suffering from a statewide depression and collapse in real estate values. Thousands of adventurous baby boomers had invested in South End property, only to see their condominiums plummet in value, making them hostage to an area of Boston that now looked down and dirty instead of up and coming.

How bad was it? It was such a tough neighborhood that in April 1991, my wife, Adrienne, spent a whole morning parked outside the building to check out the foot traffic before we committed to the purchase. It was not encouraging. She noted, among other details, that drug dealers hid their stash underneath loose sidewalk bricks so they would be clean if searched. Another aspect of South End living was revealed by a long-time resident across the park, who told us of the day she returned home with her groceries. She found her back door blocked by a working girl pursuing the world's oldest profession with a local customer. She asked them politely to move over so that she could get into her house; they grudgingly complied. A few years later, we were told about a resident of West Newton Street who decided to move when he came out one morning to find blood all over his Toyota—a man had been stabbed on the hood during the night. This same street had, for many years, boasted of a mobile car repair service; the mechanic worked on your car where it was parked, scavenging spare parts from other cars around the neighborhood.

My immediate impetus for the move was a call in January 1991 from an old friend who had recently purchased *East West Journal* and was looking for a partner to come to Boston and transform the publication from a money-loser to a money-maker, a process that took two years and a name change to *Natural Health*. Meanwhile, I was learning a bit more about the South End. The good news was that hundreds of buildings had been untouched since the Victorian era—that is, the owners had lacked sufficient funds to modernize or otherwise destroy the original interior structure, and the exteriors were protected by law. Most of the South End was built in the late 1850s and 1860s, the larger homes being close to Washington Street, the main thoroughfare into Boston in the old days, with five full stories plus a basement. Smaller homes with a narrower footprint were built closer to the center of town and Back Bay.

After showing us a series of smaller homes in better neighborhoods, our Realtor finally, and somewhat reluctantly, drove us down to a square adjoining Boston City Hospital. At the time, this was the worst part of the South End, and so close to Roxbury that the post office, to this day, labels our mail as "Roxbury," rather than "Boston." As we turned into the square from depressed and hard-luck Washington Street, the first thing we noticed were the gutters layered with compressed trash and the narrow park in the middle of the square that was windswept with coffee cups, loose papers, the odd used condom, and the contents of garbage bags that had been eviscerated by razor-wielding homeless seeking deposit bounty. Putting aside the forlorn and abandoned look of the square, which was in reality a long, narrow oval, the good news was that a new fountain had just been installed and the park was dotted with massive Dutch elms, some of them reaching almost as high as the five-story Victorian townhouses that ringed the park. It was easy to see former glory here, although a wasting disease had clearly set in decades before and the patient was on its last legs.

But then, all of a sudden, we were standing in front of our home-to-be, and it was love at first sight. It was a classic Boston redbrick Victorian: a bowed front taking up two-thirds of the width of the house and then a flat face for the rest, with two dormer windows on the top floor built into an angled slate roof. A steep procession of steps led up to the main entrance on the second floor, with a small arched-top entrance tucked under the stoop.

Adrienne and I climbed the length of steps and then passed through two sets of double doors into the second-floor parlor level. We had, in just a few steps, traveled back a hundred years. The foyer was small, the house dark and quiet, the air stale as if the windows hadn't been opened in years. To the right were the stairs with a curving mahogany wood banister; light filtered down softly from the fifth floor through a skylight positioned over the stairwell. There was a short hall straight ahead, and to the left were a pair of magnificent dark walnut doors that opened into the front parlor. This room featured twelve-foot-high ceilings, curved front windows overlooking the park, and a fireplace with marble mantels and carved surrounds. Two pocket doors with etched glass panes led into the dining room, which had its own fireplace and double windows. The plaster ceiling moldings were elaborate with medallions and cornices. Chair rails ran around the walls. The only detail that required immediate attention was the raspberry eggshell paint—a color that must have been chosen by someone who was blind drunk during a blackout.

We climbed one set of stairs to the third floor, where we discovered a library, also facing the park, with a working fireplace, high ceilings, and Corinthian columns on either side of the doors. As we kept moving up, we saw that the two top floors had the same basic floor plan: a large room in the front with a small dressing room or bedroom off to the side and a slightly smaller bedroom in the back of the house with an adjoining bathroom. The top floor had dormer windows, and the basement still contained two original soapstone sinks for doing the wash, plus an intact coal bin enclosed by massive stone blocks. There was two-car parking out back, and since none of the former owners had much money, the house was more or less intact, with the exception of locks cut into doors and the first and top floors having been walled off as rental units. Over the years, as we removed the two apartments and restored the house to its original plan, we had a total of five bathrooms, six bedrooms, a library, an office, a large playroom on the fifth floor, a full basement, a large living room, a good-size dining room, a butler's pantry, working sinks in two of the bedrooms, and plenty of closets—all for the price of a one-bedroom condo on the Upper West Side of Manhattan.

Clearly, this was the perfect home to raise four kids. The five-story layout provided plenty of privacy, but there was one problem: we felt like prisoners in our own home. The neighborhood offered the constant scent of personal danger: screams in the middle of the night; gangs of young kids constantly moving through; prostitutes, drug dealers, and the sense that nobody who could afford to live somewhere else would be here.

The first six months was like a first-time tour with the Peace Corps— we had a severe case of culture shock. We served on the board of the local neighborhood organization, where, on one memorable evening, I almost got into a fistfight with a neighbor who told me that if we did not like heroin needles sticking out of the fences around our parking area, we should never have moved to the South End in the first place. Hey, the drug addicts were here first! We threatened local drug dealers with exposure, hung out with off-duty detectives who gave us the lowdown on recent crimes, got tricked by numerous kids who knocked on the door and asked for contributions to various totally fictitious school projects, and watched prostitutes climb up fire escapes in the alley to an abandoned fifth-floor rental unit, which they were using as their "office." We participated in the annual spring cleanup run by longtime local and ward chief Steve Green, who smoked cheap cigars and drove his pride and joy, a Subaru station wagon with two hundred thousand miles on it. Adrienne and the kids attended one of the first legalized gay weddings in the state. And on a more memorable occasion, Adrienne and our son Charlie were held up at gunpoint by a drug addict. Adrienne told him off, grabbed our son, and then threw a few twenties at him, telling him to get lost. That's what city living does to you.

We also began our education about all things Victorian by joining the South End Historical Society, housed in a private building just off of Massachusetts Avenue on Chester Square, a few blocks from our house. We learned that the Victorians, including Fannie Farmer, made a distinction between private and public spaces within a house. (This is in stark contrast to current homeowners, who will give you a tour of their entire house, including the bedroom, at the drop of a hat.) The second floor, with its large front and back parlors plus a small music room off the back, was for entertaining. This is why the ceilings were high and the architectural finish was so elaborate. Downstairs, the family dining room was in the front of the house and the kitchen was in the back. The third floor front, what we ended up calling the library, was also a public space, given its detailed ceiling and door moldings—a place where the woman of the house might entertain a friend or two. However, the rest of the house was private. If there was live-in domestic help, they were housed on the top floor, the hottest space in the summer. Victorians were also less apt to invite friends over for dinner. Dining in someone else's home was an intensely personal event, and an invitation was the "highest form of social compliment."

These 4,500-square-foot homes were heated with coal furnaces that ran hot air up the flues and out into the room through vents in cast-iron fireplace inserts. These were not wood-burning fireplaces as originally conceived, although some houses did offer coal grates in the large second-floor parlors. Heavy drapes were one hallmark of the Victorian era; they were highly functional, keeping out cold air in the winter. In summer months, drapes were removed and cleaned, leaving simple lace curtains that allowed for the flow of fresh air. The kitchen was always on the ground floor in the back of the house; our original brick hearth was still intact. Cooking would have been done on a small coal cookstove with two ovens located above the cooking surface on either side of the flue.

About 1860, the South End had begun life as a rich man's alternative to Beacon Hill. A few wealthy residents had even built mansions that took up an entire city block, complete with stables and circular driveways. But most dwellings did not last as true single-family homes for long. By the time Fannie Farmer had moved into the South End in the 1890s, the neighborhood was already well on its way down the slope toward urban decay, since Back Bay, which was built in the 1880s, was now the more desirable location. The rich moved out, real estate values dropped, and by the 1960s, many buildings could be had for as little as $10,000. The Pulitzer Prize—winning book *Common Ground* detailed the struggle of young families in the South End in the 1970s during the busing crisis, trying to start their own schools, chasing drug dealers down the street with baseball bats—the sort of thing that was not uncommon deeper in the South End in 1991, the year that Adrienne and I moved in. Although the portion of the neighborhood closer to Back Bay had now become gentrified, our home in St. Elsewhere was still at the very beginnings of a turnaround. It was a hodgepodge of mixed-income apartment houses, Victorian townhouses, a large gay population, and a vibrant ethnic mix. That was, in our opinion, its charm, although the area was so poor that it could not sustain a half-decent restaurant, drugstore, bakery, coffee shop, bookstore, or supermarket. It was like living on runway 3 out at Logan Airport—you were a long way from anywhere familiar.

But by the late 1990s, we had settled in and come to love our slowly improving neighborhood, and my interest in Fannie Farmer had surfaced once again. I discovered that during her tenure at the Boston Cooking School

Fannie Farmer had lived no more than twenty feet from my early-morning walk to the bus with my two girls, Whitney and Caroline, at 87 West Rutland Square. (The 1900 census shows that the house at 87 West Rutland Square was full. The entire Farmer family had settled in: Frank and Mary with their four daughters, Fannie, Mary, Cora, and Lillian, plus Cora's husband, Herbert, and their son, Dexter. There was also one servant, Ellen Macadam, who was twenty-four years old, and two lodgers, both schoolteachers: Harriet Bolman and Fanny Batchelder. By 1910, the extended family had moved to Huntington Avenue, just a few blocks away. Both of Fannie's parents were still alive at the time of the 1910 census.)

Living in a house constructed in 1859 does one of two things: Either it makes you hungry for modernity, so you rip out most of the interior and install glass floors, two-story ceilings with skylights, and a thoroughly modern granite-counter kitchen. Or you fall in love with the past and become intensely curious about what life was like the year the house was built. Adrienne and I fell into the latter category. I started to ask basic questions: What kind of town was Boston in 1896? What was it like to step out the front door on a Monday morning and go to work? Whom would you see on the sidewalk? What about the stores, public transportation, and the other buildings? Was it an earnest backwater or a sophisticated, lively place to live and work?

For starters, Boston had 448,477 residents in 1896, including 8,590 "colored" and 158,172 foreign-born, half of whom were Irish, 5,000 of whom were Italian, and 20,000 of whom were Jewish. The Boston Social Register listed 8,000 families, of which a mere dozen were Catholic; only one person, Louis Brandeis, was Jewish. The *Boston Globe* of that era accused Lizzie Borden of killing her parents in Fall River on August 4, 1892; in the early 1890s, a great financial panic set in—the greatest since 1873—and the economy didn't rebound for almost five years. In 1895, with city finances again on the upswing, the Boston Public Library opened in Copley Square at a cost of $2.5 million. Designed by McKim, Mead, and White, it contained paintings by Sargent and Whistler.

The average life expectancy was forty-nine. The workweek was fifty to sixty hours; most people worked on Saturday, and annual income in 1900 was about $800 per year, higher for state and local government workers and lower for teachers and those in the medical fields. Domestic servants were paid less, between $350 and $500 per year, depending on the region of the country. Butter was 25 cents a pound, and so were a dozen eggs. A bicycle would set you back about $17. The value of a dollar was about twenty-five times what it is today, so a quarter in 1900 might have been worth over $6 in today's money, showing just how expensive basic food-stuffs were to a poor working-class family.

What sights would a visitor to Boston have seen? Boston was full of train stations, from the massive Union Station to the Old Colony Station, so there was no problem getting into town using public transportation. By that time, the streetcars were electrified, and one could also take excursion steamers up to the north and south shores. The subway (now known as the T) was just being built, at a cost of $5 million, and one could view the first section under construction at the corner of Boylston and Charles streets.

The *Boston Daily Globe* of July 10, 1895, suggested that tourists might do one of the following: walk around the ethnic neighborhoods of interest, including the Chinese, Hebrew, and Italian quarters; visit Trinity, the Old South or the Park Street churches; or head out of town to Nantasket Beach, Provincetown, Plymouth, Gloucester, or Salem ("home of the witches"). Landmarks included the Old Corner Bookstore, King's Chapel, Paul Revere's house, Increase Mather's house, the site of the jail where Captain Kidd was held in 1699, and Liverpool Wharf, where the Boston Tea Party took place. One of the more unusual features of Boston even today is the Emerald Necklace, a series of parks connected by a seven-mile walking path, designed by Frederick Law Olmsted with the intention of linking the Boston Common and the Public Garden with the country estate known as Franklin Park. And there were always the dime museums and "objects of wonder." Boston sounded like a great place to visit.

※

JANUARY 2008. WHERE DOES ONE START PLANNING A TWELVE-
course Victorian menu? By the late nineteenth century, home dining was a
culinary mishmash, from a simple supper of leftover cold meat and prunes
to birds in potato cases and gâteau St. Honoré. It was the end and the beginning of an era—everything was up for grabs. But I wanted this menu to
be extreme: lots of courses with elaborate dishes, plenty of technique, and
recipes that would give us a clear window into the higher echelons of cooking in 1896.

Culinary adventurism was not unknown in this period; in fact, it was
frequently enjoyed by the rich and powerful. It was no surprise, then,
when I came across a January 21, 1917, article in the *New York Times* entitled
"Roosevelt Party Dines on Roast Lion." The Roosevelt in question was
Samuel M. Roosevelt, accomplished portrait artist and distant cousin of
Theodore Roosevelt, and the dinner, held at the Beaux Arts Club, was attended by seventeen of Mr. Roosevelt's fellow artists. The lion was a baby,
and roasted whole. It seems that a young man brought the still extant
young lion with him to New York from the Salisbury School in Connecticut, where it had been used as a mascot for the football team. The lion had
been left loose about the school, destroying property and scaring the students. Something had to be done.

That something was to bring it to New York, place it in a cage in the
kitchen of the Beaux Arts, and feed it tenderloin steaks, which, given their
cost, was only a short-term solution. It was finally decided that making a dinner out of it—roasting it whole, in fact—was a good return on investment.
This was acted upon forthwith, the lion killed, roasted, and served with numerous sauces, along with Monaco soup (tomato soup), bisque d'écrevisse
(crawfish bisque), riz de veau (veal sweetbreads), and then the various parts
of the baby lion: tenderloin, chops, etc. Just three years later, Samuel Roosevelt died of a massive brain hemorrhage at the Knickerbocker Club while
stooping over to pick up his dropped cigar after yet another massive feast.

The pièce de résistance of the gilded age, however, was the Pie Girl Party of 1895 given by Stanford White, the famous architect, in his brownstone just off Fifth Avenue. The guests, all society gents, were seated in pairs at small tables when a line of seminaked young girls marched in, carrying "saucisson chaude." They were clothed only in "a scarf clasped at the shoulders, wound under their breasts, and then down across their thighs." After the last meat course had been consumed, there was a faint tinkling of bells, and the young girls, some of them reportedly teenagers, reappeared wearing nothing more than sleigh bells attached to their ankles and castanets on their fingers. After a bout of dancing, they disappeared and then reappeared once more, wearing red, white, and blue liberty caps and "gauzy veils clasped at their waist," bearing a large trestle holding an enormous pie. The pie was opened and out flew a bevy of canaries, doves, and nightingales, plus an extremely young naked female cherub, who was swept up by the host and taken upstairs. News of the scandalous party soon leaked out and reached the newspapers, including a famous illustration of "The Girl in the Pie," in which the naked virgin was, for the sake of modesty, both completely clothed and depicted as a woman more advanced in years.

Boston was a tad more conservative in its tastes, but still offered elaborate menus. An example from the 1880s: oysters; turtle soup; bisque of crawfish; chicken halibut; dauphine potatoes; cucumber salad; saddle of venison; brioche potatoes; brussels sprouts; supreme of quail; terrapin Maryland; pâté de foie gras; lettuce salad; sherbet with rum punch; canvasback duck; fried hominy; tutti-frutti ice cream; gorgonzola and brie cheese; fruit; coffee and liqueurs. Finally, we were in the land of the overstuffed gourmand—just where I wanted to be.

At the back of *The Boston Cooking-School Cook Book* I found a menu for "A Full Course Dinner," consisting of twelve courses as follows: oysters; clear soup; rissoles; fish; roast venison or mutton; a lighter course of meat, fish, or poultry; a vegetable course; punch; game; cold dessert; cake; and finally, crackers, cheese, and café noir. In an elaborate Victorian meal, the first course was almost always oysters followed by a clear, not a cream, soup. The next course was often something fried, such as rissoles, although at times a bisque would have been substituted. Fish was next, followed by venison, then game or poultry, a vegetable course, frozen punch (much like a sorbet), and then desserts that may have been preceded by a jelly course. Finally, the dinner concluded with coffee, cheese, and crackers, followed by liqueurs. More elaborate dinners may have also served a fresh fruit course followed by nuts, raisins, sugar plums, and dried ginger. Bonbons and demitasse would be served in the drawing room. The menus sampled all levels of the food pyramid here, although they did seem a wee bit short on salads and grains.

In order to actually prepare this gastronomic extravaganza, my test kitchen director, Erin McMurrer, and I would need to start sourcing ingredients. The first course was no problem: I knew an oyster farmer, Island Creek Oysters, just down the coast from Boston, who supplied many of the restaurants in town. Although consommé was typical as a second course, we decided to try something a bit more adventurous: mock turtle soup, made with a calf's head rather than actual turtle meat. This raised the issue of where we were going to find a half dozen calf's heads for testing, but more on that later. Rissoles—stuffed and fried puff pastry—were the third course, and the fourth course was to be a fancy fish recipe, lobster à l'Américaine, a dish offered by Escoffier and the famous New York restaurant, Delmonico's, as well as by Fannie herself. This presented a good opportunity to find out if Fannie, who had never traveled abroad, could handle a serious French recipe.

Per Fannie's instructions, we were onto roast venison next, knowing that the meat would have to be larded, a technique that I was eager to test. For a lighter fish or meat course, we decided on fish, although Fannie had truly horrible recipes in this department, most everything having been cooked to death and stuffed with heavy, uninspired ingredients. Knowing that salmon was a common item in the late nineteenth century, we decided on a simple dish of grilled salmon, hoping to try out a grilling insert that was made for our coal cookstove. For vegetables, we had fried artichokes, a typical recipe from the time. Following that, a simple frozen punch, Canton sorbet, which simply meant ginger-flavored. The game course was to be roast stuffed goose, and then we were on to desserts.

Jellies were high on our list, since they were spectacular, with many layers of color and flavor. A lot of technique was involved here, for example, creating natural food coloring, and they would present well at the table. (I was to learn that red food coloring, cochineal, was made from small bugs—great!) The next to last course would be a cake, and here Fannie and her contemporaries were rather unimaginative. She suggested a French cream cake, which was made from a light *choux* paste and filled with pastry cream. The good news is that the French were serving spectacular cakes at the time, usually baked in molds. One particular recipe, the Savoy Cake with Oranges, had made it to the United States and was published as Mandarin cake in Charles Ranhofer's incredible 1895 book *The Epicurean*. This looked promising.

Dessert would be followed by, as Fannie instructed, crackers, cheese, and coffee. Phew. And all of that had to be tested, perfected, and then orchestrated for a sit-down dinner for twelve. Could we do it? I was hopeful, but uncertain.

The last piece of the puzzle, at least as far as the menu went, was the wines. They tended to be overly sweet—sauterne, hock (a generic term for German wines from the Rhine regions, after the town of Hochheim), sherry, liebfraumilch—while a great deal of champagne was being served. The only exceptions were claret (bordeaux) or burgundy, which were wines that might actually have been rather good. I tracked down a former sous-chef at Hamersley's Bistro in Boston who was quite knowledgeable in this area, and he set out to pull together samples for us to try with each course as they were being developed. Ah, the joys of recipe testing!

I also contacted John Abbott, president of WGBH in Boston, about the possibility of filming the dinner and its preparations, creating a television special about the history of Victorian cooking. He was on board and I was thrilled. Now I really had to get going on planning the twelve courses, but first, I wanted something alcoholic to serve the guests as they arrived. Although cocktails and whiskey were usually not served at home, punch seemed to be a nice way to launch the evening. And I was lucky enough to know just the man to help us: Donald Friary, an expert on punch and punch bowls and a fellow member of Boston's St. Botolph Club.

✿

BEFORE ATTENDING FRIARY'S ST. BOTOLPH LECTURE ON THE history of punch, we sampled his personal recipe, given to him by an established Boston family, and realized what we had been missing. As with almost everything else in the culinary world, the history of punch is a messy business. The conventional wisdom is that the word *punch* is derived from the Indian word *panch*, which means "five," referring to the five basic ingredients of a good punch: alcohol (often rum), water, sweet (sugar), sour (lemon or lime juice), and spice. A more likely explanation is that punch derives from the term *puncheon*, which was a cask for liquids: the type of container used on board ship, for example.

Punch was well established as of the seventeenth century, the recipe having been introduced to Britain by the East India merchants. Punch bowls were common at most taverns, and the punch was made up well in advance. Donald mentioned that he once drank four-year-old punch and indeed found it to be much improved through aging. At the very least, making punch a day ahead of time seems like a good thing, not just a nod to convenience.

Some punch recipes would indeed deliver a punch, if not a ripping headache. A recipe for Thirty-second Regiment of Victoria Punch from the 1862 edition of *How to Mix Drinks* by Jerry Thomas offers the following ingredients: 6 sliced lemons, ½ gallon brandy, ½ gallon Jamaican rum, 1 pound white sugar, 1¾ quarts water, and 1 pint of boiling milk. The lemons are steeped in the brandy and rum for twenty-four hours and then mixed with the other ingredients. The punch is strained and can be served hot or cold. The recipe served twenty, which works out to be about three-quarters of a cup of brandy or rum per guest, plus two tablespoons or so of white sugar, to say nothing of the combination of lemon and milk. The British infantry must have had hard heads and strong stomachs.

By 1880, a New Year's punch started with a sugar syrup made from the juice of six lemons and oranges, five pounds of loaf sugar, two quarts of water, five cloves, and two blades of mace. This liquid was simmered to make a flavored sugar syrup, and small amounts were used to sweeten a punch. The punch itself was made with a pint of green tea, a pint of brandy, one quart each of rum and champagne, and one teacup of Chartreuse, which is mixed and then sweetened to taste with the reserved syrup. It is served in a punch bowl containing a large block of ice, along with three sliced oranges and lemons.

Things started to go seriously wrong with punch recipes in the early twentieth century. What had been a simple, strong alcoholic drink became a rather revolting cooler, the sort of thing that a modern teenager who was trying to achieve alcoholic oblivion might appreciate. In fact, the term *punch* came to have very little meaning, much like the word *cocktail*. By 1907, for example, a recipe for Victoria punch appeared in a cookbook by Paul Richards, who was writing for the hotel and catering trades. The recipe included a gallon of orange ice frozen with a pint of white wine, beaten egg whites (most recipes suggested beating them "to a froth"), and then a cup of kirsch plus a pint of arrack, or Javan rum. By 1919, Victoria punch was served with a topping of meringue, made from three egg whites beaten with a whopping half pound of sugar. Another recipe, this one from around the turn of the century, suggested adding sliced bananas to the punch bowl. No words can describe the horror.

So we decided to stick with the earlier, British recipe for punch, a simple alcoholic drink made from rum, water, fruit juice of some sort, sugar, and a spice or two. We made a few minor revisions and added five drops of bitters just to add a hint of bite to the foundation of the drink. It was now perfect. In fact, it is so good that we have been drinking it ever since.

VICTORIA PUNCH

This recipe, with a few minor changes, is courtesy of Donald Friary and, I am told, improves with age. I suggest that you make it a day or two ahead of time. Serve chilled, although it does not need to be refrigerated for storage.

4 tablespoons sugar

8 tablespoons lime juice

1 cup rum

1 cup water

Pinch nutmeg

5 drops bitters

Combine ingredients and pour over ice to serve.

Oysters

✿

Fannie Farmer Is Born, Survives Polio, Takes Over the Boston Cooking School, and Sells Over 360,000 Copies of *The Boston Cooking-School Cook Book*

Who was Fannie Merritt Farmer? Was she a cook first and a teacher second, or was she perhaps more promoter than culinary wizard? For starters, she was middle-class at best, and her view of the world, one that evidently suited her audience at the time, was parochial and narrow. To tart up a recipe, she would simply give it an ersatz French name to lend an aura of adventure and good living. Recipes such as Gâteau de Princesse Louise or Potage à la Reine fall into this category. In her worst moments, more Food Network than serious cooking school, she invented cloying recipe names such as Heart's-Ache Pudding for Valentine's Day. In fact, Fannie understood, much like any modern food celebrity, that food is, in large part, entertainment. The fact that Fannie herself was not well traveled or particularly sophisticated mattered not a whit, since her audience was even less urbane than she was. To truly appreciate her marketing and packaging skills, one need only look at the origins of the Boston Cooking School, in which she would turn a sow's ear into a silk purse.

The Women's Education Association was a post–Civil War institution founded by reformers and philanthropists, and it was the precursor to the Boston Cooking School. "The school gave women of modest means an entry into professional work at a time when more women needed employment and few had career options." This effort was funded by subscribers (similar to today's public television model) and larger gifts from philanthropists.

The first classes were given in March 1879 with seven pupils. The school quickly became popular, so it hired Mrs. David A. Lincoln to teach—her husband had recently suffered a financial setback so she headed off to work—and by 1882 she was handling over two thousand pupils. The school had expanded to teaching nurses the art of sickroom cookery, as well.

Mary Lincoln was to author the *Boston Cooking School Cook Book* in 1884 and the *Boston School Kitchen Text-book* in 1887; cofound the *American Kitchen Magazine*; lecture widely; write a newspaper column entitled "From Day to Day"; and author five additional cookbooks, the last in 1910. She was a vigorous endorser of products, including the White Mountain Ice Cream Freezer and Jell-O, and she was a principal in Mrs. Lincoln's Baking Powder Company of Boston. She is also credited for laying the foundation for Fannie Farmer's *Boston Cooking-School Cook Book* in 1896.

The school quickly added accredited classes to train cooking school teachers under a Miss Maria Parloa, who was a well-known culinary figure of the period. She had authored *The Appledore Cook Book (1872), Miss Parloa's New Cook Book: A Guide to Marketing and Cooking* (1880), and *Practical Cookery* (1884). She also wrote for the *Ladies' Home Journal*, of which she was part owner. Parloa's course included instruction in chemistry, given at the Women's Laboratory. Students received instruction on anatomy from a Dr. Merritt. Chemistry? Anatomy? The Women's Education Association and the Boston Cooking School were taking a very broad view of the culinary arts, and one that seems extremely modern. The President's Report of 1884 included the following language in describing the goals of the school: "to lift this great social incubus of bad cooking and its incident evils from the households of the country at large." This was a social, not just a culinary, movement.

By January 1884, the Boston Cooking School was now independent of the Women's Education Association, and it soon became clear to those running it that the original goal—giving free lessons to the poor and training women to become professional cooks—was difficult to achieve, although they were determined to pursue their original charter. The money was to be found in giving lessons to the rich, not the poor. People wanted to be entertained; they wanted fancy cooking and did not want to be lectured about economy, health, hygiene, and science. Good cooking was easier to sell as a means of impressing one's social peers than as a path to correcting the ills of society. Within a few years, a new teacher had shown up at the Boston Cooking School, a woman who understood the tastes and needs of Boston women. By the early twentieth century, this woman had gone out on her own, put the Boston Cooking School out of business with her own school, and published a cookbook that would sell a staggering four hundred thousand copies by the time of her death in 1914. The woman was Fannie Merritt Farmer.

Fannie was born in Boston in March 1857 and grew up in Medford, Massachusetts. She was one of five daughters: Sarah died in infancy, leaving Fannie and three younger sisters, Cora, Lillian, and Mary. (Fannie was also a distant cousin of Diana, Princess of Wales.) Summers were spent in Scituate, the home of her mother; in the evenings they played cribbage or skat; on Sundays they attended church, and sometimes pulled taffy. Her father, John Franklin Farmer, was a former newspaperman, a Unitarian, and a printer who stuck to the hand press while times were changing. As a result, his business prospects slowly deteriorated, as did the family's modest income. According to his grandson, Dexter Perkins (the son of Cora, the only sister to have children), John Farmer was also a smooth talker who managed to get in to see plays without paying and sneak a second helping of Aunt Jemima pancakes that were being given for free to attendees at Boston's annual food fair. Fannie's mother, Mary Farmer, was of an independent nature, knitting quietly, for example, after her husband had declared that he was going down to the basement to kill himself. (After a decent interval, he returned and inquired as to her sang froid. She replied, "There wa'nt anything I could do about it.") As the family fortunes waned, John came home one day with a new buggy inscribed with the letter *F* in gold. Mary commented, "*F* stands for Farmer, and *F* stands for fool." When, in 1925, she was asked to opine on the wonderful qualities of her first grandchild, Mary replied tartly, "I've known his father longer." Fannie had one other distinctive relative, her aunt Ella, who once took a football that bounced into her yard, cut it up, and threw the pieces back over the fence. She also cut Dexter Perkins out of her will, so Dexter's less than fond memories of Great Aunt Ella may be suspect.

Fannie was stricken with polio while at Medford High School. This meant abandoning further education and also greatly reduced her chances for marriage. She was an invalid for the better part of ten years and always walked with a limp. The family moved back to Boston, first to Rutland Square and eventually to Back Bay, a more upscale neighborhood. Mary became a schoolteacher, and Cora married and bore a son, Dexter, for whom Fannie had a great fondness. (After Fannie's death, Dexter's wife would edit future editions of the cookbook.)

After a brief stint in retail Fannie worked as a mother's helper in the Cambridge home of Mrs. Charles Shaw, where she managed to do a great deal of cooking. At the age of thirty-one, Fannie enrolled at the Boston Cooking School and graduated a year later, in 1889. She was offered the position of assistant to the principal, a woman named Carrie Dearborn, and became principal in 1893, when Dearborn left school to pursue the lecture circuit. Under her tutelage, the Boston Cooking School became considerably more popular and successful. (It has been noted, however, that the Boston Cooking School always had difficulty meeting its expenses because Fannie was so insistent on using the best possible ingredients.) In 1902 Fannie went out on her own, founding Miss Farmer's School of Cookery at 40 Hereford Street. The Boston Cooking School closed its doors within a year and donated its equipment to Simmons College.

Was Fannie regarded as a good cook in her own time? According to one source, "She was too apt to let the pots burn as she ran enthusiastically from one recipe to another." It was said that her sister Mary was a better cook, and that Maggie Murphy, the woman who ran the Farmer household starting in 1874, "outdid them all with delicate pastries and chowders."

(Murphy was also known to anonymously enter cooking contests judged by Fannie. Frequently, she won.) And looking at many of her recipes, one does find thick, floury sauces, an addiction to sugar, even in salad dressings and baked fish, and a mixed bag of recipes. Her niece, Wilma Lord Perkins, referred to her as "a great executive, food detective, and gourmet, rather than a great cook herself." H. L. Mencken reviewed a 1930 edition of her cookbook; he commented that it represented "middle-class British notions of cookery" and deplored Fannie's recipe for soft-shell crabs as "an obscenity almost beyond belief." But let's not blame Fannie for an edition of the cookbook published well after her time.

What she may have lacked as a talented cook she made up for with a keen sense of showmanship, marketing, and giving the public what it wanted. In fact, she often referred to herself first and foremost as a businesswoman. Here is a description of Fannie by Elizabeth Schlesinger, wife of Arthur Schlesinger: "Her bright blue eyes, red hair, and vivacious personality made people overlook her rather plain face and the pince-nez she always wore. She was plump and had no interest in dress, but a maid who accompanied her on lecture trips saw that she always looked well." Zulma Steele, a biographer and magazine writer, described Fannie's costume as follows, "Her piqué skirt hung full to the floor, protected by yards of gathered apron. Her gossamer shirtwaist had the daintiest of organdy fichus, and tiny hand-hemmed ruffles embellished her collars and cuffs." Marjorie Mills, longtime food editor of the *Boston Herald*, described Miss Farmer as "limping briskly about her platform kitchen, teaching some 200 students. She was a prim girl with vibrant enthusiasm who arrived early at school laden with market supplies and was the last to leave at night." Of course, she was always attended by an assistant and a maid or two, so much of the actual cooking was not done by Fannie. One later biographer commented, "Fannie Farmer refused to sully her own white fingertips in kneading up a flaky piecrust." Likable, energetic, intelligent, and a wonderful show woman—this was the Fannie Farmer who energized the public and the fortunes of the Boston Cooking School.

Since I had started this process reading *Mrs. Lincoln's Boston Cook Book*, and since Mary Lincoln seemed to be a thorough professional, the obvious question surfaced over and over again: Did Fannie simply steal Mary Lincoln's work and make it her own through force of personality and strong marketing skills? Was Fannie more of a promoter and organizer than a creative culinary force? Did she simply take a body of work created by others at the Boston Cooking School and run off to the bank with it?

For starters, Fannie's *Original 1896 Boston Cooking-School Cook Book* was without question a rewrite and update of Mary Lincoln's original text from the 1880s. The key difference was who owned the copyright. Little, Brown, displaying a lack of confidence in the work, made Fannie responsible for the publication costs, acting only as distributor and agent. This meant that Fannie owned the copyright, and therefore the profits—not the first time a book publisher has misread the market. This also raised Fannie's profile since she was the author, not the Boston Cooking School; in fact, the book was soon referred to as the "Fannie Farmer Cookbook." The initial printing of 3,000 copies sold out quickly; it was reprinted twice in 1897, and once per year thereafter until 1906, when a revised edition came out, enjoying a first printing of 20,000 copies. From then on, the cookbook was reprinted annually and also translated into French and sold as *Le Livre de Cuisine de l'Ecole de Cuisine de Boston*. In 1915, at Fannie's death, over 360,000 copies had been sold, and the average press run was up to 50,000 copies. It was by far the best-selling cookbook of its age. (By comparison, *Ben Hur*, perhaps the best-selling book of the late nineteenth century, had sold 400,000 copies in its first nine years of publication, falling just short of the Bible but outstripping *Uncle Tom's Cabin*, *Quo Vadis?*, and *Little Women*.) Fannie published other books as well, including *Chafing Dish Possibilities* (1898), *Food and Cookery for the Sick and Convalescent* (1904), *What to Have for Dinner* (1905), *Catering for Special Occasions* (1911), and *A New Book of Cookery* (1912). None of them came close to the success of the original volume.

Although we think of Fannie Farmer as having penned one of the few major cookbooks of her time, large cookbooks authored by well-known cooking school teachers and contemporary celebrities were nothing new. The first American cookbook of note was a reprint of *The Compleat Housewife*, which had been originally authored in England in 1727 by Eliza Smith and then reprinted for the American audience. Early recipes were vague hand-me-downs with sometimes silly directives such as this "receipt" for Indian pudding from the *Plimouth Colony Cookbook*: "Let the molasses drip in as you sing 'Nearer My God to Thee,' but sing two verses in cold weather." The most popular cookbook during the American Revolution was Hannah Glasse's *American Cookery Made Plain and Easy*, but perhaps the most famous early American cookbook was Amelia Simmons's work, *American Cookery*, which is readily available today in a facsimile edition and was the first cookbook to be protected by the Copyright Act of 1787. In the first half of the nineteenth century, the cookbook business started to heat up, with 160 titles published, including *The New England Cookery*, *A New System of Domestic Cookery*, *The Universal Cook Book*, *The American Frugal Housewife*, *Miss Beecher's Domestic Receipt Book*, and *Modern American Cookery*. These books were often more than cookbooks; they also had sections on medicine as well as household hints and management.

By the mid-1800s, cookbooks were also being published by social groups: for example, the *Woman's Suffrage Cook Book* and *The Temperance Cook Book*. Churches also became involved, with *Mother Hubbard's Cupboard*, published by the Young Ladies Society of the First Baptist Church, and *Tried and True Recipes 1897*. The rise of cooking schools also resulted in more cookbooks, for instance, *Miss Parloa's New Cook Book* and *Mrs. Rorer's New Cook Book*. Other important cookbooks of the era included *Miss Corson's Practical American Cookery*, *Marion Harland's Complete Cookbook*, *Buckeye Cookery*, *The Carolina Housewife*, *The Kentucky Housewife*, *The Virginia Housewife*, *The White House Cookbook*, *The Complete Cook*, *Good-Living: A Practical Cookery-Book for Town and Country*, *Favorite Recipes*, and, most notably, *The Epicurean* by Charles Ranhofer, which was by far the most thorough and professional cookbook of the nineteenth century.

Always with a keen ear for marketing and publicity, Fannie claimed that when she dined at a famous New York or Boston restaurant and the chef would not provide a recipe, she would secrete a dab of sauce or other victual in a handkerchief and "analyze it at the cooking school." (This sounds like utter claptrap; it was clear from her attempts to reproduce dishes from, say, Delmonico's, that the "dab of sauce" wasn't doing her much good, since her versions fell a mile short of the original. Yet her students felt that they were getting the most cutting-edge food—the secrets of the great chefs of the day.)

MAY 2008. FOR OUR DINNER PARTY OF THE CENTURY, WE HAD to establish some rules about food preparation. My first thought was to ban the use of appliances, including mixers and food processors. A few months later, however, I was visiting friends in Andover, Maine, at the family "big house," one of those massive eighteenth-century colonials, with winding passageways, cobbled-together additions, and a huge three-story-high main room. The kitchen was primitive at best, with a wood cookstove, complete with brass water heater. In a nod to the twentieth century, there was also a cheap electric range. There were no electric mixers, so I had to beat twelve egg whites by hand to produce the morning pancakes. That got me thinking—a twelve-course meal without plug-in appliances? This was looking grim.

We had decided to use refrigerators and freezers for food safety as much as anything else, plus hot water out of the tap for cleanup. The management of the cooking process, including how to hold foods until they were served, was going to be one of the biggest obstacles. I only had two ovens plus one cooktop on the coal cookstove. I hoped that modern ovens would not be necessary, but that would depend on the timing and order of the courses. Another large concern was the sheer quantity of food that had to be served perfectly hot, such as the rissoles (fried and filled puff pastry) and the fried baby artichokes. Was I going to have to give in to convenience and use the high-powered commercial wok hiding in my back kitchen, or would we be able to manage the heat of the stovetop and the space available to simultaneously fry enough food for a dinner party of twelve? (I finally decided to do almost all of the cooking on the wood cookstove, other than the baking of cakes; and that electric mixers and food processors would be used only for the baking.)

There were other considerations as well. For our jellies, commercial food colorings were out, so we had to reinvent the art of using natural ingredients to create a range of different-colored layers. And there were to be no shortcuts in making the puff pastry. For starters, we had to make the dough, fashion it into a 6-inch-square flour and butter mixture, and roll it out to 12 inches. This "paste," as they called it in Fannie's time, was then rolled into a 24- by 8-inch strip that was folded letterlike and refrigerated. This was repeated four or five times, and then refrigerated overnight before being rolled into a perfect strip one-sixteenth of an inch thick. No store-bought puff pastry here.

In addition, old recipes often call for odd measurements that had to be translated to modern terms. For example, a *gill* is five ounces, the same size as a *teacup*. A *dessert spoon* is half a tablespoon. We also came across a *breakfast cup*, which is half a pint.

The saddle of venison had to be larded on both sides using a larding needle, and we had to make a stock from an actual calf's head for the soup. The lobster à l'Américaine required both homemade lobster and fish stocks; we would have to master regulating the cookstove in order to perfectly grill the salmon on the grilling insert; a hand-cranked ice-cream machine would be necessary to freeze the Canton punch; and the elaborate Mandarin cake required two separate cakes, a filling of Bavarian cream, a fondant icing, and tangerines filled with ice cream and two different jellies. And how much of this could be prepared ahead of time? We had to test the frozen punch (more or less a sorbet)—would it still be soft and refreshing if made the day ahead, or would it would turn dense and hard? And I knew from experience that jellies tend to stiffen over time: the gelatin keeps on working, so there might be a small window of time when our elaborate, towering jellies had the perfect texture. If they were too loose, we could not serve them properly; if too stiff, they would lose much of their flavor and be unappealing to eat. There were smaller, more finicky issues as well—for instance, how does one cut into a tower of jelly and serve it cleanly?

We also had to consider the issue of service. As in all Victorian households, our kitchen was downstairs and the dining room was upstairs. We had to serve twelve courses, many of them with more than one recipe on the plate, and keep the service well paced to get through the entire dinner in one evening. (One course every twenty minutes would mean a four-hour dinner; Victorian etiquette called for a two-hour time limit on formal dinners, a time frame that appeared impossible to meet.) Given a lack of space and our preference for performing carving and plating out of the view of our guests, we would have to figure out how to warm plates and move quickly to get the food to the table while it was still hot. We would also have to carefully orchestrate the silverware, the wineglasses, and the plates, since we would have to do a large amount of recycling during the dinner. Washing up had to be an ongoing activity, and well paced to provide the cutlery and flatware for upcoming courses.

We had eighteen months to test and refine the recipes, assemble a kitchen and waitstaff, pull together a dozen high Victorian table settings plus period table decorations, create a blue-ribbon guest list, figure out how to use an authentic Victorian cookstove, choose and taste-test the wines, and become experts on the cooking of Boston in the 1890s.

MY FIRST SERIOUS AND MOST EMBARRASSING ENCOUNTER WITH oysters occurred in the mid-1990s when Julia Child called to invite me over to cook dinner together. This was nothing special for Julia; she invited virtually everyone in the food world in Boston over to her home frequently since she loved company and she loved to cook. For me, it was nerve-wracking and, as it turned out, a near disaster.

I had met Julia a number of times at industry events and had driven to Boston back in the 1980s to interview her and her husband Paul for *Cook's Magazine*. On that memorable occasion, we had an oyster stew and a warm crisp baguette that was yanked from the oven and ripped into hunks—delicious. And, like most of her viewers, I thought of Julia as a kindly teacher, a patient, accepting educator. What I did not realize until that evening was that Julia was playful and quite competitive, often putting others on the spot to see how well they would respond.

So a few minutes into our evening together, she sidled up to me with a large plastic tub and issued the challenge: "Would you mind shucking a few oysters?" using her inimitable and slightly challenging voice. Ten minutes later, by which time I had two oysters open and one slightly bloody finger, she came back and asked, with more than a hint of pixie humor in her query, "Do you need some help, dearie?" I thought for a moment and then threw caution to the wind. "Just get me the biggest glass of wine you can find, and then you shuck the oysters while I cook the rest of dinner!" We were good friends after that. I guess I failed the cooking test, but had passed the character part of the evening's entertainment.

Despite this experience, the first course on our elaborate menu was to be, of course, oysters, the reason being that oysters were almost always the first thing served at any feast or serious dinner party. They were easy and abundant and Victorians loved them. Oysters were so popular that the beds at Wellfleet were fished out as early as 1775, so enterprising fishermen dumped oysters from Buzzard's Bay into Wellfleet in the spring, thus ensuring fat, valuable "Wellfleet" oysters come fall. Eventually, hundreds of tons of oysters were dredged up from the Chesapeake and dumped onto New England beds so that they, too, could be given local names and higher prices. Oystermen also had a clever trick up their sleeve—"floating" oysters, which meant placing them on floats in low-salinity water. The oysters sucked in this fresher water, plumped up, and therefore weighed more, commanding higher prices. This process was banned in 1909, since the floats were often located near large population centers with polluted waters that offered the risk of contamination, resulting in outbreaks of typhoid.

In eighteenth-century Boston, oysters were sold door to door—the oystermen would open the oysters right there, throwing the shells into a large shoulder bag. Later, handcarts came into use, as they did with other food items. The first cooked oysters were sold by Peter B. Brigham at the head of Hanover Street, and he quickly amassed a fortune. Oyster houses soon sprang up—they were most popular between 1810 and 1875—and became a convenient, all-purpose meeting place since there were no lunch counters in Boston or other fast-food establishments. Oysters were cheap, required little to no preparation, and the oyster houses stayed open late at night. All told, there were about a thousand establishments in Boston that served oysters by the mid-nineteenth century.

Early oyster boats were as small as sixteen feet long, no more than dugouts made from white pine. In 1874, the oyster business came into the steam age when a small steam engine was installed in the sloop *Early Bird* owned by Peter Decker of Norwalk, Connecticut. By the early 1900s, the steam-powered oyster boat had started to decline in favor of gasoline engines, which took up less room and so could be used on smaller boats. Dredging an oyster bed in a sailboat required fairly advanced skills. The key was to drift over the bed, starting upwind with the centerboard down, and then to let the wind and tide take you over the prime real estate. The jib was trimmed to just short of luffing, and the main had to be trimmed just enough to keep the bow headed into the wind. Small hand dredges were used by oystermen standing on the side of the boat. The smaller sailboats were often outfitted with a hand-winder dredge (these were eventually run by steam power when steam engines came into use), but that meant one dredge per boat, a less efficient method than having four or five workmen, standing at the gunwales, using hand dredges. Once the industry moved away from sail power, larger boats used bigger hydraulic dredges.

In Fannie's time, virtually every menu started with a large platter of oysters served on a bed of crushed ice or a large block of ice that had a hollowed-out center trough. Special oyster plates that held four to six oysters and platters that usually held a dozen were also used, with a bed of ice covered with a doily, the rims decorated with holly or fern. Oysters were also fricasséed (served in a slightly thickened cream sauce), creamed, battered and fried as fritters (eggs, milk, and flour were used for the batter), or put into a stew (made from water, oyster liquor, and cream) or stuffing. Fannie also suggested serving oysters with brown bread, so we tested her recipe and made a few minor alterations. It was served in small rounds spread with salted butter.

So our first course, oysters, was simple enough. Our second course, mock turtle soup, would test the limits of our culinary adventurism.

CHAMPAGNE MIGNONETTE

1 cup champagne vinegar

2 tablespoons minced shallot

½ teaspoon coarse ground black pepper

Combine ingredients and serve with oysters.

BROWN BREAD

Since we served this bread with oysters, it is less sweet than many other recipes and, of course, contains no raisins, a common ingredient at the time. You will need two 12-ounce coffee cans for baking.

4 tablespoons melted butter, plus extra for preparing cans

1 cup rye flour

1 cup whole wheat flour

1 cup fine ground white cornmeal

2¼ teaspoons baking powder

1 teaspoon salt

½ cup light molasses

2¼ cups buttermilk

2 12-ounce coffee cans, washed and dried

1. Grease the bottoms of the coffee cans with butter. Line the sides of the coffee cans with parchment paper (cut to fit), and grease with butter. Place a steamer rack on the bottom of a large pot that is tall enough to accommodate the can with the cover on. In a large saucepan, boil enough water to fill the steaming pot about halfway.

2. In a medium bowl, whisk together flours, cornmeal, baking powder, and salt. Stir in the molasses, buttermilk, and butter, and mix until combined.

Spoon batter into prepared cans; do not fill cans more than two-thirds full. Cover tightly with aluminum foil. Secure foil to cans with a rubber band or twine. Place can on rack (or on bottom of pot), and pour boiling water to about halfway up the coffee cans. Return water to a boil and lower to a simmer. Cover the pot. Steam for 2 hours, adding more boiling water as needed, until bread is firm and a cake tester inserted into the center comes out clean.

3. Place cans on a cooling rack, allow to cool 10 minutes, then unmold. Allow to cool for 1 hour before slicing.

Mock Turtle Soup

A Walking Tour of Fannie Farmer's Boston

I t's one thing to read about the history of a place from books and quite another to actually live in the same neighborhood as the object of your investigation. My first question was, how much of Fannie Farmer's Boston was still left a century later? I called up a friend and my researcher for this project, Meg Ragland, and, a few weeks later, we met at the site of Fannie's former home on Rutland Square to follow her footsteps to the Boston Cooking School, which was located on Tremont Street, right off the Boston Common. Since she had suffered from polio, Fannie probably took the trolley that ran down the center of Columbus Avenue. Could we still see the same sights that she had seen more than a hundred years before?

But first, we examined the ward maps from 1895, which offer detailed accounts of every building in Boston, as well as listings of commercial enterprises they contained. By far the biggest categories included grocers (about 1,200 listings), hotels (700), produce dealers (250), restaurants (500, but these included coffee and oyster houses), confectioners (about 80) and, of course, liquor stores (500). So, Boston was full of people with a taste for liquor and sweets, living in lodging houses and hotels, eating and drinking out a lot. Most of the shopping was done in small, neighborhood grocery and produce stores. More interesting establishments listed in the ward maps of that year include two potato chip companies, a butter color supplier, cold-blast refrigerators, one color photography establishment, four suppliers of counting-room furniture, cracker bakers, and a half dozen manufacturers of grate bars, which pointed to the need for security.

We began at Columbus Avenue and Claremont Park, a spot only a couple of blocks from Fannie's residence. This part of Columbus included myriad hotels as well as private residences and lodging houses. It was just a block from the railroad, so hotel accommodations were in high demand.

As we moved down Columbus, toward downtown, Meg pointed out that, originally, the South End had few storefronts. As the fortunes of the neighborhood declined, it became more commercial, and street-level storefronts were added onto the brownstones, sticking out like tacked-on shanties. Today, you can see that, architecturally, the ground-floor retail spaces have swallowed up the steps leading to the second-floor parlors, the stores themselves appearing to be nothing more than crude afterthoughts. The experience of walking down Columbus Avenue in Fannie Farmer's day would have been much grander.

The big difference between Rutland Square today and one hundred years ago is that Fannie's house would have been adjacent to the Boston and Providence train tracks running into the city. The streets that intersect the railroad line were, for the most part, named for towns that the railroad served along the line: hence street names such as Worcester, Springfield, etc. Of the 169 streets in the South End, 84 were named for cities and towns chiefly in New York and western Massachusetts, all places served by the railroad. Today, because of an urban renewal project, the trains run underground and the area has been turned into green space named the South End Corridor. However, the railroad still provides a barrier between the South End and Back Bay because most of the streets on either side of the corridor are dead ends, with no through traffic, just as it was in Fannie's day.

By taking a short detour to Copley Plaza, Fannie could have walked into the major food retailer of the day, S. S. Pierce, located across the street from the Museum of Fine Arts, a fabulous, highly ornamented terra-cotta brick Gothic Revival building designed by John Hubbard Sturgis, which was torn down in 1909. A few blocks later, at Clarendon Street, the Albermarle Hotel building still exists and offers a stunning example of Gothic architecture and, like many other Boston hotels at the time, the "French flat," a continental system also called family hotels in which a tenant would occupy part or all of a floor rather than several floors in a house. Before the areas around Boston were built up, our city was said to have been the most densely populated urban area in America, and therefore these large, high-occupancy hotels were a natural development.

Across the train tracks headed toward South Station, in the next block on the left, there are two buildings of note, the first being the Pope Manufacturing building. Albert A. Pope started his career in the 1870s by exporting bicycles from England. His first bike, and the first model ever made in the United States, was the Columbia in 1881. In the late 1890s, Pope began manufacturing electric cars as well, five hundred of them between 1897 and 1899.

The next block would have been entirely devoted to the New York, New Haven & Hartford Railroad passenger depot. This large area also contained a freight house, as well as a few small buildings fronting Columbus Avenue. Because of the proximity to the depot, there would have been a run of restaurants. Finally, we walked across Tremont Street and into the Boston Common, past the old cemetery, and then up to the site of the Boston Cooking School, now occupied by a large Loews Multiplex. Fannie lived in a vital, thriving neighborhood, filled with boardinghouses, creameries, fruit sellers, small grocers, butchers, confectioners, and even a good selection of restaurants closer to town.

JANUARY 2009. THE TESTING WAS PROCEEDING SLOWLY. WE DE-cided to make an authentic turtle soup as a frame of reference for our mock turtle version. Would the ersatz version taste anything like the original, and why would Fannie and other cooks of the period use a calf's head instead of turtle meat? We finally managed to snag five pounds of frozen turtle meat, but getting hold of a calf's head was more difficult. After calling around, we finally found a supplier, Previte's Meats, who charged $9.99

per head (the feet, by the way, were a steal at just $1.99 each). The head had a "hole" in it, presumably a bullet hole. This was getting gruesome. When we picked up the order, we also noted that the employees took quite an interest in who was buying the head, peeking around corners, trying to be inconspicuous. Sort of like picking up one's custom-made leather bondage suit—you know, the one with the bat ears and cape. The next week, we showed up at the store to pick up an order for two brains and found a huge box waiting for us. I asked, "There are just two brains here, right?" I was assured that this was the case. I opened the box, just to be sure, and found a total of ten brains. This made us think that calf's heads were nothing out of the ordinary for these guys, since they were selling them in bulk. Was this for some ethnic specialty perhaps, an Ecuadorian feast or a Cambodian stew? Were they being used in some sort of bestial ritual, voodoo or some darker, more sinister rite? Finally, we contacted a butcher who had helped us out with test kitchen orders for years, Scott Brueggeman from DiLuigi Sausage Company. He supplied the rest of our orders, including the calf's feet for making homemade gelatin.

We were curious, however, as to why the brains that came with the calf's head purchased from Brueggeman were creamy white, firm, and healthy-looking, whereas the brains that we had purchased separately looked grayer, tinged with darker lines like coral and requiring more delicate handling so they did not dissolve into a puddle. The answer was that the brains purchased separately were probably ten days old and came from an older animal, whereas the calf's head and brains from Scott were fresh, just twenty-four hours old, and the animal was probably only two to four weeks when slaughtered. So, more proof that the older we get, the more our brains turn to mush.

Brains, as explained in many nineteenth-century cookbooks, require very delicate handling or they quickly turn to custard. On more than one occasion, I was holding a plump, firm mound of brains in my hand only to have it liquefy into a rich goo as I transferred it to a plate. I wondered whether we should inform our celebrity guests of the nature of our soup garnish—we had decided to serve "brain balls," which were offered in a number of contemporary cookbooks—or simply allow them to consume one or two balls first and then tell them what they had eaten. The true urbane gourmet would hardly flinch at the revelation—after all, brains are not uncommon in many cuisines—but the term *brain balls* has a satisfying ring to it, as if something fat and heavy just plopped from the gullet into the bottom of the stomach, where it promised to dissolve slowly, like cold bacon grease stuck in the S curve of a drain.

THE CALF'S HEAD HAD BEEN STUFFED INGLORIOUSLY INTO A large stainless stockpot, its bared teeth grinning hideously upward, the tongue slack, lolling out of the mouth into the now opaque broth. It reminded me of the popular glass-fronted carts I had seen in the streets of Istanbul when I had visited as a student in the early 1970s, the ones that held goat's heads, teeth bared and vicious, the small skulls nestled on a bed of parsley, the Turkish equivalent of roasted chestnuts. I removed the head, reduced the stock, shredded the cheek meat, and placed it back into the pot for serving. A final adjustment of seasonings and then the taste test. The soup was at once gamey and slick with a gelatinous back-of-the-throat scum of fat, exotic but sufficiently off in flavor and texture to produce the first tentative signs of gagging: short bursts of throat clearing followed by deep swallows of ice water. I had just eaten something that was best left still attached to a nervous system. So much for the classic Victorian-era recipe, mock turtle soup.

Weeks later, after further research and to my great horror, I discovered a common but rarely explicitly stated fact about this recipe: the brains had to be removed before cooking. I had spent days tracking down a whole calf's head, done weeks of research, and then cooked all day to produce nothing more than brain soup. This dish was going to be a lot harder than it had at first appeared.

Mock turtle soup is part of a great tradition of "mock" dishes that began in medieval times and were always a cheap knockoff of the real thing. In this case, that would be a soup made with real turtles, which, in Britain, were initially shipped from the West Indies, and were therefore expensive. And, of course, mock turtle soup was a time-saver; one didn't have to boil the live beast, slough off skin, remove toenails, etc. Sea turtles could run up to one hundred pounds or more, whereas a diamondback terrapin, the turtle of choice for nineteenth-century American cooks, was tiny by comparison, running just four pounds. (The largest turtle ever eaten weighed 350 pounds, and was baked and served at the King's Arms Tavern in Pall Mall.) Once it was discovered that sea turtles could be transported in a ship's hold, the turtle feast became a signifier of wealth and success for the British and American merchant elite.

It took little time for this expensive dish to be mocked. The first recorded recipe for mock turtle soup appeared in 1758, in the fifth edition of Hannah Glasse's *The Art of Cookery Made Plain and Easy*, just three years after her recipe for an authentic turtle soup was published.

But why turtle meat to begin with? Well, such fare was considered quite the delicacy, and diamondback terrapins were de rigeur as a mainstay of many nineteenth-century menus. Around 1800, taverns served terrapin for supper for a modest two shillings, usually boiled in its shell. Terrapins were so abundant that they were even used as food for pigs. In Philadelphia, they were sold from wheelbarrows, as were oysters. But they were also highly prized around the Chesapeake, especially toward the latter part of the nineteenth century, when they had been overfished. By 1900, the price had risen to a high of $125 per dozen for counts—legal turtles that were at least seven inches wide.

By the 1890s, Fannie Farmer was still suggesting that home cooks prepare and serve terrapin, the directions for which would make even an avid hunter and preparer of wild game slightly queasy. To begin, boil a live turtle for five minutes, remove the skin from the feet and tail by rubbing with a towel, then draw out the head with a skewer and rub off the skin. (One Philadelphia cook, Mrs. Rubicam, suggested that the terrapins be put alive in boiling water, "where they must remain until they are quite dead." Yes, I think that there would be unanimity of opinion on this point.) This is only the initial preparation. To cook it, Fannie suggests placing it in a kettle and covering it with salted, boiling water plus carrot, onion, and celery. The turtle is cooked until tender—the test was pressing the "feet-meat" between thumb and forefinger—estimated to take up to forty minutes. Then, Fannie instructs, remove the turtle from the water, cool, draw out the nails from the feet, cut the body under the shell close to the upper shell, and remove. Finally, empty the upper shell and remove the gallbladder, sandbags (a remnant from the Triassic period), and the thick, heavy part of the intestines.

Fannie was not offering anything new in the turtle department. Her basic recipe for Terrapin à la Baltimore was well known to any cook of the period and had been published in numerous cookbooks. The terrapin is boiled, the meat and selected entrails are removed and placed in a chafing dish, where it is finished with a roux, egg yolks, and Madeira. Wine, brandy, cream, and sherry were also used to finish the dish.

We finally hunted up some frozen turtle meat, but I wondered about the diamondback terrapins and thought that a fishing trip to the Chesapeake might be in order. I called the Maryland Department of Fisheries to determine when the season opened and what the legal limit was. A hasty return phone call from Diane Samuels made it clear that I had made a terrible gaffe, as if I were inquiring joyfully about the season for clubbing baby seals. After being informed that there was *no* season for the turtles of the Chesapeake—she used the words "strictly prohibited"—I asked how long the ban had been in effect. "Oh, one year," was the reply. Well, it's always the last sinner in church who protests the loudest.

To get a better sense of other preparation methods for turtle, I selected two recipes, one from Commander's Palace and the other from Arnaud's. They both used a stock—beef or veal—and roux for thickening. The Commander's Palace recipe reminded me of a traditional terrapin recipe in which the turtle meat is sautéed in butter, seasonings are added, and, in the case of this soup, the stock is then thrown in and simmered for half an hour. The roux is whisked in, the soup thickened, and lemon juice, chopped hard-boiled eggs, and parsley are added. A teaspoon of sherry for each soup plate is the final touch. Arnaud's recipe is much lighter and, I might add, stranger. In separate pots, three-quarters of a pound each of turtle meat and ground veal are cooked at length—forty-five minutes—and then the meats are chopped and set aside. Veal stock is heated with seasonings along with two halved lemons and, to finish, the meats are added, along with sherry, chopped eggs, and some roux to thicken. Delicious, you ask? The good news is that turtle meat does have a distinctive flavor: slightly gamey, rich, almost as if the meat had been hung for a few days to ripen. It is also varied. Some bits are much like white meat, and other pieces are quite dark, almost like duck. The bad news is that both of these recipes were disappointing: the Commander's Palace recipe was heavy because of the large amount of roux, and the Arnaud's soup wasn't much better: thin, watery, and overwhelmed by the acidity of the lemons.

Now that we were singularly unimpressed with the real thing, we moved on to the mock version, which required a calf's head. Two cups of brown stock are thickened with large amounts of butter and flour; the head stock is then added, with tomatoes, the face meat, and lemon juice. Madeira is used to finish. (A word about Fannie's penchant for massive amounts of flour and butter for thickening sauces: she thickens six cups of stock with one-quarter cup butter and a whopping half cup of flour. We found a similar attraction to pasty sauces when researching other Fannie recipes. I checked Escoffier to see if it was merely the prevailing method of her era or Fannie herself. In this case, Ms. Farmer is to take the blame. Escoffier's rule of thumb—his book was first published in 1902, just six years after Fannie's cookbook—was three ounces of roux to thicken four and a half cups of liquid so, in this recipe, one would use about half the amount of flour that Fannie calls for. Did she actually test these recipes?)

The problem, in retrospect, was the definition of "clean and wash calf's head." For Victorians, this may have been common knowledge, but for the modern cook, the directive is a bit vague. Almost nobody said, "Take out the goddamn brains, you idiot!" since this would be like saying, "Before logging on to Facebook, be sure to turn on your computer." Well, I was in need of remedial calf's-head preparation training, which I finally found in the pages of *The Complete Cook*, authored by J. M. Sanderson in 1846. In it, we finally achieve specificity: "Get the calf's head with the skin on [another query of mine], the fresher the better, *take out the brains* [italics mine] and wash the head several times in cold water. Let it soak in spring water for an hour." Thanks—now my computer is on! (As I continued my research, the refrain "take out the brains" kept appearing—a mantra of sorts to my abject stupidity. But it was noted that the brains must be removed "without breaking them," a warning that implied a memorable scene from *Young Frankenstein*.) The tongue, however, was to remain in the water during cooking and then "cut into mouthfuls, or rather make a side dish of the tongue and brains." Well, whatever. Then the head was cut into tiny pieces, five pounds of knuckle of veal were added, "and as much of beef," and then a stock was made by boiling for five hours. Other recipes, I noted, also added salt pork, ham hocks, trotters, anchovies, smoked tongue, or bacon.

As my research continued, mock turtle soup took on a life of its own, being an all-purpose starting point to which one added all sorts of culinary backflips and flourishes. My favorite was the following, which appeared in *Jennie June's Cookbook*. "Brain-balls or cakes are a very elegant addition, and are made by boiling the brains for ten minutes." A recipe from the 1877 *Buckeye Cookery* suggested that the brains be removed to a saucer. They are used later to make forcemeat balls (that would be brain balls to you), which started with a paste of hard-cooked egg yolks, to which the brains are added "to moisten."

As I started piling up recipes for mock turtle soup, other details came to light. The butcher was to remove the hair by scalding and scraping. The teeth and the eyes were also goners. One was also supposed to scrape "the interior of the nasal passage and the mouth." The tongue was supposed to be removed as soon as it was tender, and the skin "stripped off."

The brains were to soak separately in salted water and then the outer membrane was to be removed, "being careful not to break the substance of the brain." In other words, "Listen, you ham-handed oaf—handle the brains gently or they will turn into custard!" Then you boil the brains gently for ten to fifteen minutes, allow to cool wrapped in a wet cloth, and keep in a cool place. You bet I will! I'm not leaving gently simmered room-temperature brains right next to my 700-degree pizza oven!

Now I had some idea of what the original recipe was like, as well as being up to speed on what to do with a calf's head without feeling like some twenty-first-century culinary nincompoop. So we ordered another batch of calf's heads, cut into large pieces, the brains reserved, presumably for brain balls. They were delivered in a large cardboard box, somewhat bloody at the bottom, and wrapped with two bands of thick plastic strapping. The first dilemma was the eyes. Since they had not been removed, I was forced to perform an eye-ectomy. Remembering the final scene of *Kill Bill*, I thought that a well-performed plucking might do the trick, but sadly that was not to be. In case you have ever worried about your eyes inadvertently falling out or perhaps being popped into midair if you were given a sharp blow to the side of the head, you may now relax. Eyeballs—at least those of male calves—are sturdily attached. I next grabbed an oyster knife, but this was hopeless for attacking the thick, rubbery connective tissue that lined the socket and kept the eye firmly in place. Only ten minutes' sawing with a very sharp paring knife did the trick, and that was just for one eye. (Don't ask which one; the head was already in pieces.) We let the head rinse in cold salted water for an hour, and then we began cooking.

With plenty of water to cover, a ham hock, five pounds of beef round, a few vegetables such as carrot and celery, and the odd spice, including bay leaves, cloves, allspice berries, and peppercorns, we simmered the pot all through the day on the cookstove, strained it, and then let it sit overnight before we defatted the stock and moved on to make the soup. This was more like a traditional Escoffier stock, and it looked a whole lot better too. At least the liquid was thin, not goopy with melted brains, and it had a pleasant French stock odor. We reheated the stock after first cooking onions in butter, and then adding a julienne of carrots and turnips as garnish. The taste? Remarkably, the flavor reminded me of the turtle soups I had made a few weeks before, but substantially more delicious. How and why a calf's-head stock would produce a flavor similar to turtle meat simmered in water is one of the culinary questions that is probably best not asked.

Thinking that we were now done, I was rudely awakened to the fact that I had forgotten about the garnish, the aforementioned brain balls. (How many authors have had the pleasure of using the phrase "aforementioned brain balls"?) To see how the standard forcemeat balls (meat loaf mix, bread crumbs, salt pork, egg white, salt, and pepper) would turn out, we tested a recipe from the 1831 cookbook, *The Cook Not Mad*. (The title of this anonymously authored cookbook refers to a rational, rather than a helter-skelter, approach to the culinary arts.) The resulting balls were coarse, rough, and tough. They also lacked flavor and interest. So, thinking that we might as well go whole hog, as it were, and use the brains, we turned to a recipe from *The Good Housekeeper* (1839). We simmered the brains for ten minutes in a court bouillon (the Victorian cookbooks were correct on this point—brains must be handled *very* gently lest they dissolve like broken custard) and then mixed them with dried bread crumbs, nutmeg, thyme, two eggs, salt, and pepper. Since the brains were still a bit warm, they turned to mush when chopped, so we took the remaining cooked brains and let them cool under a damp towel to firm up the texture. (We thought that soaking in cold water might make them looser and more watery.) When shallow-fried in a skillet, the crisp exterior retained its texture even when floating in the soup and the inside was uniform and tender. Brain balls were a success! (The final adjustments included allowing the brains to rest in the refrigerator to really firm up, and frying the brain balls in 350-degree oil, not in butter.)

MOCK TURTLE SOUP

The "mock" in mock turtle soup is a calf's head, which is simmered to make a stock for the soup. Be sure to remove the brains first (and the eyeballs), and have the head cut into pieces. Preferably, this is done by your butcher, not you. (Eyeballs are firmly attached—they won't just pop out!) The recipe for Crispy Brain Balls can be found at www.fannies lastsupper.com.

STOCK

1 calf's head

1 cup white wine

1 smoked ham hock

5 pounds beef round, cut into 2-inch pieces

2 bay leaves

5 cloves

6 allspice berries

24 peppercorns

4 onions, chopped rough

4 carrots, chopped rough

4 ribs celery, chopped rough

1 head garlic, halved across the equator

8 sprigs parsley

4 sprigs thyme

1. Split calf's head in half, remove the brains (reserve for the Crispy Brain Balls recipe) and eyes (discard), cut out the tongue, and clean well, including the nostrils. Cut the head into pieces, soak for one hour in a 20-quart stock pot in slightly salted water.

2. Drain, cover with 6 quarts cold water, and add wine, ham hock, beef, bay leaves, cloves, allspice berries, peppercorns, onions, carrots, and celery,

garlic, and herbs. Simmer for 3 to 4 hours or until the calf's-head meat is tender, skimming foam as necessary.

3. Transfer bones, meat, and vegetables to colander set in large bowl. Pour broth through fine mesh strainer (adding any liquid given off through colander), let sit for 10 minutes, skim off fat, and use as needed (or cool quickly to room temperature and refrigerate until needed, removing fat from top before using). Yields about 4 quarts. Reserve the meat from the head along with the ham hock and tongue; shred into small pieces; this should yield about 3 cups. Discard pieces of beef round.

SOUP

4 tablespoons butter

2 large onions, diced medium (about 3 cups)

2 tablespoons sage, chopped fine

3 tablespoons flour

2 quarts calf's-head broth

¼ cup dry white wine

1 bay leaf

Salt and pepper

1 medium carrot, 2-inch julienned (about ¾ cup)

½ turnip, 2-inch julienned (about ¾ cup)

1 medium leek, white only, cut into 2-inch lengths, cut in half lengthwise, and julienned (about ¾ cups)

1 tablespoon sherry

¼ cup chopped chives

1. Heat butter in large heavy-bottomed saucepan over medium heat; when foaming subsides, add onions and sage and cook, stirring frequently, until softened, about 8 to 12 minutes. Add flour and cook for 1 to 2 minutes. Whisking constantly, gradually add broth and wine; bring to boil, skimming off any foam that forms on surface. Reduce heat to medium-low, add bay

leaf, partially cover, and simmer, stirring occasionally, until flavors meld, about 20 to 25 minutes. Strain through fine-mesh strainer. Season to taste.

2. In two batches, blanch julienned vegetables in 2 quarts seasoned stock, 1 to 2 minutes each. Shock in ice water. Reserve.

3. To serve: Reheat soup base and finish with sherry. Prepare Crispy Brain Balls. To each bowl add equal portions of room-temperature vegetables, 1 to 2 tablespoons pulled meat. Pour hot soup over garnish. Finish with 2 to 3 brain balls per serving and chopped chives.

Rissoles

❀

Fannie Farmer Sexes up Her Food:
Was She Really the "Mother of Level Measurements"?

The Boston Cooking School at 174 Tremont Street had four kitchens and a staff of ten teachers, the students being either young women planning to marry or older women running their own homes. There was also a big draw from cooks in private homes—there were often over one hundred career cooks each week in these demonstrations. You could take how-to-shop courses, including visits to Faneuil Hall, and there was a crash course—daily lessons for a month—for folks who wanted to get up to speed fast. For the most part, these classes were designed for a family of six with no more than one servant; the recipes were, at least in the beginner's classes, easy to follow. Farmer knew her audience and packaged courses to suit their needs.

A friend of ours, Bob Brooks, had a grandmother, Mary Brooks, who came to Boston from County Galway in 1910 and then took courses from Fannie herself at her new school. According to her diary, the tuition was $125, a huge sum for that time, but there were just eight students and these private classes were held one day per week in the mornings, from 9:00 A.M. to 12:30 P.M. Fannie also gave two weekly demonstration classes, one for homemakers and one for professional cooks, which attracted audiences of between one hundred and two hundred students. She often employed a screen around the teaching platform to conceal the fact that she was teaching from a seated position. According to the diary, "Fannie Farmer . . . was confined to a wheelchair for more than seven years," and died while Mary was still a student there. Mary always regretted that Miss

Farmer died before she learned to make candy. An odd requiem for the departed.

We know a great deal about Fannie's original set of courses, since they were printed in her *Original 1896 Boston Cooking-School Cook Book.* Farmer offered three sets of cooking courses as a promotional gambit from 9:00 A.M. to 12:30 P.M. for the plain cooking (evidently what Mary Brooks had signed up for), and at 2:00 P.M. on Friday for the second and third course of instruction.

She began with how to manage the fire (the school did have gas stoves as well, but one assumes that most of her students were still dealing with coal). The plain-cooking basics include the obvious choices: bread baking, mashed and boiled potatoes, soup stock, boiled eggs, beef stew, frying fish and potatoes, apple pie, roast beef, macaroni, and plain lobster. Other staples of nineteenth-century cooking were included as well: clarifying fat, bread pudding, Indian pudding, hoe cake, and wine jelly. Of more interest, although rather mundane, are the following items, since they paint a good picture of the everyday late Victorian menu: water bread (stale bread dipped in water and buttered), blanc mange (a very plain milk-based pudding made with Irish moss, a thickener made from seaweed), and snow pudding (gelatin, water, and sugar with beaten egg whites, usually served with a boiled custard). This penchant for puddings was clearly middle-class English in origin. Even today, on many menus in London restaurants, the dessert section is usually labeled "Puddings."

The "richer-cooking" courses covered an odd mix of items from French (Charlotte Russe and Lyonnaise Potatoes) to English (Stuffed Leg of Mutton) to classic American (Parker House Rolls, Chicken Croquettes, Cream Pies) to a few rather odd choices, including Curried Lobster and Apple Snowballs. Finally, the "fancy-cooking" classes were where the recipe names became longer, the food felt continental, and Fannie started to pull out all the stops. In the French classics department, one got Veal Birds, Potage à la Reine, Vol-au-Vent, Gâteau St. Honoré, Birds in Potato Cases, macaroons, floating island, Bombe Glacée, Sweetbreads with Peas, and

Gâteau de Princesse Louise. But, look out—you also got Pigs in Blankets and Cabinet Pudding (a molded mishmash of gelatin-thickened custard, lady fingers, and macaroons, served with a cream sauce and candied cherries). This seemed as if middle-class suburban Boston women were trying to be sophisticated without having spent any time eating the food on location, in Paris, for example. If that sounds a tad condescending, well, Boston was still rather provincial in 1896, and Fannie's cooking classes reflected that limitation.

Fannie also understood that home cooks wanted impressive food, restaurant food, continental food—anything that she could dress up, sex up, rename, or make tantalizing. She knew that the larger audience were middle-class and upper-middle class women who had sufficient time and income to make their dinner table a place of distant locales, of experimentation, of the new and progressive. This meant puff paste, lobster Newburg, Baked Alaska, and any recipe with the word *Delmonico* or *Reine* in it, rather than Boston baked beans and gingerbread. It is quite telling, however, that Fannie could teach the basics of making a cake at one moment while in the next she might be explaining the finer points of preparing charlotte russe. If anyone needs confirmation of America as the ultimate melting pot or Fannie's keen ability to give her students whatever the hell they would pay for, this was it.

When Fannie got too cute with her food, she ran into culinary trouble. Butterfly Tea was a puff paste cookie in the shape of a butterfly and decorated with chopped nuts, glaceed cherries, angelica, cinnamon, and sugar. Russian Eggs were boiled, peeled, set into puff paste cases, and then covered with a creamed mushroom sauce. A Valentine's Day menu was pink and white: Lover's Sandwiches (salmon) and the Heart's-Ache Pudding, both in the shape of hearts, with an addition of cream cheese-and-olive-stuffed walnut halves for Cupid's Deceits. For St. Patrick's Day, she tied popcorn balls with green ribbons, upon which were glued the words "St. Patrick" in letters made of macaroni dyed sauterne green. She was, in some way, a budding Martha Stewart, but lacking the benefit of good taste and sophistication. As Laura Shapiro aptly stated in *Perfection Salad,* this was "socially ambitious cookery." Fannie had put "high-class food within the reach of ordinary housekeepers and made up-to-date novelties accessible as well—all in the context of progress."

This was all going on at the same time that Auguste Escoffier was doing the exact opposite, trimming back the excess frivolity of classic French cooking to focus on the foundations of a higher, more refined culinary experience; everything on the plate must serve the purpose of good taste and good sense without elaborate garnishes and unnecessary complexity. Just for a moment, consider the level of culinary training the best chefs acquired in France, compared to the handful of years Fannie spent as a student at the Boston Cooking School. Escoffier had served a six-year apprenticeship starting at age twelve at his uncle's restaurant in Nice and then worked five years at Le Petit Moulin in Paris. After a stint in the army, he returned to Le Petit Moulin, and then was asked by César Ritz to become chef at the Grand Hotel in Monte Carlo, a partnership that was to become instrumental in the development of his career. They took over the Savoy Hotel in London in 1889, opened a hotel in the Place Vendôme in Paris in 1896, and then the Carlton Hotel in London in 1896. There was simply no comparison between the culinary worlds of the United States and France in the 1890s. Fannie Farmer could not have held a candle to Auguste Escoffier.

But the news is not all bad; some of her culinary advice, information, and recipes seem more than reasonable. Fannie stated that a modest 68 degrees Fahrenheit was the proper temperature for bread fermentation. Bone marrow was often used for browning meat, especially when making soups. Beef was supposed to be best when it was from a steer that was four or five years old. (Today's beef is from animals no more than two years old.) The Victorians let it ripen for two to three weeks in the winter for best flavor. Onion juice was a common flavoring ingredient, one that we often use today. Poultry was roasted with a flour coating, which created a nice crust and helped to keep in the juices. (We tested this recipe, and it actually worked; see page 141.) Several vegetables in a salad ought to be marinated before serving. (This is something that we thought we had discovered in our test kitchen—demonstrating, once again, that there is little that is new in the culinary world.) There were five different types of batters used for frying—Fannie mistakenly thought fried foods were healthy. (Frying was popular, since it could be done on a stovetop without worrying about managing the heat of an oven.) Dissolved gelatin was added to mayonnaise to make it set up when it was used for decorative purposes. All in all, she was a pretty smart cook when it came to the basics, although prone to tarting up the fancier dishes without a deep understanding of the underlying subtlety and technique of the original.

The one claim that is repeated endlessly in books about Fannie Farmer is that she was the "mother of level measurements," a label that was earned through her devotion to precision. This is the typical one-note tagline that historians love to bandy about. Here is a typical quote: "Her particular innovation was the refinement known as level measurements, which she promoted forcefully with every recipe she published. Previously even the strictest use of measuring implements retained the old notions of a 'rounded' spoonful and a 'heaping' cupful. . . . To Fannie Farmer, it seemed simpler and more rational to dispense with the imagery entirely and call a tablespoonful a level tablespoon, using a knife to level the surface after the spoon had been filled."

Reportedly, the great turning point in Fannie's cooking career, akin to Newton watching a falling apple, was when she was asked by Maggie Murphy, her cook, to define "butter the size of an egg" as well as "a pinch of salt," leading to the revelation that precise measurement was the key to culinary perfection. Perhaps if we started with Mary Lincoln's cookbook, first published in 1883, and then referred to Fannie's work of 1896, we might finally get to the bottom of this claim.

We need to keep in mind that in Mary Lincoln's time, the cookware industry was just starting to provide standardized measuring spoons and cups for general home use, the silver teaspoons and tablespoons sold at retail being the accepted units of measure. By 1896, when her cookbook was published, Fannie refers to "tin measuring-cups, divided in quarters or thirds, holding one half-pint, and table spoons of regulation sizes—which may be bought at any store where kitchen furnishings are sold." So, Fannie had the benefit of a cookware industry that had adopted and advertised more precise, standardized measuring cups and spoons. In a May 1887 edition of *Table Talk* magazine, Sarah Tyson Rorer comments: "A small tin kitchen cup has recently made its appearance in our market. They are sold in pairs at various prices; one of the pair is divided into quarters and the other into thirds." In 1894, Mrs. Rorer included measuring spoons and measuring cups in a list of essential kitchen furnishings. So Fannie showed up at just the right time, whereas Mary Lincoln, writing in 1883, was a bit ahead of the cookware industry.

A close examination of *Mrs. Lincoln's Boston Cook Book* (I refer to my 1890 edition; the first edition was 1883) reveals a very different story than the one painted by historians. The first observation is that late-nineteenth-century cookbooks often discussed methods or ingredients that were never actually used in the recipes. This is because the world of home cooking was changing so rapidly that the authors felt they had to cover all their bases, from old-fashioned to modern. So, for starters, Mary Lincoln defines an even teaspoonful the same way Fannie did. She did, it is true, include discussions about heaping teaspoons and butter the size of an egg, but she almost never used those measurements in any of her recipes. Her standard units of measurement, the ones found in 99 percent of her recipes, were a "teaspoonful" and a "tablespoonful," defined as follows: "Dip into the sifted material, and take up a heaping spoonful, shake it slightly until it is just rounded over, or convex in the same proportion as the spoon is round." Her other definitions for measurements were also precise. She noted that "most cups are smaller at the bottom," so her rather ingenious method was to fill one cup full of water and then to pour out enough liquid into another, empty cup so that both stood at the same level. That was a half cup. Clearly, she was doing the best anyone could with the tools available to most home cooks. She was also precise when it came to a "scant cupful," which she defined as "within a quarter of an inch of the top." Not bad, considering that even modern recipes refer to a "pinch" or a "scant" half cup.

Fannie, to be fair, did remove everything but level measures from her cookbook. She noted in italics, *"A tablespoonful is measured level. A teaspoon is measured level."* This is hardly a watershed moment in home cooking, nor is it justification for her moniker, the "mother level of measurements." This was evolution, not revolution, and Lincoln's rounded teaspoonfuls were simple enough to use. She was still stuck, as was Mary Lincoln, with measuring spoons that did not have half, quarter, or eighth sizes, so she offered the same solution that Lincoln had used—dividing a tablespoon in half lengthwise for a half, divided once again crosswise for a quarter, and the "quarters crosswise for eighths." (Cooks in the nineteenth century did not have liquid versus dry measuring cups either. Fannie points out that to measure liquids, "a cupful of liquid is all the cup will hold.")

Perhaps the most astute comment about the two cookbooks is Laura Shapiro's observation that "Fannie Farmer did help herself, generously and without acknowledgment, to Mrs. Lincoln's work; but she stamped the material with her own personality, or perhaps it is more accurate to say that she drained it carefully of Mrs. Lincoln's."

As for introducing modern cookery, a fresh wind had already been blowing, and its name was Home Economics. At the 1896 Boston Food Fair, Dr. William T. Harris, the U.S. commissioner of education, proposed elevating the home arts, mostly cooking, into a science—one that could be studied, analyzed, perfected, recorded, presented, and taught. So Fannie was part and parcel of a national movement, with less than stellar culinary skills, but a keen sense of marketing, a forceful personality, and a sharp eye for making money and giving the public what it wanted.

❋

FEBRUARY 2009. GIVEN THE CENTRAL ROLE OF THE COOK IN the Victorian household and the rather primitive conditions under which she worked, I quickly became intrigued with the details of her life, starting with the details of getting dressed in the early morning. One historical expert, Tames Alan, was particularly useful in describing the lives of household servants, since she regularly provides "living history" lectures on this period and others, dressed in period costume.

In a large private household, the kitchen maid was always the first to rise, cleaning the stove, firing it, scrubbing the floor, making tea, and then bringing a cup to the cook, who might request help in getting dressed. The first article of clothing donned in the morning was a set of split drawers followed by a camisole: cotton in the summer, wool in the winter. The lady of the household, however, wore a one-piece version that was made of silk or extremely fine cotton, so thin that it could pass through her wedding ring, much like a handkerchief. This distinction in the quality of clothing between employer and cook was continued within the household hierarchy: kitchen and housemaids wore even coarser fabrics than the cook. The same inequality was also true between households of different social status: a wealthy family provided better garments for its cook than did one of merely middle-class stature.

Next were the wool stockings, held up by ribbons or, toward the end of the nineteenth century, elasticized garters. The cook would then slip on a petticoat: red flannel in the winter, cotton in the summer. The corset was next, loosely laced and ending above the hips so that the cook would bend easily while working. (Her mistress wore a tightly laced corset to appear as narrow-waisted as possible; a thin cook was never a good sign. Corsets also provided bust support since brassieres were not invented until the 1920s.) The stays were made of a springlike steel, rather than whalebone, another contribution of the Industrial Revolution. One inevitably wonders how one tightened a corset when dressing alone. One clever solution was to install a metal ring on the wall of a servant's bedroom. The wearer would tie the corset strings to the ring and simply walk away to tighten it.

A cook was likely to wear a corset made of coarse material and therefore a sleeveless corset cover was often slipped on next; this protected the petticoat or dress that rubbed up against it from chafing and wear. The dress was the final piece of clothing; it would still have had a high neckline in the 1890s—no low scoop—and long sleeves that had to be pushed up for cooking. Fabric colors were solid and muted: a light blue or gray, perhaps. The final touches were sensible shoes, perhaps boots, hair pushed into a mobcap or cook's cap, and a spotless apron. (Women almost never cut their hair and therefore a cap was necessary. In fact, a short-haired cook applying for a job would be regarded with suspicion. A woman had her hair cut for just two reasons: to remove lice or to sell hair for money.) According to a 1904 *House Beautiful* article, outfits were often changed midafternoon to provide a more formal appearance for the evening.

As the century progressed, however, social equality became the cry of the working class and so the workmen, maids, and cooks often chose clothing that mimicked that of their employers. *Harper's Bazaar* noted this trend in 1867, pointing out that crinoline and a flowing train of silk have no place next to a red hot stove or dirty kitchen floor. Instead, they promoted looser, more practical clothing, preferring the flowing blouse of the French workman to the tight-fitting coats and pants often worn by the lower classes in imitation of their masters. This smacked of putting the working class in their place, however, as in this printed admonition: "Let her take the advice of the tasteful, who will tell her that the rude freshness of natural beauty appears to the greatest advantage in a plain setting."

The pay was modest—a few hundred dollars per year—although cooks in wealthy households were at the high end of the scale and were usually treated well, since a good cook was hard to come by: poaching within one's social circle was not uncommon. (Cooks had their own menu books—collections of personal recipes—and the mistress of the household would choose among them to create menus.) Life with a middle-class family, however, was often a nightmare; the mistress of the house often had little experience with managing servants, so they were often poorly treated and paid. To get by, then, the cook had her own bag of tricks. When interviewing for employment, she would ask if she could choose the tradesmen. This was crucial, since she often asked purveyors to mark up their prices, paying her the difference. She would also inquire as to the dispensation of the pan drippings and candle ends, both of which could be sold for ready money. On the other hand, servants, including cooks, had their quarterly pay docked if they broke a plate or burned the pudding. In some cases, the servant owed the household money at payday.

As for washing, undergarments, including petticoats, would be laundered either commercially or in-house, but dresses would only be spot-cleaned, since they were usually made of finer, more expensive material and could not withstand constant soap and water. One could purchase "double-motion" hand-cranked washing machines, fashioned from galvanized iron and white cedar tubs. Also for sale were endless designs for racks to dry clothes outside (including one model that attached to a window frame), wash benches, ironing tables, ironing boards, and bosom boards, designed specifically for ironing shirts.

By the early 1900s, however, a private home was often no longer staffed by numerous household servants but reduced to employing just one all-purpose maidservant. In the 1904 *The Expert Maid-Servant*, the mistress of the household is cautioned that cooking would be just one of the maidservant's many duties and therefore one had to inquire whether the potential employee understood plain cooking and could follow a simple recipe. "More elaborate accomplishments can rarely be looked for in a maid-of-all-work." By 1920, after the devastation of the First World War and the influenza epidemic, and the increased availability of factory and other nondomestic jobs, the era of the well-staffed Victorian household was at an end both here and in England.

❀

THE THIRD COURSE WAS TO BE RISSOLES, SMALL FRIED AND filled pastries; this presented the problem of making and rolling out thin sheets of puff pastry. I had never made puff pastry from scratch using the old-fashioned French method, but I was about to get an education.

Rissoles and Boston were perfectly suited for each other, since the original notion was frugality, a kitchen where every scrap was saved, even the water used to boil vegetables. By Fannie Farmer's era, the de facto rissole was a small puff pastry turnover filled with cooked meat, moistened with a classic French white sauce, and then deep-fried and served on a folded napkin. The term comes from Latin, *pasta russeola* (later translated as *ruissole* in Old French; *rissoler* means "to brown" in modern French as well), which, roughly translated, means "reddish paste." The fillings were made from just about anything, including peacocks (pheasant, rabbit, and chicken were also offered in descending order of desirability), as one recipe from Apicius, the famous Roman gastronome, attests. Over the centuries, rissoles (sometimes called "rissables" as well) have also been made from fish, lobster, veal, beef, game, tongue, lamb, sweetened fruit, and vegetables.

The puff pastry of Fannie's day is, of course, a French invention and her nod to being continental, but this sort of rissole was nothing new, a similar recipe having already been offered in *The White House Cookbook* by Fanny Lemira Gillette. Earlier nineteenth-century versions, however, were nothing more than chopped meat, bound with eggs and bread, then fried in a pan with perhaps a simple bread crumb coating. Over time, the bread crumb variety became known as croquettes.

Rissoles could be dainty, made from puff pastry cut into two-inch squares, or gargantuan, the pastry cut to the size of a dinner plate and folded over a mound of minced meat, fried, and served with a garnish of fried parsley. The fillings could be fashioned from chicken or other poultry, lobster, raw oysters, boiled clams, Indian corn, leftover veal, ham, tongue, lamb, sweet stewed fruit, or mincemeat. Many cooks used lemon zest as a seasoning as well as spices such as cayenne, mace, and nutmeg. Like hash, rissoles were more of an idea than a recipe, one that made good use of whatever happened to be on hand.

Fannie's recipe did have one unusual aspect. She writes, "Roll in gelatine, fry in deep fat, and drain. Granulated gelatine cannot be used." I had never heard of using gelatin as a coating for fried foods, but was game to try it. We used the chicken-and-ham combination that she offered as a filling choice, then moistened it with different amounts of béchamel, the "thick white sauce" that she referred to in the recipe. For the gelatin coating, we purchased agar-agar (a dried, tasteless seaweed that was also used in Fannie's time), rehydrated it, cooled it to room temperature, coated the rissoles, and then fried them up, finding that 360 degrees was just right. To our surprise, the agar-agar coating made the surface blister, and it yielded an extraordinarily crisp coating. This was one of those rare moments when a technique from the foggy culinary past comes back as a true revelation. The filling, however, was bland and creamy, and did not stand up to the wonderful puff pastry on the outside. The moisture in the filling also made it difficult to cook the puff pastry all the way through.

A flavorful chicken-duxelles mixture seemed like a better option. In addition, we thought that cutting out two-inch circles of puff pastry, filling them, and then laying a second circle on top was a better approach than cutting out three-inch circles and folding them over. Our theory was that the folded edge was too thick, making it difficult to cook the pastry all the way through. We also wanted to test using sheet gelatin in place of the agar-agar; we were curious whether frozen rissoles were better than refrigerated in terms of frying and whether a two-step process, similar to the way french fries are cooked, made any sense.

The chicken-duxelles mixture was a winner since it held less moisture and had more flavor, although we thought we could reduce the amount of fat slightly. Adding more chicken also made for a drier, and therefore better, filling. We tried a very thin sheet of puff pastry, just a sixteenth of an inch thick (older recipes speak about "the thickness of a penny"), and this worked a bit better, but the pastry was still not cooking through properly. The sheet gelatin worked pretty much the same as the agar-agar, although both will thicken even at room temperature. Since it is easier to coat rissoles with a liquid than a solid, we used sheet gelatin in a lower concentration.

Chilled rissoles are much better than frozen for frying; the latter sank to the bottom of the pot and one side never cooked properly. The notion of pressing together the circles of puff pastry was indeed better than the "foldover" method, since the folded edge in Fannie's recipe never cooks through properly. A two-frying method was not necessary.

One other trick: we found that constantly basting the rissoles with the hot oil as they fried made a huge difference—they puffed up immediately and seemed to cook through better. This meant that one could fry only two at a time, but the results were worth it.

As for the remarkable effect of the gelatin, edible coatings were nothing new when applied to fried foods, egg whites being a prime example. The theory is that proteins tend to inhibit oil absorption. The use of gelatin, however, was not part of the culinary repertoire until just before Fannie's era; the first published example that we were able to find was in 1869. (In addition, gelatin had been used as a preservative. Meat was dipped into hot gelatin, allowed to dry, and then dipped again.) Even today, patents from the 1980s include gelatin used in formulas for frozen pastries. This method promotes a "crisp, unsoggy texture and contributes to mouthfeel." In our testing, however, the big difference was an immediate blistering effect, the puff pastry exploding like a hooked blowfish, making the rissoles incredibly light and crispy. The result was visually spectacular and was not primarily an issue of absorbing too much oil.

MASTER RECIPE FOR RISSOLES

Yes, this recipe is a lot of work and, yes, you do have to roll out the pastry until it is a mere ¹⁄₁₆ inch thick. Despite these hurdles, this is a fascinating recipe. The little dumplings fry up quickly with a crackly, blistered coating because of the hot oil and gelatin coating—all in all, a spectacular first course. If you want to cheat, just purchase a good-quality frozen puff pastry and the recipe will come out just fine: simply roll it out to a thickness of ¹⁄₁₆ inch and then into 2-inch squares. Proceed with step 3. Our recipe for Homemade Puff Pastry can be found at www.fannieslastsupper.com. In terms of commercial puff, we prefer Dufour Classic Puff Pastry, but Pepperidge Farm also works well.

> 2½ sheets gelatin
> Cool water (for soaking sheets)
> 1 cup water (for simmering)
> 1 package frozen puff pastry sheets (or use ⅓ of the Homemade Puff Pastry recipe)
> 1 recipe filling (see page 68)
> 2 to 3 quarts frying oil

1. Cover gelatin sheets with cool water to soften, about 5 minutes. Remove, squeeze or drip dry, and add to 1 cup simmering water to dissolve, about 20 seconds. Remove from heat, transfer to small bowl, and let cool to room temperature.

2. Roll puff pastry into a rectangle about ½ inch thick, being careful not to press dough too hard with rolling pin. Cut in half, parallel to the short side. Working one at a time, roll each half gently, flipping and rotating piece until ¹⁄₁₆ inch thick. Square off edges of each half with a sharp knife; cut into 2-inch squares, about 18 per sheet. Keep puff pastry refrigerated as much as possible during this process to keep the butter firm.

3. Working with three rissoles at a time, add 1 teaspoon of either the Chicken Liver filling or Duxelle and Chicken filling (recipes at www.fannies lastsupper.com) or ½ teaspoon of Onion-Cherry Chutney Filling plus 1 pea-sized piece of blue cheese (see recipe on page 68) in center of each cut-out puff. Brush edges lightly with water or gelatin mixture. Top with second piece of puff, pressing air out before completely sealed; press edges to seal. *It is important that puff pastry is chilled, and handled as little as possible while assembling; if dough warms up too much, it won't puff properly when fried.* Repeat with remaining puff and filling. Cover tightly with plastic wrap. Refrigerate.

4. When ready to fry, heat oil to 375 degrees. Check each rissole to make sure that the seal is secure, pinching gently as necessary. Working two at a time, brush with room-temperature gelatin. *Gelatin texture should be the consistency of thin egg whites. If it is too firm, microwave for 2 seconds at a time, until correct consistency.* Fry two to three at a time, basting each constantly with hot oil until the rissoles turn light golden brown and puff and blister, about 45 to 60 seconds. Flip until cooked through, about 30 to 45 seconds. Remove with slotted spoon, transfer to paper-towel-lined baking sheet and then to wire rack placed in rimmed baking sheet; hold in warm oven while frying remaining rissoles. Season rissoles with salt. Serve.

For the Chicken Liver Filling and the Duxelle and Chicken Filling, go to www.fannieslastsupper.com.

ONION-CHERRY CHUTNEY FILLING
WITH BLUE CHEESE

Of the three, this is my favorite filling, since the balance of sweet and pungent marries well with the blue cheese. It knocks your socks off when served in a thin, crisp, hot shell of fried puff.

2 teaspoons vegetable oil

1 large onion, diced medium, about 1½ cups

¼ teaspoon kosher salt

⅛ teaspoon fresh ground black pepper

2 teaspoons sugar

2 tablespoons white wine vinegar

¼ teaspoon minced fresh thyme

½ cup dried cherries

½ ounce blue cheese, broken into 12 small pieces the size of peas

1. Heat oil in medium saucepan over medium heat until it begins to shimmer; sauté onion until soft, about 3 to 4 minutes. Add salt, pepper, and sugar and cook until bottom of pot begins to brown, about 6 to 8 minutes, then deglaze with vinegar and cook until pan is dry. Add thyme and cherries and cook until softened and fragrant, about 2 minutes. Remove pan from heat. Transfer mixture to a plate. Refrigerate.

2. Once onion mixture is chilled through, finely chop. Check for seasoning. Refrigerate until ready to use.

Lobster à l'Américaine

Eating out in Boston and
Why the Tavern Club Owned a Bear

Boston has never been, until recent years, a restaurant town. The high and mighty frequented private clubs when they ate out, with the bulk of the dining occurring at home. The 1889 edition of *King's Hand-Book of Boston* noted that the number of restaurants and cafés in Boston numbered "nearly 500" at the time, about the same quantity as in 1800. But commented King, "excepting those connected with hotels, there are not many worthy of particular mention." One might have dined well at the Parker House Café, or at Frost and Dearborn's, which opened in 1873.

Boston might not have been in the same league as New York in terms of fine dining, but we did have a lot of coffeehouses. Their appeal was less the quality of the coffee than the other, stronger libations. Apparently, the drinking vessels in the coffeehouses "were not especially adapted to that beverage." But long before coffeehouses, there were taverns in the English tradition; the first tavern in Boston was opened in 1634 by Samuel Cole on Merchants Row.

Chophouses were also popular, for instance, the Coolidge Café, opposite the Paul Revere House. The steaks and chops were cooked over a hot coke fire on "silver grills" that were grooved to drain the fat away from the fire. (Coke was coal that was heated in the absence of oxygen, making it both purer and able to produce higher temperatures. Coke was used primarily in steelmaking.) Locke-Ober, at 3 Winter Place, originally named the Winter Palace tavern, was a merger of Frank Locke's wine bar (established

1892) and Louis Ober's French restaurant (established 1868). There were many French dining establishments as well, usually named after their proprietors, and heartier fare was served around the markets for the men and women who worked there. By the late 1800s, there was a group of little French restaurants in Van Rensselaer Alley (later called Majestic Alley), next to the Majestic and Colonial theaters.

There were a number of oyster houses, as well as establishments that sold pies in Pie Alley. The selling of small pies was a common practice in Boston—one of these establishments was Henry's Hole in the Wall, which sold small meat pies called "cat pies" for 10 cents. Another favorite food of the time was—yes, it's true—baked beans served with coffee for a modest 6 cents.

Club life was, and still is, an important part of the social and culinary scene, and no club in Boston has more history than the Tavern Club, which had, albeit briefly, a live bear cub as its mascot. Boston's private clubs were also a key part of the cuisine of the city, many boasting French chefs and long menus. It all started with the Old Colony Club in Plymouth, which met for the first time on December 22, 1769, whereupon the members consumed a feast of Indian whortleberry pudding, succotash, clams, oysters, codfish, venison, sea fowl and eels, apple pie, cranberry tarts, and cheese made in the colony. Perhaps the most prestigious establishment was the Saturday Club, founded in 1855; its members included James Russell Lowell, Ralph Waldo Emerson, Henry Wadsworth Longfellow, Oliver Wendell Holmes, and Nathaniel Hawthorne, among others. Another early club was the Porcellian Club, founded by Joseph McKean, later a Congregational clergyman, who once smuggled a roast pig into his rooms at Harvard. The most powerful club in Boston is still the Somerset Club, located on Beacon Street about halfway up the Common.

Women's clubs flourished in the latter part of the century, including the Mayflower Club (named for the flower, not the ship), which was founded in 1893, and the Chilton Club, founded in 1910. Dining at the club was, for many, much more socially acceptable than eating at a public restaurant, and for a long time, much club food was actually superior to the fare at most Boston restaurants. The Somerset Club, in particular, was known for its variety of choices. The chef had fifty-nine ways of preparing tournedos, sixty-seven chicken dishes, and eleven ways of cooking calf's brains. However, the clear winner was the egg category—they offered one hundred different egg dishes. Club menus in the Victorian period often offered a dozen different courses.

The true eccentricity of the Boston character is revealed through club life. The Tavern Club bear, who was housed for a few weeks at the club before being sold back to a vaudeville show, was walked by a waiter who was forced to dress in a highly picturesque "Spanish costume for the special purpose of leading the bear on a chain into the Common and exercising him there." Another club, the Wharf Rats, uses the reproductive member of a whale as a gavel. When the original gavel was consumed in a fire and no longer usable, a visiting admiral learned of their loss and procured a substitute through naval connections in Japan. Clubs were famous for their entertainments, and one of the strangest was a late-nineteenth-century event entitled "Darkest Africa." Since Mr. Stanley (as in "Doctor Livingstone, I presume?") had declined the club's invitation to speak, a member assumed the role of the explorer. A contemporary review commented, "Curtis Guild, Jr., the lecturer, came forth as a black Stanley in white duck and then gravely took off all his clothes and delivered his lecture as a savage, in black tights with a yellow codpiece and a necklace of leaves." Finally, the Somerset Club refused to accept the bequest of Admiral Byrd's stuffed penguin, "mainly on the grounds that it looked too much like some of the members."

Understanding the essence of club life in Boston is understanding the difference between life within the walls of the club and everything else. To a true Bostonian, hell can freeze over, Rome can burn, and technology can run amok all it likes, but here in Boston, nothing changes. A Cambridge don who had invented an ingenious mathematical theorem once said, "The best thing about [the theorem] is that no one can make any use of it for anything . . . this uselessness is the highest kind of use. It is kindling and feeding the ideal spark without which life is not worth living."

This notion of uselessness, of inquiry with no higher purpose, of pursuit for the sake of pursuit, is a Victorian ideal, one that was soon to be crushed under the boot heel of science, practicality, and the pursuit of the common good—all ideals carried under the banner of Fannie Farmer and many other such modernists.

MARCH 2009. IT WAS TIME TO FIND OUT IF FANNIE KNEW HER way around French cooking, so we chose lobster à l'Américaine, a dish that requires subtlety, stock-making skills, and a delicate balance in flavors. How did Fannie do? Fannie's recipe was certainly competent, if a bit ham-handed, with a heavy, floury sauce. We had to look to Escoffier, Julia Child, Jasper White, and, finally, Gordon Ramsay to come up with a recipe that was sophisticated, rich, and capable of being served to a dozen guests in a demanding time frame. Fannie might have been a marketing genius, but her command of French cuisine was lacking.

This was also a dish for which my status as sous-chef and kitchen assistant was made painfully apparent. Erin, my test kitchen director and a longtime friend, was heading up the recipe development. Erin appears solid and practical, which is ideal for long, hot days spent in a Victorian kitchen, yet she is also blessed with the face of a classic beauty, the fiercely handsome qualities of a Hepburn married to the energetic bright-eyed humor of a Mickey Rooney, all framed by acres of long, curly black hair. She cons you with a sweet, gentle smile, but woe to the cook who disappoints, who falls short of the finish line. In her kitchen, excellence and energy are not suggestions; they are requirements. So, over a two-year period, we spent days and weeks at the stove getting to know each other's culinary skills and personality quirks. The routine never changed. The day started with cranking up the massive cast-iron cookstove before dawn, a waffle breakfast, a review of the schedule (much like a football coach prepping his team for the big game), and then a headlong rush into a full day of boiling calf's heads, poaching brains, roasting venison, or baking cakes. Visitors or my kids would look in occasionally, hoping for a slice of cake or spoonful of jelly, but they were most often offered a bite of fried brain ball, a chewy slice of rare goose breast, a small bowl of ripe-tasting turtle soup, or a slurp of calf's-head stock. To make up for the lack of desirable tidbits, we soon decided to mix up a fresh batch of rum punch around midafternoon; this ameliorated the heat of the stove and made us more popular with adult kitchen visitors.

But it was clear from these cooking sessions that Erin was the boss. She had made her bones as a real sous-chef at Hamersley's Bistro in Boston. Yes, I actually cooked all the recipes over the two years that we worked on this project, but she took the lead, and I was often left to mince the carrots, make the stock, or lard the venison. My inferior culinary skills became painfully apparent when the time came to dispatch live lobsters. She instructed me that the best way to kill a lobster was to hold it from the top at a 45-degree angle, the head touching the cutting surface. Then, using a large, very sharp knife, whack down hard and cut off its face.

Cut off its face? I immediately suspected a prank and suggested that she show me. She did, and it seemed to work, so I grabbed a lobster and brought the ten-inch chef's knife hurtling down. Unfortunately for this, the world's unluckiest lobster, my knife only got halfway through the face, which caused the poor beast to writhe in agony, the tail closing and opening convulsively, the claws reaching out instinctively for something to attack. This caused me to lose my grip, drop the lobster, and start all over again.

Sweating, nervous, and a bit in shock, I finally did the dirty deed and left the lobster on the cutting board in its own death juices, the legs rowing back and forth, the tail still flapping in postmortem spasms. For the next one, I reverted to my tried and true method, severing the spinal cord behind the head with a sharp thrust of the knife. (I still think that I was had. Erin experienced her own moment of lobster fear late one night while testing the recipe alone. The tails had been reserved and refrigerated while she was making the stock. She removed the tails, salted them, and then, incredibly, the meat started to pulsate, almost dancing in the shell. There is something very odd about lobster.)

ALTHOUGH FANNIE WAS TRYING TO CREATE A VERY SPECIAL REC-ipe, the underlying ingredient, lobster, was relatively inexpensive at the time—the 1800s witnessed huge catches, including 350,000 pounds sold in just one day—and was not yet considered a gourmet food. In May 1895, lobsters from Nova Scotia were plentiful, and they sold for just $5 per crate of 140 pounds. When they became scarce later in the year, they sold for $18 per crate. These, of course, were wholesale prices, the actual retail price varying from a bit less than 15 cents per pound up to 25 cents or so. This compares as follows to other seafood: halibut, 15 cents; scallops, 35 cents per quart; fresh Oregon salmon, 35 to 50 cents. All in all, lobster was on the low end of the price scale. This did not mean, however, that the industry was unregulated. There were fines of $5 per lobster under 10½ inches in length and $25 for every "seed" lobster found onboard. It was also common for rogue fishermen to break off lobster tails and sell them illegally to seaside resorts.

Lobster preparation was not much of an art, at least before Fannie's time; by 1890, canned lobster was also an option. A quick glance at Mrs. Lincoln's cookbook tells the story. The basic cooking method was twenty minutes in boiling water, with a few variations using the cooked meat: Plain lobster is removed from the shell, arranged on a plate, and served with salt, pepper, vinegar, and oil, or melted butter. Stewed lobster is placed into a stewpan with a little milk or cream. Creamed lobster is made with one pint of lobster meat to one pint of béchamel. Curried lobster is simply lobster meat heated in a curry-flavored béchamel. Scalloped lobster is creamed lobster placed back into the shells, covered with cracker crumbs, and then baked until the crumbs are brown (Lincoln suggests placing two tails together, ends out, to imitate a canoe, and then laying the small claws over the side to represent oars). And deviled lobster is prepared with the addition of salt, pepper, and cayenne plus chopped parsley, onion juice, mustard, and Worcestershire sauce. One could also find lobster soup, chowder, cutlets, croquettes, and salad as well.

By 1896, Fannie included all of Mrs. Lincoln's preparations but offered a few more adventurous recipes, including lobster à l'Américaine, which was cooked in a large omelet pan. She sprinkled the split lobster with a bit of onion and cayenne and cooked it for five minutes. Then she added a half cup of tomato sauce and cooked it for three minutes; then she added two tablespoons of sherry, covered the pan, and placed it in an oven for seven minutes. Then she made a sauce of the liver using wine, tomato sauce, and melted butter. The lobster was served with the plain sauce. For our Victorian dinner, this seemed like a good place to start.

So how was Fannie's lobster à l'Américaine? The cooked tomato sauce was heavily thickened with a roux, but loosened up a bit with the addition of the sherry. The lobster was cooked perfectly, and the flavors were rich (browning the butter and then the roux added a nuttiness to the sauce). The sauce was full-bodied but borderline grainy, and too thick and muddy for modern tastes. So, nice idea, but the recipe needed a lighter, more sophisticated approach.

The obvious next step was Escoffier, since his *Guide Culinaire* was published about the same time, in 1902. Here we find quite a different recipe, lighter and more in keeping with the main ingredient. He sprinkled the lobster tails with shallot, garlic, white wine, fish fumet, a small glassful of burnt brandy, one tablespoon of melted meat glaze, three small fresh pressed tomatoes, a pinch of chopped parsley, and a very "little bit" of cayenne, covered it, and cooked it in the oven for eighteen to twenty minutes. The lobster was removed, the sauce reduced, and then reserved bits were chopped and added along with butter. The sauce was strained, reheated, a bit more butter added, and then served over the lobster.

This seemed a tad more promising, so we looked to Julia Child to give us a more modern version of this recipe, as well as to the 1995 edition of *The Joy of Cooking*, which had a more streamlined version. These versions were much better, although the sauce was still a bit grainy and the lobster overcooked. We then turned to a colleague, Jasper White, who is a well-known Boston chef and author of *Lobster at Home* (1998), since he based his recipe on a homemade lobster stock made from roasted shells. The dish was vastly improved, but we still had a big problem—and this goes back to a basic rule of lobster cookery, well known a century ago. Once a lobster is killed, the meat deteriorates rapidly. Since we were using the shells to make stock and then reserving the raw meat for up to two hours, the results were disappointing.

That meant that we needed a different approach to the stock, one that would take minutes, not hours. We searched our cookbook library and came up with Gordon Ramsay's quick lobster stock base. Unfortunately, this provided a rather grim experience, even for those who have removed the brains and eyes from fresh calf's heads and field-dressed rabbits. His approach was to freeze the lobsters for thirty minutes to "make them sleepy," and then plunge them into boiling water for a mere one minute. After cooling them briefly, he rips into them with savage abandon, removing the head and claws and extracting the meat with scissors or poultry shears to "cut through."

Let me provide you with our firsthand testing notes: "We have to say that is a horrendous way to cook/kill a lobster. We boiled lobsters for 1 minute and began to remove them, but they were like burn victims, still writhing in choppy, halting movements, so we immediately dropped them for another minute, hoping they would die, but no such luck." Clearly, if heartless test cooks such as ourselves were becoming queasy, this was not going to fly in the typical American kitchen.

We started with three 1½-pound lobsters, then boiled the claws and knuckles separately in heavily salted water and removed and reserved the meat. The remaining carcass was chopped into pieces; the tails were reserved and refrigerated. We also reserved the tomalley and the roe for the sauce. Then we made the lobster stock using the chopped shells, pretty much following Ramsay's guidelines, a method that is done very quickly in a skillet. The reserved tails were then sautéed quickly and flambéed, and the sauce was reduced and seasoned. The result? By far the best lobster dish you will ever eat if you have the will and the wherewithal. This is not a recipe for the casual cook.

LOBSTER À L'AMÉRICAINE

This recipe was printed in Fannie's original cookbook in 1896, along with more pedestrian recipes for lobster. It featured a heavy, floury tomato sauce, which is typical of much of her cooking. We wanted a lighter, fresher version and looked to Escoffier, Julia Child, and even Gordon Ramsay for inspiration. Although not a quick Tuesday night dinner, this method of preparing lobster is spectacular, if we do say so ourselves. The claws and knuckles are boiled in water as a first step, but the tail meat is separated and left raw, stored in the refrigerator no longer than one hour. It is important to make sure that your butter is at 70 degrees before mixing with the tomalley to ensure that it gets fully combined. The recipe for fish stock can be found at www.fannieslastsupper.com.

3 female lobsters, 1¼ pounds each

4 tablespoons butter, softened (70 degrees)

Vegetable oil

1 small carrot, finely diced, ½ cup

1 small leek, finely diced, ¾ cup

1 small celery stalk, finely diced, ½ cup

1 small bulb fennel, finely diced, 1½ cups

1 28-ounce can whole tomatoes, drained, liquid discarded, tomatoes broken into large pieces

1 tablespoon tomato paste

Pinch cayenne

3 sprigs fresh tarragon, plus 1 tablespoon chopped

¼ cup brandy, plus 2 tablespoons

½ cup dry white wine

2 cups fish stock

1 bay leaf

8 peppercorns

(CONTINUED)

Salt and pepper

1 lemon

6 sprigs chervil (for garnish)

1. Split lobsters in half lengthwise. Remove claws and knuckles and boil them in heavily salted water until cooked, about 5 minutes. Remove cooked meat from shells, reserving meat and discarding cooked shells. Cut each lobster in half crosswise, separating the body from the tail. Remove intestinal tract from each tailpiece and discard. Refrigerate tails (meat should still be in the shells). From the body halves, remove tomalley and roe and reserve separately. Roughly chop legs and body (these will be used to make the sauce base). Make tomalley butter: pass 4 tablespoons softened butter and 2 tablespoons of reserved tomalley through fine mesh strainer, stir to combine, and chill.

2. *For the sauce base:* Heat 2 to 3 tablespoons vegetable oil in 12-inch sauté pan over medium-high heat and sauté shells until bright red. Stir in carrot, leek, celery, and fennel, and cook, stirring occasionally, for 9 to 12 minutes, until nicely caramelized. Add drained tomatoes, tomato paste, cayenne, and tarragon sprigs (reserving chopped tarragon) and stir well to combine. Cook, stirring occasionally, 4 to 6 minutes until contents are sticky and well caramelized. Add ¼ cup brandy (reserving the 2 tablespoons), flambé, and cook until it evaporates; add wine and cook until syrupy, about 2 minutes. Add fish stock, bay leaf, and peppercorns, and simmer until it reduces by half, about 6 to 8 minutes. Remove pan from heat and allow to cool for 10 minutes. Strain through china cap or large sieve or fine colander, squeezing and gently pressing solids with tongs to remove all liquid and until shells are dry—you should have 2 cups liquid. Whisk to combine; reserve.

3. *For the lobster:* Heat 2 tablespoons vegetable oil in 12-inch skillet over medium-high heat until shimmering. Season tails with salt and pepper, add to pan, shell side down, for about 3 minutes until bright red. Flip each piece and cook about 30 seconds; add remaining 2 tablespoons brandy

and flambé, cooking and swirling pan until liquid cooks off, about 5 to 10 seconds. Add reserved sauce, bring to gentle simmer, cover, and cook until lobster is cooked through, about 2 to 4 minutes. Transfer lobster tails to platter, cover with foil. Reduce sauce to ½ cup, about 2 minutes. Add cooked claws and knuckles and heat through, about 1 minute; transfer to plate and cover. Whisk in chopped tarragon, chilled tomalley butter, and lobster roe. Season with salt and pepper. Add a couple of drops of lemon for brightness. Spoon sauce over lobster. Garnish each plate with chervil sprig. Serve.

Serves 6 as a first course.

Saddle of Venison

The Old Boston, the New Boston, and Social Nudism

My favorite Boston anecdote dates from the 1920s, when a Chicago banking house asked for a reference from the Boston investment firm of Lee, Higginson & Company with regard to a young Bostonian it was considering hiring. The young man was vouched for in a letter, noting that his father was a Cabot, his mother a Lowell, and his extended family included Saltonstalls, Appletons, Peabodys, etc. Several days later, a curt acknowledgment arrived stating, "We were not contemplating using the young gentleman for breeding purposes."

Although Fannie Farmer did represent change in Boston's culinary world, the city itself had resisted change for more than two centuries, and had done so rather effectively. In fact, the very essence of the Boston character remained well into the twentieth century. Simply put, there was a proper way to behave and everyone else be damned. In one story, a tall girl was passing by the house of Mrs. Jack Gardner. She heard a tapping on the pane and saw a beckoning finger. She knocked on the door and was admitted to find the mistress of the house facing her in a dark room. Mrs. Gardner noted that the girl was not carrying herself properly and stated flatly, "Walk erect," then rang for the maid to have the girl ushered out. Life was a series of rules and habits that had been refined over the centuries, and woe to those who thought otherwise.

This worldview is not unique to Boston but is very much part, I think, of the Pilgrim culture. My maternal grandmother, whose maiden name was Blanche White, was not much different from Mrs. Gardner. At the tender age of ten, I was summoned upstairs to her daffodil yellow sitting room, located in a stately brick home on Kalorama Road in the nation's capital, and given "the talk." This was to be a succinct transfer of wisdom from one generation to another, a summation of what she had learned in over seventy years of living. She looked me in the eye and said, "Now, Christopher, always remember—wash your fruit!" Well, I admit to having been quite taken aback. Until that time, I had no reason to suspect my fruit but, I can assure you, I took her advice to heart, and have repeated her mantra to each of our four children.

But Boston did change, at least a bit, from its original staid provenance to something slightly more modern, although still steeped in the past. Senator Henry Cabot Lodge once remarked, "The year 1850 stood on the edge of a new time, but the old time was still visible from it, and indeed prevailed about it."

The reasons for this move into a new century were both population—the 1840s saw a huge influx of immigrants, many of them Irish—and the growth of transportation, which opened up Boston to a much wider swath of New England. In 1847, there was not even one "horse car line" in Boston, just stagecoaches. Lower Chestnut Street on Beacon Hill had so many stables that it was once named "Horse-Chestnut Street." But things were starting to change. There were eight railroad stations in town, most of them opening in the 1830s and 1840s. One sure way to check the modernity of a city is to track the introduction of natural gas. The Boston Gaslight Company was established in 1827 and built in the North End. In 1828, the price of gas was $54 per thousand feet, but it had dropped to a mere $1.80 by later in the century.

Throughout this tumultuous age, however, Boston was to retain its unique character, one forged by its religious beginnings and married to its wildly successful run in the nineteenth century as America's busiest port. It might be summed up as a reverence for the family name, old money (money was to be gathered, not spent), and old ways. And custom was all-powerful, as this story about Judge John Lowell portrays. One morning when he was at home in suburban Chestnut Hill around 1900, seated at the breakfast table, his wife and a nervous maid arrived and Mrs. Lowell confided nervously, "There isn't going to be any oatmeal this morning, John." The maid had burned it, and there was none left. He responded, lifting his head out of the paper, "Frankly, my dear, I never did care for it."

Being placed in the public eye, especially for commercial purposes, was to be avoided at all costs. In 1933, when Mrs. Powell Cabot and Mrs. John Gardner Coolidge II agreed to promote Camel cigarettes in the press, Boston society regarded it as an act of "social nudism." (One of the print ads showed Mrs. Cabot lounging on a yellow sofa with a modest décolletage, saying, "Flavor is just as important in tobacco as it is in food, don't you think?")

Given its emphasis upon and love of custom, Boston was still far from cosmopolitan. Speaking of the Cabot family, a historian declared they were "a strange dynasty, with customs but no manners." One's word was indeed gold in Boston, since the best families used few written agreements, even when a large amount of business was at stake. Boston's Russell & Company and the famous Chinese merchant Houqua had no written agreements other than one small slip of rice paper that was discovered many years later. It said, "Forty thousand dollars. Houqua." Perhaps the most concise definition of what it meant to be a gentleman in Boston was this: "A Boston gentleman never takes a drink before 3:00 or east of Park Street." Translated, this means that one did not drink before the close of the stock market or anywhere in the business district. When Oscar Wilde visited in 1899 and attended a debutante ball, he commented that the lack of feminine pulchritude was so overwhelming that he understood why Boston artists were reduced to painting "only Niagara Falls and millionaires." Charlie McCarthy had similarly unkind words for the Boston debutante, whom he compared to a groundhog in spring "who comes out, sees her shadow, and goes back in again."

Boston culture might not have been changing with the times, but by the end of the nineteenth century, gas stoves were being introduced in many Victorian kitchens, replacing coal stoves, which took considerable time to heat up and clean, and required much advance planning for cooking. However, most cooking in Boston was still done on the coal cookstove. If I was going to turn back the kitchen clock for our own Victorian feast, I would have to find and install an authentic stove.

Fortunately, in the early 1990s, I had joined the St. Botolph Club on Boston's famous boulevard, Commonwealth Avenue. It was there that I finally—almost fifteen years later—discovered the perfect Victorian cookstove, a massive sixty-three-inch-wide affair, one that had been sitting in the basement of the club unused for decades.

APRIL 2009. THE HISTORY OF FOOD TEACHES US MANY THINGS, but first and foremost, it teaches us that what we eat is based on supply and demand, and, second, that no matter how silly or odd the demand, someone will quickly find a way to supply it. One of the strangest examples of the marketplace at work is cockscombs, a garnish for vol-au-vents and other classic French preparations, as well as a delicacy that is eaten on its own, battered and fried.

Since cockscombs were in much demand as a nineteenth-century garnish, there was a large discrepancy between the supply and the actual inventory. An 1878 book entitled *Wholesome Fare* by Edmund and Ellen Delamere took a sharp look at this problem. "Some years ago it was calculated that not less than five and twenty thousand chicken entered Paris every morning. Ten thousand of these appeared on the tables of private families; the other fifteen thousand fell into the hands of restaurateurs, pastry cooks, rotisseurs, and their colleagues." The authors go on to make the point that a much larger number of cockscombs were being served daily in Parisian restaurants and therefore, the question was, where did they come from?

It turns out that someone had invented a method for making artificial cockscombs by taking the flesh from the palate of a cow, cooking it, and then, using a custom-made stamp, punching out ersatz cockscombs. One could tell the difference, however: "Nature's cocks'-combs are studded on both sides with papillae, or little warts; Lecoq's, and his imitators', on only one." If one could not obtain a beef palate, one could also use the "white parts of a calf's pluck." (Pluck usually referred to the lungs, but it could also mean the heart, windpipe, or liver.) It was also noted that any blacksmith could fashion a decent stamp and then one would be in business. So even ersatz cockscombs were being invented to satisfy the strange desires of the consuming public.

This process of supplying the needs of consumers tends to start benignly enough, as in the case of the late nineteenth century. By 1896, there was already talk about homemade versus store-bought. Some items were considered better when purchased at a store, including water crackers. As one correspondent to the *Globe* commented, "Don't waste your strength in making water crackers when you can buy them so easily and so much nicer than homemade." And who would disagree? Industry can make life better and easier. But even a casual glance at the S. S. Pierce catalog from that era gives one a taste of what is to come, whether it is something as seemingly harmless as Bell's poultry seasoning or Aunt Jemima's pancake mix, or harbingers of future foods, like canned soups and vegetables, potted meats, and bottled sodas such as ginger ales and lemonades. Convenience always starts out as a good idea.

The perfect, and most egregious, example of commercialized food production is the promotion of margarine, a product that turned out to be substantially less healthy than the product it was replacing. It was invented in France in response to a challenge by Napoleon to create an inexpensive butter substitute. Original recipes included cow's udders, sheep stomachs, and beef suet, but by the late nineteenth century, French margarine was using imported animal fats, cheap by-products of the Chicago meatpacking industry. Meanwhile, in 1910, American scientists had perfected the hydrogenation of vegetable oils—the process of turning them into a solid at room temperature. Even as early as the 1870s, margarine manufacturers made their product look more like butter by adding a yellow dye. (The dairy lobby pressured Washington to tax dyed margarine; as a result, many manufacturers sold the yellow dye separately to avoid surcharges.) The watershed moment came in the 1960s, when margarine was promoted as healthier than butter, a claim that turns out to be absolute nonsense. (This claim was based on butter's seven grams of saturated fat per tablespoon, versus two grams for margarine; but margarine has three grams of trans fats per tablespoon, an ingredient that is highly suspect.)

OCTOBER BRINGS NOVEMBER, WHICH IS KNOWN IN NEW ENGLAND less for Thanksgiving than for deer season, when the .306s, .308s, and .32 specials get cleaned and sighted in once again. Gear is checked, including thermoses, walkie-talkies, four-wheelers, the supply of Doe-In-Rut Lures, and cold-weather garb. We look for and then test out our Buck Roar deer calls and hunting hats with the built-in flashlight under the cap. We spend half days here and there up in the woods looking for scrapings and hookings, hoping to find the perfect spot to place a deer stand—not too close to a deer run and with a good range of view over a hollow or field. And then we plan to meet, that first morning, at 5:15 A.M., down at my neighbor Tom's garage—he's the one with the 1950s style hat festooned with orange hunter's tape—where he makes the coffee and fires up the kerosene heater. By 5:45 A.M. we are off, headed up to the top of the mountain. In the predawn darkness, you can hear four-wheelers climbing the sides of mountains and see pinpricks of headlights worming their way slowly uphill. Then we sit in our stands, cold but excited, hoping that this year will bring us the big buck that we dreamed about during the off-season.

Last year, a large buck with a spreading rack and thick, muscled shoulders did walk up under my stand while I was facing the other way, photographing a flock of wild turkeys. I heard a soft crunch, turned slowly, and almost—well, let's just say that it is a good thing that I have a strong sphincter muscle. Life offers a few defining moments, crises that require clear thought and strong action. What was my response? I did nothing for five seconds and then, stunned, slowly put the camera away in my bright orange hunting vest, then silently reached for my gun, which was straddling my lap. Meanwhile, the buck had gotten a good snoutful of my scent. He pivoted and took off like a freight train, straight behind my tree. I stood, twenty-five feet up in the air, turned, and unloaded all five shells in my .308, hitting the odd birch and poplar and doing no damage whatsoever to the once-in-a-lifetime trophy deer. I did, however, get some nice photographs of a flock of wild turkeys. My two hunting buddies, Tom and Nate, heard the shots and came running, expecting to see a carcass. When I related what happened (leaving out the camera part), Tom said with an almost straight face, "Well, maybe you should have invited him up into the stand next to you!"

Hunters like Tom and Nate always think that the glory days are behind us; that a hundred years ago, there was plenty of game to be had. Well, think again. In 1897, Vermont had the first open season it had had for twenty years. Massachusetts had had restrictive hunting laws in place since 1693, when John Winthrop first forbade deer hunting between January and July. By 1898, killing deer was completely illegal in Massachusetts as well as in Connecticut at *any time of year*. Deer farms were starting to pop up in Connecticut, Georgia, and other New England states. Another proposal, this one from 1895, suggested that watersheds near large cities, used for supporting the urban water supply, be used as breeding grounds for deer, in essence becoming municipal game farms. According to an 1896 article in the *Boston Globe*, venison was selling for a very expensive 35 to 40 cents per pound (turkey and beef were roughly half this price), and the supply was scarcer than it had been in forty to fifty years. In Faneuil Hall around 1888, there were 128 stalls for vendors, and only two of them sold venison; whereas there were nineteen stalls for pork, forty-five for beef, and twenty for fish. One might also find bear, selling for up to 30 cents per pound, as well as raccoon and woodcock. Much of the venison supply, such as it was, was derived from illegal sourcing.

One promising note was that the deer were, generally speaking, larger than the animals running around the woods of New England today. Females were 90 to 200 pounds, and males weighed in at 150 to up to 300 pounds. (Today, a buck weighing over 200 pounds is rare, while just two deer shot in the 1897 season in Maine weighed in for a combined total of 700 pounds.) Much of the venison sold at Faneuil Hall was probably provided by individual hunters, mostly from Maine—in 1897, a local Maine guide estimated that there were 150,000 deer "waiting to be shot" (but this was probably just local boosterism). Maine was clearly a major source of the wild venison supply for Boston, New York, and other large New England markets. We know this since the *Boston Globe* published articles detailing the shipments of venison and listing the names of the hunters along with the number of deer that they provided for the shipment, which was never more than two.

Venison was not just a New England specialty; it had been a prized dinner table item for centuries. In fact, the phrase "to give the cold shoulder" originated in a practice once common in France as well as during the Norman rule in Britain. When a guest had outstayed his welcome, he was not served the expected warm haunch of venison. Instead, a dinner of a cold shoulder of mutton was placed before him as a sign that it was time to leave.

Early recipes for venison discussed spit-roasting for hours ("at least 5 hours," according to one 1840 recipe). As for cooking times in an oven, recipes were all over the place, from two hours for an eight-pound saddle to just forty minutes in 1889 for a five-pounder. Just as today, there is little agreement about anything in the kitchen. The meat was frequently basted, sometimes with claret, other times with melted butter and currant jelly. By the late nineteenth century, most saddle of venison recipes were larded, which did not mean inserting long strips of fat deeply into the meat. What Victorian cooks had in mind was something rather different. Here is a description from the *White House Cook Book* of 1887: "Use a saddle about ten pounds. Cut salt pork into strips two inches and 1/8th inch thick, lard saddle two rows in each side." The short thin pieces of salt pork were stitched into the meat shallowly, with both ends sticking out. Other approaches were simply to "bard" the meat, using strips of bacon or salt pork draped over the top during roasting.

Recipes for roasts often suggested wrapping the meat in a double thickness of paper, including white paper, brown paper, coarse paper, or writing paper. The paper was usually buttered or oiled, and it was often used for just part of the cooking—it was removed to allow the exterior to brown properly before the meat was cooked. It is clear that this method derived from cooking over a fire, either on a spit outside or next to a fireplace inside. The heat was often fierce, and one needed to shield the meat from burning. This is still true, but less so, in a cast-iron cookstove from the nineteenth century. Unlike ovens today, the level of radiant heat was much higher (cast iron retains heat much better than other metals), and therefore the browning ability of these ovens was greater. I know this to be true, since we roasted a larded saddle of venison both in a conventional modern oven and in my large coal cookstove. The former did not render any of the strips of salt pork; the wood cookstove, however, did a vastly better job of rendering the fat and browning the exterior. (However, a good convection oven set at 550 degrees will do a more than decent job.) So paper may have been useful under those conditions, although when tested in my wood cookstove, the paper simply reduced the browning and crisping.

Since my hunting expedition came up short, we purchased venison saddles from New Zealand at a specialty food store in Boston. They weighed fifteen pounds and measured over two feet in length, and were just too big for our wood cookstove (we had to use a conventional oven). But we made the best of it: we larded one side with salt pork and left the other plain, then roasted the meat in a conventional oven at 425 degrees. (We were to discover that the design of the needle was key—the thicker needles with a hinged jaw at the back end to hold onto the salt pork were vastly better than the thinner sewing-style needles with a small rectangular notch cut out of one end.)

The meat did not brown well, the salt pork did not render, and when cooked to 115 degrees, the outside meat was moist and tender, but the rare interior was fleshy and unappealing—not a success. A second test was similar, but we brought the internal temperature up to 130 degrees; the texture was chewy, the meat tasted livery, and the salt pork still had not melted.

We then stepped back and decided to more closely approximate the venison that Fannie would have cooked with. Happily, we found a purveyor, UnderHill Farms in Moundridge, Kansas, which could provide us with Fallow deer, which are similar in size to what one might have purchased in 1896. These saddles weighed in at eight pounds, which is the same weight described in Fannie's cookbook. (There is a discrepancy between the sizes of deer shot in Maine and then delivered to the Boston markets and what Fannie calls for in her recipes. It makes me wonder if the Boston markets were already selling farmed deer, since an eight-pound saddle would be from a relatively small specimen.) This time, we used the wood cookstove (the saddle was small enough to fit in it), and the results were much improved—the salt pork had partially rendered and the exterior had taken on a richer, deeper color. The meat was also moist and tender and had great flavor.

Next, we cranked the cookstove to over 550 degrees, hoping that this would provide even more rendering of the salt pork and a better crust. We roasted the saddle for just thirty-three minutes, until the meat was 108 degrees at the bone and 150 degrees at the thin end, removed it from the oven, let it rest, and then carved it into thin slices. The crust was even better; the tips of the salt pork were crisp and brown, and the meat now had better flavor from the pork.

ROAST SADDLE OF VENISON

You will need to use a larding needle for this recipe. The best design uses a hinged "mouth"—SCI makes one for about $6—which holds the strips of salt pork in place as they are sewn through the meat; once the needle is pulled through, the hinged "jaw" on the back end opens up, releasing the salt pork. The more classic design, the ones that look like a regular sewing needle with a large eye through which the salt pork is drawn, is pretty useless. It is hard to pull the salt pork through the eye, and it does not release easily. We did find that freezing the strips of salt pork for about fifteen minutes was a good idea as warm strips are very mushy and hard to work with. Also, a conventional oven does not provide as much radiant heat as a cast-iron stove, which means that the salt pork will not render as well—so just crank up your oven as high as it will go.

> 1 saddle of venison, 7 to 8 pounds, trimmed of fat and silverskin
> 60 strips salt pork, 2¼-inch pieces, ³⁄₁₆ inches wide and deep
> 1 tablespoon vegetable oil
> 2 teaspoons kosher salt
> 1 teaspoon coarsely ground black pepper

1. Adjust rack to lower-middle position. Heat oven to 550 degrees or the highest possible setting. (A convection oven is the best bet here, but it will be less effective at crisping the salt pork than cast iron.)

2. Lay one strip of lardon in the trough of a larding needle. Starting at one end of the saddle, going with the grain of the meat, hold needle at a 45-degree angle, push needle half an inch deep and back up through the surface of meat, pulling salt pork through and releasing from needle. There should be about half an inch of salt pork protruding on each end. Repeat at half-inch intervals with remaining salt pork to cover surface of meat. Rub meat with oil. Season with salt and pepper.

3. Place in oven for 25 to 35 minutes, rotating halfway through, until meat reaches 125 to 130 degrees. Check temperature carefully and frequently. The thicker end of saddle will be rarer than thinner end. Rest 20 minutes. Carve and slice on bias into ¼-inch slices.

Currant Jelly

My wife is a jam maker and enthusiastic currant lover. She has now planted dozens of bushes, and our root cellar is full not only of currant jam, but of a vast inventory of raspberry, blueberry, wild blueberry, apricot, strawberry, and sour cherry. A recent count uncovered over one hundred jars—we are well provisioned in the event there is ever a nationwide jam shortage.

Collecting berries has a certain ritual to it. Many years ago, we discovered a patch of blackberries on a ridge about a half-hour walk from our Vermont farmhouse. It was next to an abandoned carriage shed, and the charm of it was that it was not always easy to find the spot—ridge lines are deceptive since they are never straight, merging into other ridges, often following a confusing, serpentine path. But each year, we finally made it and collected a small pailful or two for jam-making.

The problem with making jam is determining when a jam or jelly is properly cooked so that it ends up neither too thick nor too thin when set. The good news is that red currants are naturally high in pectin, which means that no commercial pectin needs to be added. Pectin can leave a gummy, hard-set jelly, which I find unappealing. However, each batch of fruit is different (slightly underripe fruit has more pectin than ripe fruit— one part underripe fruit to three parts ripe is a good rule of thumb if both varieties are available), and if one tries to make large quantities, the mixture is not all at exactly the same temperature. This often causes one to overcook part of the jam or jelly in order to bring up the entire mixture to the right temperature.

The first solution is to work with smaller batches. Second, I finally purchased a copper pan for jam-making from a store in England. It is 11 inches wide at the bottom, 14 at the top, and 4½ inches deep, with a nice sturdy handle. Since copper is such an excellent conductor of heat, we find that the jam mixture cooks more evenly and more quickly. Also, the flared sides mean that boilovers are not an issue, something that has to be watched when cooking in a straight-sided pot.

Older recipes are insanely sweet, but the Victorians were primarily concerned with long-term storage, and therefore higher sugar amounts—sugar is a preservative—were practical. Modern cooks, however, will find that one part sugar to two parts fruit is about right. One can also use much lower amounts of sugar if the jam or jelly is stored in a refrigerator for no more than a few months. My suggestion is to start with one part sugar to two parts fruit and then increase the sugar as you taste the mixture. Again, refrigerator storage is the best bet for lower-sugar jams and jellies. As far as canning goes, there is no need if the jam is to be stored for a few weeks in the refrigerator, but it is absolutely necessary when kept at higher temperatures and for longer periods.

Fannie suggests picking currants between June 28 and July 3, noting that they should not be picked directly after a rain. She picks over the currants without removing the stems, then washes and drains them. Mash a small quantity in the bottom of the saucepan and then repeat until all the berries are done. Cook until the berries appear white, strain through a coarse strainer, and then let the mixture drain through a double thickness of cheesecloth or a jelly bag. Measure the liquid, bring to the boiling point, and boil for five minutes, then add an equal measure of sugar. Boil for three minutes, skim, and pour into glass jars. She suggests that they be placed in a sunny window for twenty-four hours, then covered and kept in a cool, dry place.

We tested this recipe starting with six cups of red currants. They never did turn white—she must have been using a different variety. We got one cup of juice, added one cup of sugar slowly, and then boiled for about three minutes. The result? A beautiful jewel-colored jar of exquisite currant jelly—although it was on the sweet side. We reduced the sugar to ¾ cup and then Fannie's recipe was spot-on.

We did wonder about the directive regarding leaving the stems on—turns out that this makes no difference. We also tried this recipe using frozen currants. They did not set up quite as well and the flavor was not quite as bright, so fresh fruit is definitely recommended.

RED CURRANT JELLY

Jelly is best made in small batches and watched carefully. Red currant jelly makes a good foundation for many meat sauces.

6 cups fresh currants on the stem
¾ cup granulated sugar

1. Over medium heat, place 2 cups currants in a large saucepan and mash with a potato masher until well broken up. Add remaining currants in batches and continue to mash until they are also well crushed. Increase heat to medium-high and bring to a boil over medium heat, reducing heat to maintain a lively simmer. Cook until all of the juice is released, about 5 minutes. Strain through a coarse strainer. Discard solids. Strain juice through a fine mesh strainer lined with a triple layer of cheesecloth, about 10 minutes; this will yield about 1 cup juice.

2. Add juice and sugar to a clean medium saucepan and bring to boil; cook until sugar is completely dissolved and temperature reaches 225 degrees, 4 to 5 minutes. Remove from heat.

3. Test liquid, using the Rodale Jelly test. Float a small metal bowl in larger bowl filled with ice water. Add a teaspoon of the jelly mixture to the bottom of the floating bowl. Let cool about 30 seconds, and run finger through mixture. It is ready when the jelly starts to run back together but stops. If it fails, cook mixture longer and test again every 2 minutes or so.

Potatoes Lyonnaise

Potatoes were serious business back in Fannie's time since they were such an important part of the diet. Contemporary cookbooks spoke about determining the quality of a potato. One such author, Thomas Jefferson Murrey, suggested the following approach: "Take a sound-looking potato of any variety—cut or break it in two, crosswise, and examine the cut surface. If it appears watery to such a degree that a slight pressure would cause water to fall off in drops, reject it, as it would be of little use for the table. A good potato should be of a light cream-color, and when rubbed together, a white froth should appear round the edges and surface of the cut, which indicates the presence of starch. The strength of its starchy properties may be tested by releasing the hold of one end, and if it clings to the other, the potato is a good one." We did test this last bit of advice and found, as with much historical kitchen advice, that it made little sense.

The "go-to" potato that Fannie Farmer would have used in 1896 was the Burbank, developed by Luther Burbank in 1876 in Lunenburg, Massachusetts. He took a suitcase-full out to California where they became widely planted; decades later, the Burbank was bred again in Denver, Colorado, resulting in the world-famous Russet Burbank. As with apple production, the number of varieties grown in the United States has diminished considerably since the nineteenth century. In Wisconsin alone, the record shows a large number of varieties that most of us have never heard of, including Alexander's Prolific, White Beauty of Hebron, Monarch, Wisconsin Beauty, Seneca Red Jacket, and Mullaly.

In terms of cooking potatoes, I was surprised to find that many cookbooks suggested boiling potatoes with their skins on (for better nourishment), a technique that our test kitchen has promoted for many years. Our reasoning, however, was based on producing lighter, fluffier mashed potatoes, since less water is absorbed with the skins on. Again, Victorian-era cooks were on to this concept as well, since they suggested placing boiled potatoes on top of the range or in the oven to allow surplus moisture to escape. Cooked potatoes were often sliced and sautéed; they were cut into small pieces and placed in a gratin pan, covered with milk, finished with cheese and bread crumbs, and then baked in a hot oven, or even cut into squares and cooked with cream and boiled salt pork, then finished "au gratin."

Potatoes lyonnaise is simple enough: onions are cooked in a skillet; precooked, cold potatoes are sliced and added; then the whole dish is finished with thyme and parsley. Not much to it, or at least that is what we thought at first. We found two recipes for lyonnaise potatoes in the *Boston Cooking-School Cook Book*. Start with one thinly sliced onion briefly cooked in three tablespoons butter. Add three cold boiled potatoes cut in quarter-inch slices and sprinkled with salt and pepper. Stir the mixture lightly and then cook until the bottom layer is well-browned. All in all, a lackluster approach. Fannie's second recipe for lyonnaise potatoes uses much less onion—a mere tablespoon, chopped—and the potatoes and onion are cooked separately. Again, a dull recipe with greasy potatoes (a lot more butter was called for here), not enough browning, and not worth the time or trouble.

We then looked to our own version of potatoes lyonnaise, as printed in *Cook's Illustrated*; one and a half pounds of russets are boiled, cooled, peeled, halved, and then cut into quarter-inch slices. Onion is sautéed in a skillet, removed, the potatoes are added to the pan and browned, and, finally, the onions are added back to finish. We still wanted more flavor so we decided to cook the onions with white wine, butter, and a little brown sugar for about half an hour rather than just for a few minutes. Finally, cooking the potatoes in two batches instead of one gave us superior browning and deeper flavor. This rather bland, greasy offering had been transformed into a rich and crisp side dish.

POTATOES LYONNAISE

Most recipes for this dish are nothing more than potatoes, onions, and parsley, and the flavors are not well developed. We caramelize the onions to add richness, which makes this a dinner party recipe, not just an everyday affair.

For the potatoes:

2 pounds russet potatoes, unpeeled and scrubbed, smaller potatoes
  preferred, roughly 2½ by 3½ inches
Salt
6 tablespoons vegetable oil
1 tablespoon unsalted butter

For the onions:

1 tablespoon unsalted butter
1 tablespoon vegetable oil
½ teaspoon kosher salt
1 teaspoon brown sugar
2 pounds medium onions, halved pole to pole, root end removed,
  peeled and sliced ¼ inch thick pole to pole (8 cups)
⅓ cup dry white wine
½ teaspoon thyme, minced
1 tablespoon chopped parsley

1. Place potatoes in large saucepan, cover with 1 inch water, and add 1 tablespoon salt. Bring to boil over high heat; reduce heat to medium-low and simmer until potatoes are just tender—a paring knife can be slipped into and out of center of the potatoes with very little resistance—25 to 35 minutes. To preserve shape, gently remove from water with tongs or slotted spoon. Refrigerate overnight until cold.

2. Meanwhile, heat butter and oil in 12-inch nonstick skillet over high heat; when foam subsides, stir in salt and sugar. Add onions and stir to coat; cook, stirring occasionally, until onions are golden brown and beginning to darken around the edges, about 12 to 16 minutes. Reduce heat to medium and cook, stirring frequently until onions are deeply browned and slightly sticky, about 14 to 18 minutes longer. Add wine and thyme; increase heat to medium high and cook, stirring frequently until dry, about 2 to 3 minutes. Remove from heat and season to taste with salt and pepper. Cover to keep warm. Reserve.

3. Once potatoes have cooled, carefully peel and cut potatoes in half lengthwise, and then slice into ½-inch-thick half-moons. Season each piece with salt and pepper on both sides, being careful not to break apart.

4. Heat 3 tablespoons oil in 12-inch nonstick (or cast-iron) skillet over medium-high heat, until shimmering. Add half the potatoes in a single layer, and cook, shaking pan occasionally until deep golden brown, about 7 to 11 minutes. Flip. Continue to cook on second side until deep golden brown, about 4 to 6 minutes; transfer to paper towel–lined plate, wipe pan with additional paper towels to remove oil. Add ½ tablespoon butter and browned potatoes back to cleaned skillet. Gently swirl to coat and then transfer contents to a rimmed baking sheet lined with a cooling rack and hold in warm oven. Wipe pan with paper towels; repeat with remaining potatoes, oil, and butter. (You can also do this simultaneously in two 12-inch nonstick skillets.)

5. Serve potatoes with onions and garnish with chopped parsley.

Serves 12 as small side dish.

Glazed Beets

Beets were not a very profitable crop, and therefore, much of what Bostonians consumed in the 1890s may have been locally grown, although they did receive root vegetables shipped in from the South in the spring.

According to *Miss Parloa's New Cook Book: A Guide to Marketing and Cooking*, "Beets, carrots, turnips, and onions are received from the South in April and May, so that we have them young and fresh for at least five months. After this period they are not particularly tender, and require much cooking." There were two type of beets, those whose seed was sown early in the spring, and those that were planted in June as a fall crop and referred to as "winter" beets.

Nobody can accuse Fannie Farmer of doing anything continental or silly with beets. Her recipe for boiled beets suggests a cooking time of from one to four hours, noting that old beets may never become tender, no matter how long they are cooked. This range of cooking times is based on whether one is cooking freshly dug beets in the summer or the winter variety, which might have been stored for months and become quite tough. To finish them, Fannie simply added a few tablespoons of butter and a touch of sugar and salt to the sliced beets and tossed the ingredients together, reheating them for serving—nothing very exciting.

The first problem with Fannie's recipe was the issue of size—we were probably using much smaller specimens than those available in 1896. The second issue was flavor; the beets were rather plain. To solve this problem, we sautéed the beets in butter, sugar, and salt rather than using these ingredients as just a coating. Further testing proved that higher heat was helpful in adding depth of flavor, as were four tablespoons of balsamic vinegar, which brought the dish into balance. A sprinkling of fresh parsley finished off a simple but flavorful recipe

GLAZED BEETS

Smaller beets tend to have a nicer flavor and are more tender. The winter beets of the Victorian time were so tough and large that they had to be boiled for hours.

8 to 10 golf-ball-sized beets (2 to 2½ inches), greens discarded, washed and patted dry

2 tablespoons oil

Kosher salt

Ground black pepper

2 tablespoons butter, cut into 2 pieces

Pinch clove, ground

3 tablespoons light brown sugar

6 tablespoons aged balsamic vinegar (10-year preferred)

2 tablespoons chopped parsley

1. Heat oven to 350 degrees, adjust oven rack to middle position. Place beets in a 9-by-13-inch baking dish. Drizzle with oil; season with 1 teaspoon kosher salt and ¼ teaspoon ground black pepper and toss to coat. Cover with foil and bake until beets are tender, shaking dish occasionally, 60 to 75 minutes. Remove foil, and continue to roast until pan is dry and beets begin to brown, about 15 to 25 minutes. Cool. Peel, cut in half, and then cut each beet into 1-inch wedges.

2. Melt butter in a 12-inch nonstick skillet over medium-high heat until foaming subsides. Add beets, clove, 1 teaspoon kosher salt, and ¼ teaspoon ground black pepper and cook until edges begin to brown, about 5 to 7 minutes. Add brown sugar and cook, stirring frequently until sugar dissolves and coats the beets, about 30 seconds. Add vinegar and cook to a syrupy glaze, so that beets are coated, about 1 to 2 minutes. Remove from heat; add parsley and toss to coat. Serve immediately.

Serves 12 as small side dish.

Wood-Grilled Salmon

How to Cook on a Short, Hot Coal Cookstove

The beast in the basement of the St. Botolph Club was an authentic Victorian-era six-burner coal cookstove with two large ovens: a Number 7, the largest model ever made for the American market. It was sitting unused in a corner of a small office, and I immediately inquired as to its future. After months of sly suggestions, petitions to the board, and promises to fully restore this black monster, it was decided that I might purchase the stove and move it to our townhouse. Unlike modern ranges or the wood cookstoves used on farms, this urban colossus is an assembly of cast-iron parts that are assembled around an existing brick structure. In other words, the stove is the outer shell and the bricks form the inner workings. Yes, there are metal ovens (they can be slid out), but when one removes one of the circular "burners," one looks down into a firebox made entirely of brick.

Almost a year later, the stove had been deconstructed, the brick foundation built, and the stove put back in its place after having been fully restored off-site. As it turns out, the problem with coal stoves is that the extreme heat of anthracite coal over a period of decades warps the top, especially the oval pieces that surround the burners. In other words, the top of the stove is not one solid piece of cast iron but made up of a series of small interconnected bits, many of which had to be recast in order to present a smooth, even cooking surface. Since heat makes metal expand, we soon discovered that the pieces had to fit rather loosely when the stove was cold since, when hot, the pieces would overlap and buckle, turning our perfectly flat stovetop into a train wreck. But over time, this was sorted out, and we began the long process of learning to cook on our Number 7.

Today, most readers would find this method of preparing food both silly and terribly outdated. The coal cookstove was in fact a modern invention, one that infinitely expanded the possibilities of the home kitchen from the limited potential of a fireplace. Cooking in and around a fireplace presented a host of problems, including lack of precise temperature control, the inability to cook a number of things at once unless one had a built-in brick oven next to the hearth, the need to constantly turn meat and game so that they came out evenly cooked, and the general difficulty of managing a cooking process that was nothing more than a campfire moved indoors with all the dirt and lack of a convenient cooking surface.

Roasts were delicious when cooked over or near an open fire, but they had to be turned by hand. A dripping pan was placed directly underneath the roast—usually a cast-iron skillet or, in England, a pan used to bake puddings, Yorkshire pudding being the most famous and also the crispiest. They had grease, heat, and a hot pan—why not simply throw in a batter and bake it up? These breads were often served as a first course, not as a side dish, and when the coal cookstove came into fashion, these puddings had to be baked in an oven, which led to the invention of popovers.

Hand-turning the roast for a few hours was not ideal, so the simplest solution was to hang the roast by a string; a kitchen helper could give the roast a turn every few minutes, and it would spin back and forth until it came to a stop. It was then given another spin by the cook. (I have seen this done with a roasting chicken over a campfire at a Revolutionary War reenactment near our farm in Vermont.) Later improvements on this system were the *clock jack*, which used a system of pulleys and levers to automate this process, and the *spit engine*, which was spring-loaded and used a horizontal spit in front of the fire on which the roast was tied. The most ingenious solution was the *smoke jack*, which automatically rotated a spit above a wood fire. It was a horizontal wheel, installed in the chimney above the fireplace and filled with metal spokes set obliquely like the sails of a windmill. The spokes turned when a current of hot air and smoke hit them, in turn rotating another wheel to which a chain was attached. The chain stretched down to a wheel fastened to the spit so that the spit rotated. The hotter the fire, the faster the jack went around.

As the process of casting iron became more refined and with the advent of a sophisticated railroad network, coal cookstoves could be easily cast and transported. Early prototypes had an open-faced fire in the center of the cookstove, which meant that the foods nearest the fire cooked more quickly. Eventually, both wood and coal cookstoves had an enclosed fuel box and built-in dampers that allowed the heat to circulate evenly around the oven(s) once the wood or coal was well lit and up to temperature (although all the country wood-fired cookstoves that I have ever used had the firebox on the left side of the stove, thus making the left side of the oven hotter). This produced more even heating, which was particularly important for the afternoon baking when the fire had been allowed to decrease a bit from the fierce heat needed for breakfast (toast, chops, bacon, and so on).

Why coal and not wood? In the countryside where wood was free and plentiful, most folks did use wood cookstoves, but in the city the issue was storage. Coal is substantially more efficient per cubic foot, and therefore took up a whole lot less space in the basement coal cellar, and required less transporting of fuel within the house as well. I have cooked on both wood and coal cookstoves, and the difference is remarkable. Just to keep a cookstove hot for an eight-hour cook day, I have had to use ten to twenty lengths of oak; the coal stove needed no more than two large shovelfuls, although coal does require jostling to stay properly lit. (Coal stoves have a handle on the side that allows one to rotate the grates under the coals, thereby knocking off excess ash.)

So what was it like for a kitchen maid at the height of the Victorian period? She would start the day by raking the ashes at 5:00 A.M., saving the cinders that could still burn. (The light, useless coals were referred to as "clinkers," since they clinked when jostled.) Then the flues had to be cleaned with long-handled brushes or a long chain tied to a stick. The stove had to be cleaned and black lead (carbon and iron) had to be applied to the front and sides. It was purchased in sticks and mixed with a drop of turpentine, then put on a brush, much like shoe polish: one brush was used to put it on, one to brush it off, and one to put on a shine. Steel or chrome on the range also had to be burnished. Wind was also a problem, causing a downdraft and a terribly smoky kitchen, but chimneys were usually built within the walls of a house in order to keep the flue warm, offering a better draw. On many occasions, I have tried to start a wood cookstove connected to a chimney mounted on the outside of our Vermont farmhouse on a cold morning, only to find it is almost impossible to warm up the air quickly enough to jump-start a good draft. We had to install an electric fan on top of the flue to help get things moving.

In the 1880s, home cooks had a wide array of fuels: wood (soft and hard), charcoal made from wood, anthracite coal, coke, kerosene oil, and gas. In cities, however, coal was the fuel of choice. To start a coal cookstove, the bottom was lined with paper, then fine pine kindling crosswise, and then hardwood, leaving plenty of air spaces. The direct draught (damper) and the oven damper were opened and the paper lit. When the wood was fully kindled, coal was added to fill the firebox. The coal was pushed down as the wood burned away, and more coal was added to keep it even with the top of the fire bricks. When the flue flame turned white, the oven damper was closed, and when the coal started to burn freely, but not red, the direct draught was also shut. Lincoln cautioned that coal was at its height when kindled and only needed sufficient air to keep it burning; when bright red throughout, however, it had lost most of its heat and was dying out.

Although the stovetops offered a variety of heat levels and were therefore quite convenient, the ovens were difficult to manage, since it took time to either increase or decrease their internal temperature. (After six months of experience on our cookstove, however, I found that I could raise the temperature of the ovens 200 degrees in about forty minutes, so heat levels could be managed more efficiently than I had thought. It is also possible that wood fire offers more rapid adjustments in heat levels than coal, which is a slower, steadier source of heat.) To deal with this, Lincoln suggested using a screen (another pan, for example) on a rack above or below the item cooking if the oven was too hot. This would moderate the temperature around the food by reducing the amount of radiant heat. Another method was used when roasting: adding water to the roasting pan in order to moderate the oven's temperature. Lincoln also suggested that the cook get to know the various points in the oven to understand their relative temperatures. (Even modern ovens have a wide range of temperatures—sometimes 40 degrees or more—depending on where one measures inside.)

In the early days, there were no built-in thermometers, so cooks had to judge their ovens from experience, using either the flour method (sprinkle flour on the floor of the oven; brown is good, but black is too hot) or the paper method (if the paper burns when thrown into the oven, it is too hot; if it turns dark brown, the heat is good for pastry; light brown is good for pies; dark yellow for cake; and light yellow for puddings). Over time, however, oven thermometers became available. Joseph Davis invented a thermometer that had the bulb inside the oven and the tube with the mercury outside, attached to the oven door. He also made a thermometer that stood inside the oven. By the 1870s, most wood or coal stoves had hot-water reservoirs either within the stove or in an attached tank; metal pipes for circulating and heating water ran from the tank to the back of the stove.

Gas cookery did not become popular until 1900, although prototype gas stoves had been invented in the 1840s. The first commercially distributed gas stove was made by William W. Goodwin of Philadelphia as early as 1879. The Sun Dial range included two to four cooking burners and an oven and open broiler below. There were problems with rapid adaptions of this technology, including the high price of gas—over $50 per thousand feet in 1850, compared to under $2 by the end of the century—and the consumer's fear that the gas itself would taint food during the cooking process. It wasn't until 1896, however, that the Massachusetts Pipe Line

Gas Company was capitalized at $5 million with the purpose of "convey-ing, transporting and distributing gas for illuminating, heating, cooking, chemical, mechanical and power purposes."

Early on, we decided to use wood instead of coal for three reasons: we had plenty of room in the basement for storage; the smell of wood burning is nicer than coal, which has a noticeably unpleasant aroma; and because David Erickson, our stove expert, had made a grill insert for our stovetop that would allow us to grill indoors over a wood fire. Our first thought was that indoor grilling would throw off a great deal of smoke, but to our amazement, the draft was so strong in our cookstove that all the smoke was sucked down into the firebox and then out the flue. So we had an un-expected bonus—an indoor grill.

So, exactly how does our stove work? The firebox is located in the cen-ter of the stove; this is ideal since it heats both sides of the cooktop evenly. To add wood, one removes one of the circular cast-iron burners with a lifter and simply slides the wood into the firebox. (To start a fire, paper and kindling are added first, as with any wood fire.) There is a door in front of the stove that allows the firebox to be used much like a fireplace, but for cooking purposes it remains closed. There is a sliding draft control under-neath the firebox at the front of the stove which is slid open for maximum air intake during lighting or when you want a rapid increase in oven or stovetop temperature. Then there are two additional controls above the cooktop and located between the two ovens. (The ovens sit fourteen inches above the stove, built into the brick surround, and are twenty inches deep by nineteen inches wide.) These are two "pulls." One is a knob that can be pulled out to adjust the opening in the flue. The other controls the direc-tion of the draft: when the knob is pulled, the hot air moves directly up the flue and out the chimney; when pushed in all the way, the heat is diverted around the ovens and heats them. These controls were also effective when grilling on the stovetop, since a few quick adjustments turned a moderate fire into a fierce source of heat.

Victorian cooks had to be remarkably inventive since the temperature of the stovetop varies depending upon location: right over the central firebox you get enough heat to boil water; off to the sides, the two burners are medium in heat; and toward the back, you get the equivalent of a hot plate or a low simmer burner—hence the origin of the expression "on the back burner." Yet this is still a rather primitive setup, since the heat of the whole unit cannot be changed quickly and the internal temperatures of the ovens is usually the deciding factor, the stovetop being less crucial. So what do you do?

For starters, you might invent the bain-marie, whose original purpose was to keep sauces just below a simmer. These were long oval pans with small covered pots that fit neatly into them, usually resting on a trivet inside. These bains-marie were also partially filled with water, and since water boils at 212 degrees Fahrenheit, the sauces would never get any hotter. The braising pan, used to cook meat on the top of a cookstove, used a similar principle. Meat and broth were put into the pan, then the lid was put on and then sealed with clay or dough. The braising pan was put on the corner of the range to simmer, and live embers or coals were put on the concave top of the pan. This was, in essence, an indoor Dutch oven, which also used heat above and below the pot. Copper cookware was lined with tin, and pots had to be constantly retinned. Anyone who has used an old copper saucepan or skillet knows that if the pan is heated while empty for too long, the tin will simply melt and puddle at the bottom of the pan.

One story recounted the fate of several gentlemen who died from a ragout that had been stored in a copper vessel that was badly tinned. In the event that one was poisoned, the Victorian remedy was to beat the whites of a dozen eggs in two pints of cold water, administer to the victim, and repeat every two minutes until vomiting was induced.

It was hard to perfectly regulate an oven in a coal cookstove, so cakes were not the easiest item to prepare. One solution was to design a cake tin with a metal cone projecting up from the bottom, a design that came into fashion in the 1880s. This conducted heat through the center of the cake to promote even cooking, much like a tube pan. One way to check if your cake was done was to take out a slice, check it for doneness, brush each side with egg white, and then slide it back into place.

The *hot closet* was a screen on one side with shelves on the other, and was used to keep cooked foods or serving plates warm. (The screen was placed near the cookstove or fireplace.) The *American oven* was an open-fronted metal box, its floor inclined to reflect heat. This box was placed with the open front facing the coal fire; the meat, smaller cuts such as chops, was positioned on a shelf halfway up the box. The oven was often stood on a chair and pushed up to the range. (One would have to open the door covering the firebox on my oven to use this device.) One could also purchase a *bottle jack* for an American oven, a small spring-loaded vertical rotisserie from which a small roast could be hung, rotating slowly in front of the fire. This was consistent with how the English roasted their meats using coal cookstoves, since they favored the notion of hanging a joint in front of the open coal box using a three-part metal screen that had a hinged opening in the middle in order to baste the meat as it roasted, with a pan beneath to catch the drippings. This was probably done for a number of reasons: that's how they used to do it when they cooked in a fireplace; they had only two ovens, so they were at a premium; and a large joint of beef simply wouldn't fit into most ovens.

What other cookware, appliances, and tools would have made up a true Victorian *batterie de cuisine*? For starters, a Victorian kitchen would include an ice chest: ice wrapped in sacking was placed in the top, and foods could be put above or below on perforated shelves. Maids would have to drain off the water from a tap from time to time. Although there is some dispute about whether ice chests were common household items by the 1890s—ice was expensive—there is no question that any upper-middle-class home in Boston would have had one. This resulted in the popularity of ice creams; crude ice-cream machines were patented as early as 1840. Ice-cream molds became extremely popular as well, wealthy households having them made to order, often with the family crest.

I wasn't going to install a true ice chest, but Adrienne did find a fully restored four-door electric Kelvinator "icebox" from a firm out in California, and we had it shipped in and installed. At least it looked the part. We also purchased a manual ice-cream machine from White Mountain—quite similar, I suspect, to the original manufactured in Fannie's era.

Cast iron had been around forever, but enameled cast iron made its debut in 1874, followed in 1892 by enameled sheet steel, which was lighter and easier to clean and maintain. This graniteware was used for tea and coffeepots, as well as for stew pans, although egg beaters and even waffle irons were eventually fashioned from it. Vollrath Ware, an American-made line of this enameled cookware, was known for its speckled or mottled blue, black, brown, or gray enamel. Of course, bread graters were everywhere, since using up stale bread was the basis for hundreds of recipes, from rissoles to puddings, from stuffings to croquettes. Other common kitchen items would have included jelly molds, patty pans (pie pans), and tartlet pans, a corned beef pan, cast-iron gem pans, muffin rings, and square biscuit pans. And, with the twentieth century right around the corner, the late Victorians were being introduced to the cookware of the future, such as the electric skillet, which was marketed in Britain as early as 1898.

❈

MAY 2009. RESEARCHING HISTORY IS A TERRIFIC WAY TO CURE oneself of taking anything for granted. Fannie wasn't really the "mother of level measurements," FDR's New Deal didn't really fix the American economy (unemployment jumped up to 19 percent in 1938 and the market had taken another header), and Salem wasn't much of a town for witches. What? It turns out that Salem deserves a solid gold Chamber of Commerce medal for taking a very short and undeniably sordid historical period, one that most normal folks would like to quietly forget, and transforming it into a year-long bonanza of tourism, ersatz Wiccan memorabilia, and huge crowds on Halloween, not to mention crappy T-shirts and greasy sausages.

First, let's get a few facts straight. Witch hunting was all the rage in Europe in the sixteenth and seventeenth centuries; the Germans, in particular, were thorough professionals, although the French also deserve an honorable mention. During this bloody period, one hundred thousand witches were put to death in Germany and seventy-five thousand in France. How did New England fare in comparison? Bloody amateurs! Only thirty-two witches were ever put to death in our part of the world, and just four of them in Boston. And the whole fervor only lasted a few years—the first witch, a Margaret Jones, was hung in 1684. By 1693, the fervor had abated. So, once again, hats off to the folks up in Salem.

The history of food is equally misleading, because how the average Joe cooked and ate is less likely to be reported than how the rich and famous dined. The Victorian dinner that we were re-creating would have been as alien to the average resident of New England in 1896 as it is to us today. The rich had refrigeration, domestic servants, silverware, access to expensive foods, a kitchen large enough to prepare a multicourse meal, and a dining room, still a rarity for most Americans at the time. We were taking a thin slice of the culinary pie here, and doing so on purpose, since I would rather research and prepare a twelve-course high Victorian menu than a plate of baked beans and brown bread.

So to come to any ready conclusions about the food of the late nineteenth century is fraught with danger. Okay, I scanned all the recipes in the *Boston Globe* of 1896, but do recipes in a newspaper really tell the whole story of the typical home cook of the era? Maybe, maybe not. Do the food pages of the *New York Times* truly reflect what New Yorkers are cooking for dinner? Most of them probably eat out five nights a week.

However, I have learned something about the Victorians after two years of cooking their food. They had one foot in the past and one in the future. They had grown up in parsimony and were now headed toward abundance. Fannie was teaching them how to make hoe cakes (a cheap form of cornbread) as well as endless recipes wrapped in puff pastry and finished with béchamel. More than in any other period in American history, the Victorians were a bipolar mix of old-fashioned and modern, and their food exemplified the coexistence of these two very different lifestyles.

In 1900, for example, one could purchase Jell-O manufactured by the Genesee Pure Food Company; or make one's own jellies using any number of thickeners, including powdered gelatin, Irish moss, or isinglass; or boil calf's feet to make homemade gelatin, as we did for our jelly course. Unlike modern times, the gap between how various New Englanders lived was extraordinarily broad, from the technology they used in their everyday life (many New Yorkers and Bostonians already had access to gas for lighting and cooking, whereas in rural areas farm wives were still cooking over inefficient wood cookstoves) to where their food came from (Château Lafite for the urban rich and cheap ale for the poor). Today, there is, for the most part, a homogenous culture; in the 1890s it was a cultural hodge-podge.

The Boston Cooking-School Cook Book reflected this disparity, from its preachiness regarding the science of nutrition, to the inclusion of basic American staples such as Indian pudding, blanc mange, or even water bread (stale bread dipped in water to refresh it and then buttered), all the way to the ersatz French concoctions like vol-au-vent, birds in potato cases, and gâteau de Princesse Louise. Cooking in the Victorian age was nothing in particular; it was everything all at once.

This mixed-up approach to preparing food was particularly true when it came to Fannie's recipes for fish cookery. As far as I could tell, Fannie was not a great lover of fish, since most of her preparations were rather pedestrian. To be fair, her instructions for broiling seemed fine, but a four-pound bluefish was to be baked in a hot oven for forty-five minutes, a three-pound halibut was baked a full hour, and one is sometimes instructed to throw a lobster sauce onto fish that turns out to be nothing more than hollandaise with a bit of chopped lobster meat added. One also finds many references to "white sauce I," which is a classic medium béchamel (two tablespoons each butter and flour, a cup of milk, salt and pepper). This would be a rather grim blanket, although it was not at all uncommon in Fannie's time as an accompaniment to a nice piece of fresh cod or halibut. There was also a basic recipe for fish stuffing—nothing more than cracker crumbs, stale bread crumbs, melted butter, hot water, salt, pepper, and a few drops of onion juice.

Fannie also suggested broiling salmon, so I decided to head in that direction: a simple preparation that would let the flavor of the salmon shine through.

❈

MY GRANDFATHER, CHARLES STANLEY WHITE, WAS A GREAT salmon fisherman, and that is probably why I have spent quite a bit of time fishing the Matapedia River in Quebec, as well as the Restigouche and Miramichi rivers in New Brunswick. The first run of Atlantic salmon starts in April or early May, when the ice lets out, and the fish that have spent the winter upstream swim down to the ocean. Then, beginning from June to July, the main run of salmon begins, the fish swimming upstream to their place of birth, where the cycle begins all over again. Fly-fishing for salmon has always been a popular sport. The rich and powerful took trains up from Boston and New York, even in the late nineteenth century, and then took up residence on small houseboats floated on rafts that were pulled upstream by teams of horses or oxen onshore toward the camps where "sports" might spend a few weeks during the season. Fishing was done, before the use of outboard engines, in wide-bottomed canoes that were poled up and down the river from one "pool" to the next.

Anyone who has been to a hunting or fishing camp knows the drill. On the evening of your arrival, you immediately inquire about your prospects. How many fish were caught last week? What is the weather report? Have the salmon started running? The answer, given by the head guide, is always hopeful but murky, something like, "There is a full moon tonight and the water should be rising and I expect a good run in the next day or two." Translation? Nobody is catching fish, but we hope to shortly.

My first salmon fishing trip to Cold Spring Camp on the Matapedia in Quebec involved ten sports and, oh, about ten thousand casts between us. The only woman among us caught the only fish, a twenty-six-pounder, on the fourth day. Other than an excursion to the local strip joint in Campbellton, the highlight of that outing was a taste of that lone salmon. The flesh was almost white, not orange, incredibly firm and light, not at all oily. It was vastly better than even the expensive wild salmon one can buy at the best fish markets.

As for cooking the salmon, I was surprised that our Victorian cookstove could be used for indoor grilling. David Erickson, the gentleman who restored our cookstove, made up an oblong grill insert that can quickly replace two of the burners and the surrounding cast-iron pieces. The beauty of this design, and what makes me think that the world is moving backward in terms of technology, is that the draft from the chimney is so strong that any smoke from the grilling is sucked downward and up through the flue. So, there we are, indoor grilled salmon.

I began by seasoning the grill with a dozen different coats of oil as it heated on the cooktop. Then we took four salmon fillets, two to three ounces each, seasoned them with oil, salt, and pepper and, over a hot fire, grilled them skin-side down until the skin was brown and crisp. We flipped the fish to finish. I found that by adjusting both the draft in front of the firebox and also the main flue, I could immediately change the heat level. Unlike a Weber or most other charcoal grills, it was much like cooking over gas—there was a high degree of control. We served them with a caper vinaigrette and an additional garnish of fried capers. This was the best grilled salmon I'd ever had, and it was cooked indoors to boot.

GRILLED SALMON
WITH CAPER VINAIGRETTE

It is true that Fannie did not offer any grilled fish recipes—they were mostly boiled, roasted, or poached—and the cooking times were ridiculously long. In addition, canned salmon was available at this time and was often used in cold salads. However, a few contemporary cookbooks did offer grilling salmon as a common preparation method, so we followed that advice. We used our wood-burning cookstove with a grill insert to cook the salmon indoors, not a charcoal grill. When grilling salmon, we find that ten separate coats of oil on the hot grill will create a nonstick surface. Brush the oil using tongs and a wad of paper towels.

Vinaigrette:

¼ cup lemon juice

¼ teaspoon Dijon mustard

½ teaspoon whole-grain mustard

1 tablespoon minced shallots

2 teaspoons capers, rinsed, dried, roughly chopped

1 teaspoon caper juice

¼ teaspoon thyme, minced

Salt and pepper

6 tablespoons canola oil

6 tablespoons high-quality extra-virgin olive oil

1 tablespoon chopped parsley

2 lemons, cut into wedges

Salmon:

12 3-ounce salmon fillets, cut into rectangles

1 to 2 tablespoons vegetable oil

Salt and pepper

1. *For the vinaigrette:* Combine lemon juice, mustards, shallots, capers, caper juice, thyme, and salt and pepper to taste in small nonreactive bowl. Whisk until thoroughly combined. Combine oils in small measuring cup so that they are easy to pour. Whisking constantly, very slowly drizzle oil into lemon mixture. If pools of oil are gathering on surface as you whisk, stop addition of oil and whisk mixture well to combine, then resume whisking in oil in slow stream. Stir in parsley. Vinaigrette should be glossy and lightly thickened, with no pools of oil on its surface.

2. *For the fish:* Prepare a hot fire for grilling. Pat salmon dry with paper towels. Make two or three shallow slashes along the skin side of each piece of fish, being careful not to cut into the flesh. Brush both sides of fish with thin coat of oil and season with salt and pepper. Place fish skin-side down on grill diagonal to grate, and cook without moving until skin side is brown, well marked, and crisp, 3 to 5 minutes. Flip fish to second side and cook, until centers of fillets are still translucent when cut into with a paring knife, or register 125 degrees on instant-read thermometer, 2 to 4 minutes longer.

3. Serve fish skin side up, and drizzle vinaigrette around and over each piece of fish, with 2 to 3 teaspoons vinaigrette. Serve with lemon wedges.

ABOVE: The Boston Cooking School at 174 Tremont Street (far left building). *Josiah Johnson Hawes. Courtesy of the Bostonian Society/Old State House Museum.*

ABOVE, LEFT: Fannie Farmer (front right) at the Boston Cooking School. *Edward L. Allen and Frank Rowell. Courtesy of the Boston Athenaeum,*

LEFT: A model kitchen from the 1898 Food Exposition in Cincinnati, Ohio. *Courtesy of the Boston Athenaeum.*

BELOW: Quincy Market, circa 1880, photographed from North Market Street looking toward Faneuil Hall. *Clinton Johnson. Courtesy of the Bostonian Society/Old State House Museum.*

ABOVE: A small oyster boat with deep-water oyster tongs attached to a winch. *National Oceanic and Atmospheric Administration/Department of Commerce. Archival photographer Stefan Claesson.*

BELOW: After growing up in Medford, Fannie moved into the South End of Boston. (Her street, Rutland Square, is the first intersection on the left.) *Courtesy of the Bostonian Society/Old State House Museum.*

1901 photograph showing Fannie seated in the hammock; her mother, Mary, in the rocker; her nephew, Dexter; and his mother, Cora, standing behind him. In the foreground is either Mary or Lillian, two of Fannie's three sisters. *Courtesy of the University of California, Berkeley Library.*

One of the most famous photographs of Fannie, since she is holding a measuring cup, symbolizing her public crowning as the "Mother of Level Measurements." *Copyright © Bettmann/CORBIS.*

Erin McMurrer, the kitchen director at America's Test Kitchen.

BELOW, LEFT: The Cyrus Carpenter Number 7 coal cookstove that we installed in our South End home. (We had the stove converted from coal to wood.)

BELOW, RIGHT: The front cover can be opened to reveal the firebox.

To add wood to the firebox, one or more of the cast iron rounds are removed.

All photographs on pages 4–8 copyright © Kate Kelley.

ABOVE, LEFT: For our first test of Mock Turtle Soup, Erin and I boiled a calf's head only to discover that we should have first removed the brains.

ABOVE, RIGHT: "Brainballs" are quick-fried in hot oil and served as a crispy garnish for Mock Turtle Soup.

RIGHT: Erin taste-tests stock for the Mock Turtle Soup.

The saddle of venison was larded: thin strips of cold salt pork are sewn through the exterior of the meat.

Fannie's Last Supper

OCTOBER 24, 2009

DUXBURY ISLAND CREEK OYSTERS
1990 Veuve Clicquot La Grande Dame

MOCK TURTLE SOUP
Lustau Rare Amontillado Escuadrilla Sherry

RISSOLES
1996 Heimbourg Pinot Gris, Domaine Zind Humbrecht

LOBSTER À L'AMÉRICAINE
2005 Saint Joseph Blanc Lyseras, Yves Cuilleron

SADDLE OF VENISON WITH POTATOES LYONNAISE, SUGARED BEETS
AND CURRANT JELLY SAUCE
1986 Château La Mission Haut Brion

WOOD-GRILLED SALMON
2005 Riechsrat von Buhl Riesling Spatlese Trocken Pfalz Forster Ungeheuer

FRIED BABY ARTICHOKES

CANTON FROZEN PUNCH

ROAST GOOSE WITH CHESTNUT STUFFING AND APPLESAUCE
1999 Leroy Beaune 1er Cru Belissands

THREE MOLDED VICTORIAN JELLIES

MANDARIN CAKE
1988 Château Guiraud 1er Grand Cru Classe

COFFEE, CHEESE, CRACKERS AND BONBONS

The printed menu for Fannie's Last Supper.

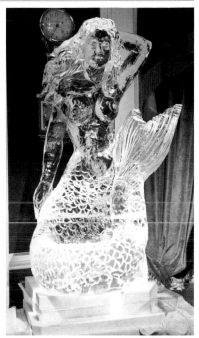

RIGHT: This hand-carved sculpture would not have been unwelcome at some of the more risqué parties of the age.

BELOW: My wife, Adrienne, setting the table in the back parlor of our 1859 Victorian home.

ABOVE: The waitstaff speaking with chef José Andrés before dinner. From left to right: Melissa Klein (foreground), Emile Arkinstall, Michael Ehlenfeldt, Jake McDowell, Debbie McDowell, and Cindy Ehlenfeldt.

BELOW: Fiona Hamersley (right) speaking with Cindy Ehlenfeldt.

Fried Artichokes

It's 1896: Let's Go Shopping

The year Fannie published her cookbook, 1896, was a shopper's paradise. One could walk through the doors of S. S. Pierce, the preeminent grocer of the day, and purchase Formosa oolong, Penang cloves, authentic Parmesan from Italy, a bottle of Château Lafite or Château Margaux (they would set you back $20 to $30 per case, roughly $1,000 to $1,500 in today's dollars), six types of preserved cherries, green turtle soup, Jamaican ginger, California peaches, hothouse cucumbers, potted ham, medicated toilet paper, Aunt Jemima pancake mix, Havana cigars, cherry blossom toothpaste, truffles, jarred French peas, and Tanglefoot sticky fly paper.

But this bounty, all neatly displayed and offered for immediate home delivery, was a far cry from Boston's beginnings—a time before Faneuil Hall and Quincy Markets, before the railroads brought oranges from Florida and canned fruit from California, before ships were unloading mushrooms from Paris and olive oil from Italy. The most venerable method of purchasing foodstuffs was through vendors—butchers, fishmongers, and farmers—who went door to door. This old English custom endured well into the eighteenth century, and many Bostonians opposed the building of central markets, since it meant the inconvenience of a shopping trip and an end to unregulated commerce. What is so vile and detestable about something so simple as a public place to sell meat, vegetables, fish, and fruit? The answer is one that explains the American Revolution, or at least the enthusiasm many wealthy colonists felt for risking their life, liberty, and possessions against overwhelming odds and the most powerful navy in the world. It is simply this: The colonists hated any notion of taxation, regulation, or central authority if these interfered with their daily lives. They came to America to be left alone.

By 1634, the city of Boston decided that it was indeed time for a central, city-funded marketplace, and the perfect spot was down at the docks. The original market in Boston was called, of course, Dock Square market, although it was also referred to as the corn market. At first, it was open only on Thursdays. It was established on the site of the old state house by order of the court, and it was not much more than an open field—it was not until the eighteenth century that Boston markets had indoor facilities as well. Fishermen could sell cod and mackerel; farmers came down the Charles River in boats with vegetables; and the farmers from Roxbury and Dorchester could transport their goods by wagon over the thin strip of land that connected Boston with the mainland.

As many of the early colonists feared, there was soon a need for a court to settle market disputes. Thus the Pie Powder Court was founded, named after the baking flour covering the feet of its members. By midcentury, however, two clerks of the market were appointed in place of the court—Jeremy Houchin and James Penn—and their job was to inspect the market for cleanliness, regulate weights and measures, and settle disputes. They were paid "one third part of all forfeit" for their efforts, with the remainder paid to the poor. By 1658, a two-story Town House was erected. It was used for public business—a court, a library, and a meeting place for an artillery company—but the ground floor was open and used for the merchant exchange. It soon became the home of the first formal New England town meeting at which officials were elected. (They used the old Anglo-Saxon term for *sheriff*, which is a contraction of "shire reeve," *reeve* meaning "peace." They kept the peace in the shire or town.)

By the end of the century, the market was open three days a week. A bell was rung at its opening, 6:00 A.M. in the summer and 9:00 A.M. in the winter months. The practices of freewheeling peddlers and door-to-door salesmen continued, since the public markets scared off many vendors because of the need for licenses, fees, rents, and fines. And consumers enjoyed the convenience of this early colonial form of the Home Shopping Network.

Over the next few decades, a series of fires closed the market, and other markets were built in the downtown area, but, all in all, Bostonians did not cater to centralized, regulated markets. In fact, in 1736, a mob disguised as clergymen (mobs in colonial Boston had a penchant for disguising themselves) destroyed the central Dock Square market. Enter Peter Faneuil.

In 1738, Peter Faneuil, a Boston merchant whose wealthy family had emigrated in 1691 from France, came into a great deal of money through his uncle Andrew, including holdings in Great Britain, France, and Holland. The will stipulated that the family fortune only pass through to someone who worked for the uncle and never married. (A brother, Benjamin, fell in love, so Peter stepped up to the plate.) In 1740, Faneuil offered to fund a market at Dock Square as long as the city agreed to authorize and maintain it. Without his knowledge, his offer was quickly written up as a petition and signed by scores of prominent citizens. Nevertheless, the proposal passed by just seven votes—a testament to the forces that supported unregulated commerce—and a petition was circulated and passed noting that peddlers were still allowed to sell their goods wherever they pleased. (Faneuil also complained bitterly that nobody could properly pronounce his family name, a problem that persists to this day. It is correctly pronounced "Fan-nel," with the accent on the first syllable.)

Faneuil attached conditions to his offer. He demanded that the hall be built of masonry to help withstand fire, and that the site be maintained forever as a market, to avoid the fate of South Market, which had been converted into a storehouse and rented. The architect was a Scottish artist, John Smibert, a friend of the Faneuil family. He designed a classic English Renaissance structure forty feet wide by one hundred long, with an arcade on the lower floor to serve as the market and a large hall above. The latter became the new public meeting room for Boston, the old Town Hall being too small for the growing seaport. It was located at Dock Square, and was therefore on the waterfront. (Visitors to modern Boston will note that Faneuil Hall is no longer on the water, due to the expansion of Boston's footprint into the harbor over the years.)

Faneuil Hall was topped with a domed cupola that housed a bell for signaling the start and end of the market day as well as a thirty-eight-pound grasshopper weather vane, modeled after a similar creature that sat atop London's Royal Exchange. The weather vane was built by Deacon Shem Drowne out of hammered copper and gold leaf; the eyes were green glass doorknobs, and it also had long metal antennae. It soon became the most famous weather vane in the country.

What is often lost in all of this grand history is that Faneuil Hall was pretty much a disaster. It took three months to rent the first stall. Finally, it was rented to Anthony Hodgson, who sold butter, cheese, and flour (the butter was from Ireland and Cheshire cheese from England). The market was actually closed twice for a year or so in its early history, owing to lack of interest from both sellers and buyers. The anti-market faction, which referred to Faneuil Hall as the "Grasshopper Market," seemed to be winning the battle against a centralized shopping center.

To add insult to injury, the hall burned in 1761, even though it was made mostly of masonry. In 1762, the new Faneuil Hall was erected and, in 1805, doubled in size by architect Charles Bullfinch. By the early nineteenth century, the market had finally come into its own. Inside the hall on the first floor, one contemporary writer described the scene. "Here are sausages in festoons; roasting pig that would have made Charles Lamb's mouth water; vegetables in parterres, and fruits from every clime. Here one may have fish, flesh, fowl, or good red herring." Outside, around the hall, there were vendors with wagons and pushcarts, sometimes as many as three hundred teams converging around the market. (The horses were sent to nearby stables while the market was open.) They paid no rent, so the colonists' vision of an unregulated marketplace had really come to life even though Faneuil Hall was a success. Actually, there was more to buy outside the hall than inside. (Some farmers, however, simply sold their goods at wholesale prices to the merchants within the hall instead of spending the day by their wagons selling to the retail trade.)

With the success of Faneuil Hall, Boston soon needed additional market space and so, in 1826, Quincy Market, named after former mayor Josiah Quincy, was erected, built of granite, two stories high and 535 feet long. Vendor stalls were installed downstairs on each side of the grand corridor (leased from the city), and on the second floor was Quincy Hall, for meetings. The entire project, including new streets around the market as well as the North and South Market Street warehouses, and stores flanking the new hall, cost the city over $1 million. At first, these surrounding establishments were more likely to sell dry goods and nonperishable items such as clothing, leather goods, hats, cigars, stoves, and snuff; sail and awning makers also rented space on the top floors of these buildings. Produce vendors appeared in the warehouses later in the century.

By 1880, Quincy Market was a huge success, one of the few public commercial enterprises in Boston that could make that claim. Produce merchants in the halls had annual sales of $20 million from cheese, poultry, meat, fish, seafood, vegetables, and fruit. Fifty to a hundred carcasses of beef, mutton, and veal were sold every day, and goods were imported from Florida and the Pacific Coast. One could purchase "a pound or a hundred quarters of beef; a pound of sausage or a thousand dressed hogs; a peck or a thousand barrels of apples; a pound or a ton of butter; a dozen oranges or a hundred boxes; a pound or a cargo of fish, fresh or salted." By the 1880s, refrigerated storage (no longer ice, but a cold brine system of refrigeration) was available at a facility near the market, and Boston vendors were shipping goods across the Atlantic and to the West Coast. Over time, other smaller markets opened up as well.

Until the mid-nineteenth century, the fruits, vegetables, meats, and poultry sold at these markets were mostly local. Small establishments and the city markets offered everything from poultry (chicken, partridge, quail, woodcock, snipe), seasonal fruit (peaches, pears, melons, "morocco" grapes), confectionary products (cream cakes, mince pie, Washington pie, vanilla jumbles, harlequin, éclairs, charlotte russe), and seafood (scallops, smelt, clams, whitefish, salt cod, haddock, shad roe, mackerel). But in the period after the Civil War, the railroads opened up the Midwest, a more fertile area than New England, and this was the beginning of a long decline for New England farmers. From 1850 to 1914, the number of farms in the New England states had not increased, nor had the number of people working on them. In fact, the amount of acreage under cultivation actually decreased.

One good example of the growth of nonlocal foods is the turkey business. By 1890, very few Vermont turkeys were showing up in Boston markets, although they were supposedly of the highest quality. By this time, the birds were being shipped in from "out west," which meant Indiana, Illinois, Kentucky, and Iowa. The reason? Corn was cheaper in the Midwest, and the turkey farms were bigger. Fannie Farmer noted a similar trend in terms of produce: "A few years ago native vegetables were alone sold; but now our markets are largely supplied from the Southern States and California." By the late nineteenth century, however, foods were not just coming from the Midwest; they were coming from all over the world.

The preeminent Boston grocer, the founder of the original gourmet market, was Samuel S. Pierce. The year was 1831, and the location was Court and Tremont streets. Samuel Pierce thought that this was a good location for a food market, since it was equidistant from the West End, the Bullfinch mansions (which were torn down to make way for, among other things, the ugliest building in the world, Boston City Hall), the residential district around Summer Street and Church Green, and the growing Beacon Hill. This same building had housed the headquarters of General Washington, and one of Mr. Pierce's early customers was Daniel Webster, whose law office was located in the same building.

The term *grocer* is a derivation of the French *groser*, referring to someone who purchases items in "gross," or wholesale. As the trade monopoly of the East India Company came to a close in the late nineteenth century, this opened up the market for local entrepreneurs—wholesalers who bought in bulk, measuring out small household units of flour, meal, molasses, tea, and spices for their customers. However, two things really set S. S. Pierce apart. The first was home delivery of groceries, originally by wheelbarrow, then by horse and cart, and finally, by teams of six matched grays that were imported from Ohio. The second was an eye toward gourmet products, since Boston was becoming a much more sophisticated and wealthy town as the twentieth century approached.

By 1896, S. S. Pierce had outgrown its original location and had to move its headquarters down Tremont Street to a spot across from the Parker House and King's Chapel. Many might suppose that this was nothing more than a small storefront, but Pierce had to employ ninety horses and two hundred men to move the four thousand types of items in his inventory. By that time, one could purchase the expected: grapes, lemons, vermicelli, vinegar, molasses, almonds, prunes, Moxie soda (Moxie was first marketed as a "nerve food" in the 1870s and was quickly transformed into a soda favored by Calvin Coolidge; it is still made today), pickles, and biscuits. But the list of available items also included the first pick of mushrooms grown in caves in old quarries near Paris, and isinglass, the precursor to modern gelatin (originally made from the bladders of Russian sturgeon, and later made more cheaply from cod). When this extremely expensive import (up to $18 per pound) was temporarily unavailable, Pierce sent his own agents to Russia for a new supply, dragging it on dogsleds through the "frozen forests" before it could be shipped back to Boston.

The extraordinary effort that S. S. Pierce spent in sourcing its products was also evidenced in its approach to customer service. The Bon Voyage Basket was a famous offering that was delivered to a ship's passenger just prior to sailing. In one famous case, however, the basket did not, in fact, reach the ship before departure. The first port of call was Bombay, where the basket was finally delivered to the customer by a representative of the company as soon as the ship reached port. A similar story involves a shipment of green turtle soup that had not arrived on the morning of a dinner party in Poughkeepsie. A Pierce employee was immediately dispatched, and he arrived with the soup in hand one hour before the party started.

Pierce was also an early adopter of canned goods; its first recorded sale of canned corn was in 1848. It should be noted that in the nineteenth century, this new method of preservation was considered a marvel, and foods sold in this manner were not necessarily looked down upon, as most canned foods are today. One happy customer wrote to S. S. Pierce noting that his grandfather's homegrown fruits and vegetables were always a source of great pride at his table, but that the canned variety sold by Pierce compared favorably to his own fresh produce. The heart and soul of S. S. Pierce was its catalog, which was entitled *The Epicure*. It contained food writing, recipes, and, of course, a description of items, including prices.

And what was for sale at S. S. Pierce in 1896? There were twenty-three pages of listings, with about 180 items per page, including tea; coffee at 40 cents a pound; maple and fruit syrups; a long list of sugars, including loaf, granulated, crushed, cut loaf, golden yellow, confectioner's, German beet sugar, maple sugar, rock candy crystals, and red frosting sugar; a range of flours, including three brands we still recognize today, Pillsbury, Hecker's, and Swan's Down; a wide selection of oats, including McCann's Irish and Quaker rolled; Aunt Jemima's pancake mix; Graham flour (the brainchild of Sylvester Graham, a health-food advocate and founder of the first health-food store); infant foods, including malted milk; condensed milk; beef extracts for making stocks and sauces; spices (Penang cloves, Java cassia, Jamaica ginger, Tellicherry, Nepaul, curry powder); herbs, including Bell's poultry dressing; chocolate and cocoa (the better brands ran up to 90 cents per pound); dried, crystallized, and glacéed fruits; nuts; crackers and biscuits, as well as American and foreign cheeses. American cheese was rather inexpensive—25 cents a pound or less—whereas the imports cost up to $1 a pound. Corn included hominy, samp, white cornmeal, and cornstarch. There were copious listings for pantry staples such as pickles; macaroni (they were only selling lasagna, spaghetti, vermicelli, and noodles at this point); catsups and sauces (including catsup made from walnuts and mushrooms, soy sauce, and A1 and Tabasco sauces); vinegars; olive oil from Italy at 65 cents per quart and labeled under the house brand; and imported vegetables, including a wide assortment of truffles, as well as Brussels sprouts, artichokes, and cepes. There were loads of pâtés; all sorts of canned meats, including potted ham, chicken, tongue, and turkey; canned soups; and American canned vegetables and fruits, many of them imported from California. Fresh fruits were put up in jars with a light syrup, and preserved fruits were sold separately in airtight glass jars, including six kinds of cherries (maraschino, canned, crystallized, fresh in glass jars, preserved, and sweet pickled). And in a nod to locally sourced foods, a Quaker community out in Harvard was contracted to raise herbs for the Boston store.

As for household supplies, there was wax, candles, soaps (Dobbins electric soap and Hoxie's mineral soap), polishes (Kimball's liquid polish and Burnishine), blacking, sardine knives, matches, twine, brooms, clothespins, and five different brands of toilet paper, medicated with aloe or witch hazel. One could find imported whiskies, including Jameson's and Canadian Club, as well as domestic bourbon, brandy, beer, rum, and gin. Nonalcoholic beverages ran the gamut from squashes (citrus juice and soda water), to lemonades, ginger champagne, ginger ales, fruit syrups, shrubs (fruit, vinegar, and water, although some were alcoholic, since they were allowed to ferment), and sarsaparillas, as well as a full range of bottled waters, including Poland, Hygeia, Manitou, Schweppes, Vichy, Saratoga, and Bethesda.

With the growth of S. S. Pierce, smaller grocery stores emerged to service local neighborhoods, the goods being mostly packaged foods, imported teas and coffees, and staples such as flour and sugar. Larger retailers were also starting or expanding their grocery sections; one such store, Bailey's, often undercut S. S. Pierce with lower prices. In time, these larger establishments put the fresh-air markets out of business, since they delivered, they were clean and orderly, they were usually closer to home, and they had larger inventories.

Back in Boston in the 1890s, most of the food shopping was done in Faneuil Hall Marketplace, where almost 1 million people came to market. However, by 1899, the market was so overcrowded that proposals were afoot to build new markets, such as the one suggested for the former railway depot site at Park Square. Unlike S. S. Pierce, these markets allowed farmers from thirty to forty miles outside of Boston the chance to set up shop and sell directly to consumers.

Shopping was not done just by professional cooks or the middle-class housewife with list in hand. By the 1890s, some upper-class women were also going about doing their own shopping, as described in a November 17, 1895, article in the *Boston Globe*. These "ladies of leisure" would go to market in carriages driven by liveried coachmen, keeping their shopping lists in "leather and gold notebooks." (Other well-to-do women came by public transportation or walked, of course.)

The experience of shopping for Thanksgiving in 1896 was recorded by one intrepid *Boston Globe* reporter, who wrote about the tremendous last-minute rush for turkeys with "sounds worthy [of] the realms of Beelzebub" as bargain-hunting shoppers descended on Quincy Market to secure the main event in the biggest meal of the year. The streets were lit with both torches and electric lights and the birds formed fences and walls along the lines of the curbstones, hung from their feet by ten-penny nails pounded into improvised wooden scaffolding. As the evening progressed, the prices fell from 20 cents a pound at 8:00 P.M. down to 15 to 17 cents by 9:00 P.M., which was closing time for the market itself. Outside, the vendors kept up their "seductive oratory" until almost midnight. By 11:00 P.M., turkey had dropped to 10 cents per pound and a vendor with just one chicken in inventory hawked it at a mere 5 cents per pound, saying, "Here you go now, ladies and gents. This is the last bird I possess in the world. He's yours for 12 cents, and if you don't find him the tenderest chicken in Boston, I'll give him to you for nothing."

One of the best accounts of life in Boston in the late nineteenth century appears in *One Boy's Boston* by Samuel Eliot Morison, who describes the types of stores found on Charles Street. There were two fish markets; a hardware store; a fruit store (Solari & Porcella); Chater's Bakery, which had a lunch counter where one could purchase a bowl of soup or a ham sandwich for 5 cents; Greer's Variety Store, which sold green pickles in a large goldfish bowl for 1 cent each; Murphy's Grocery; John Cotter's saloon; a shoe repair shop; and a tailor. Morison goes on to talk about food shopping, indicating that the "man from Pierce's" would show up every morning to take an order. Staples such as flour, sugar, potatoes, and apples were brought by the barrel, and all the breads and cakes (except for parties) were baked in the house. Meat, poultry, eggs, and fish were ordered by his grandfather personally at Faneuil Hall or Quincy Market on Saturday mornings. As it was in Europe, food shopping was a daily affair, in part due to the lack of cold storage space; iceboxes were still rather small in the late 1800s, and many households did not even own one.

Victorian Boston was, all in all, a vastly better and more convenient place to shop than Boston today. The farmer's market was not a small-time, anything-but-mainstream concept, but the bread and butter of food shopping. And vendors had the benefit of faster and refrigerated transportation, so they could import fruits, vegetables, and even fish from across the country, and also purchase mushrooms, olive oil, pasta, chocolate, and many other delicacies direct from Europe. It was a wonderful time to be a home cook, especially if one had sufficient disposable income.

JUNE 2009. WHILE I WAS WORKING ON THIS PROJECT, A NUMBER of books and magazine articles had appeared saying, in effect, that cooking was dead. I would inevitably get sucked into reading these diatribes, the virtuous food writer either waxing poetic about the past or launching into a polemic about the evils of fast food or the effect of agribusiness on the American dinner table.

I kept thinking, don't my Vermont neighbors count? They not only do a lot of cooking but also do a lot of canning and preserving. I also knew that the magazine *Taste of Home* had over 3 million subscribers and its pages were filled with recipes, not long lifestyle pieces. These were mostly midwestern cooks who baked more than their share of cookies, breads, pies, and cakes. So was this the bicoastal food mafia talking—people who ate out at least five nights a week—or was home cooking really dying? And what was I doing cooking a twelve-course, twenty-eight-recipe menu in an age when the media had declared the culinary arts to be purely a spectator sport? What was next, the death of sex?

There is no question that the time spent cooking at home has gone down a lot over the last hundred years. The key driver of this decrease is the movement of women out of the home and into the workplace. In 1900, only 20 percent of women were in the labor force, versus over 60 percent in 2000. For most women, life at home was neither easy nor pleasant. In Fannie's day, a woman spent on average forty-four hours a week making and cleaning up after meals and another seven hours in general cleaning; and then, on top of that, there was child care. Families were larger—20 percent of American households had seven or more family members— thus more to cook and clean up for. Another big factor in time spent cooking was the availability of electricity. As late as 1930, only 10.4 percent of farms were electrified. A wood cookstove and no electric appliances translated to a great deal more time preparing food.

By 1950, however, this picture had changed dramatically, with over 90 percent of rural areas now having electricity, thanks to the Rural Electrification Administration. Electricity also meant the availability of mechanical refrigerators: by 1950, 80 percent of American households owned one. By midcentury, the typical American cook was spending only twenty hours per week cooking, down from forty-four hours in 1900.

Given the huge technological changes since 1900, much of this reduction in time spent cooking was probably a very good thing indeed. And why the hell don't food writers ever admit that spending six hours a day cooking and cleaning in the kitchen is not ideal? Hey, I love from-scratch cooking as much as the next cook, but I am extremely grateful for many of the technological wonders of the modern kitchen. For starters, we have gas or electric stoves and ovens, which require a whole lot less time, thought, planning, and maintenance than a wood or coal cookstove. And how about dishwashers for reducing cleanup time?

Food preservation is not an issue at all these days, owing to electric refrigerators and the ability to purchase small portions of almost anything. Cooks in Fannie's day were still spending a lot of time breaking down or preserving large quantities of seasonal foods for use later. Much of our food has already been sorted out, cleaned, and packaged; for example, turkeys no longer require plucking. We can purchase foods that reduce cooking time enormously—who among us would really like to spend half an hour shucking peas for dinner? Or beating egg whites by hand or even with a mechanical, hand-turned Dover eggbeater? And that is not even considering what the food processor, the microwave, electric knife sharpeners, blenders, pressure cookers, bread machines, and electric deep fryers have done for us in terms of reducing preparation and cooking time.

So unless one believes that six hours a day in the kitchen inevitably leads to moral superiority—it needs to be said that the Victorians were absolutely thrilled to spend less time in the kitchen—then using technology to cut down on drudgery should be a plus, not a minus. Is washing dishes by hand innately more virtuous than using a dishwasher? (I do admit, however, to an irrational belief in the moral superiority of those who take time to prepare their own food as opposed to eating out all the time— but I am still not going to use a wood cookstove on a daily basis, and am deeply grateful for hot water out of the tap.)

Perhaps of even more importance is the fact that the cost of food has dropped enormously since 1900. Back then, the average household was spending about 30 percent of its total annual income on food, 20 percent in 1960, and about 10 percent today. When food is cheap, you spend less time preserving and reusing it—it is no longer a scarce resource. (This does have a curious dark side, however. From 1985 to 2000, the price of fruits and vegetables rose 118 percent, whereas sugar and sweets have risen just 46 percent, fats and oils, 35 percent, and carbonated soft drinks just 20 percent. For households that are watching their food dollar, the cost of fresh produce is outpacing the cost of fats and sugars, the foundation for most convenience foods.)

Another common yardstick for decrying the lack of home cooking is the amount of money spent on dining out. Fifty years ago, 25 percent of the food dollar was spent outside the home; today, just under 50 percent. So one can claim that expenditures on eating outside the home have increased 100 percent! Conversely, one might say, over half of all food dollars are still spent inside the home. That sounds better. Americans are still spending slightly more on food consumed at home than at restaurants.

Drilling down into the statistics, one finds that of the expenditures outside of the home, 22 percent goes to food purchased at snack bars, movie theaters, amusement parks, and sports arenas. These are hardly replacements for meals. In fact, one might note that we are simply eating a lot more food outside of the regular three meals per day. The point is simple: although the percentage of the food dollar spent at home is dropping, the distribution of those expenditures is over a larger number of choices, snacking being a major category. That means that the percentage of food dollars spent on food consumed at home may not paint as disastrous a picture as we think.

Other trends further queer the statistics. Let's take midday dinner, which, in the late nineteenth century, was still the big meal of the day (as it still is in some parts of Europe). With women moving quickly into the workforce and the rise of industrialization, the midday dinner disappeared; folks were now eating at lunch counters and food carts. This was not a matter of Americans choosing to cook less; it was simply a matter of fewer women left at home to do the cooking during the day. Commuting also destroyed the midday meal, since it became increasingly difficult to go home for lunch. So the time spent cooking may have dropped considerably since 1900, but with absolutely no loss in quality or pleasure in terms of the one large meal of the day.

In a July 29, 2009, article in the *New York Times* Michael Pollan says that only twenty-seven minutes a day are spent cooking at home, plus another four minutes for cleanup. And the Bureau of Labor Statistics' *American Time Use Survey 2008* reports that the average amount of time spent cooking during weekdays is about thirty minutes. But wait a minute! The bureau also found that roughly half the American population over age 15 does no cooking whatsoever—meaning that the average time spent cooking, for those who *do* cook, is roughly sixty minutes. Since 2003, this amount has only changed by three minutes. So we have gone from cooking six hours a day in 1900 to just one hour today, but much of that decrease is simply because it takes a whole lot less time to prepare food and clean up afterward than it used to and because, for all intents and purposes, we have gone from three meals a day prepared at home to one.

So let's put aside the "time spent cooking at home" discussion, since it is almost impossible to judge cooking time from one century to the next. Sure, we are cooking less, but much of this may be due to increased efficiency and the focus on just one meal per day. And how many of us would like to spend one-third of our waking hours just getting food on the table? That's what cows and horses do—they have to spend most of their time grazing just to get enough to eat. Maybe that's why they don't read books, go to movies, or spend time on Facebook.

Of course, anyone can play the "cooking is dead" game. Here are some carefully selected statistics that make the case. From 1999 to 2005, there were huge increases in prepared foods sold at supermarkets, including salads (52 percent), frozen prepared meals (32 percent), and desserts (25 percent). In this period, flour sales were way down (46 percent), as were sugar and chicken (16 percent). Pretty clear that the sky is falling, right? Well, now let me argue the opposite side: that cooking is holding its own very nicely. Spending on baking ingredients has actually *increased* 18 percent from 2000 to 2005—butter alone went up 1 percent. Frozen prepared foods actually declined by 15 percent during this period—a hopeful sign. Sales of lettuce, tomatoes, and potatoes all fell by less than 10 percent.

And if I were asked about the huge decrease in flour sales, I would simply point out that the French buy their bread and pastries at retail, so why shouldn't we?

Sales of cookware have also been on the upswing. In 2004, American cookware manufacturers shipped $992 million worth of product; in 2008, the total was $1,269 million. This is after a steady decrease during the prior five-year period. The International Housewares Association's Consumer Advisory Board conducted focus groups in 2006 indicating that consumers eat dinner at home five or more times per week, and half the participants said that they were eating at home more often than they did a year ago. Internationally, cookware sales rose 9 percent in 2008. One industry analyst commented, "The growing interest in cooking and cooking programmes has had its influence specifically by changing people's behavior, as 'dining-in' becomes the new 'eating-out.'" This was even true in Poland, where cooking shows are extremely popular. This trend will probably be extended by the prospect of a long-term weak world economy.

So in the spirit of a renewed interest in home cooking, we moved on to the vegetable course. Fannie had a few suggestions: asparagus tips with hollandaise sauce, celery salad, dressed lettuce with cheese straws, string bean and radish salad, or a simple preparation of mushrooms, cauliflower, or artichokes. (This vegetable course may, in fact, be the precursor to the inevitable salad course that is, these days, currently sandwiched between the main course and dessert.) The notion of artichokes was appealing, since they were the most unusual choice. Frying battered artichokes was the most compelling recipe offered by Fannie, the others being stuffed artichokes (stuffed with a chicken forcemeat and topped with a "thin white sauce") and boiled artichoke bottoms, also served with either a hollandaise or béchamel. It seems that every time Fannie was confronted with a plain, simple ingredient, she threw a white sauce or hollandaise on it. Hardly *cuisine minceur*!

We had also put together the kitchen team for the dinner. Erin, my test kitchen director, was to be *chef de cuisine*. Four of our editor-cooks from

America's Test Kitchen would be joining Erin, including Keith Dresser, Andrea Geary, Dan Souza, and Yvonne Ruperti (Andrew Janjigian would bake the brown bread off-site); Marie Eleana and her son Ryan would handle cleanup. The waitstaff was chosen by Mike Ehlenfeldt, who had worked at Hamersley's Bistro with Erin. His wife, Cindy, would work the room, along with Jake McDowell, Debbie McDowell, Emile Arktinsal, and Melissa Klein. A rehearsal was planned for Saturday, October 24, so that we could cook through the whole meal to sort out timing and orchestrate the actual serving of the courses.

IN 1896, THE GLOBE ARTICHOKE WAS BOTH RARE AND EXPENsive in Boston. At a February 1896 meeting of the Massachusetts Horticultural Society, Anna Barrows, managing editor of *American Kitchen Magazine*, commented, "Many of the wealthy find in the expensive varieties of fruit and vegetables, like the mushroom, the globe artichoke, and the products of the hothouse, an opportunity to spend money lavishly and to gratify their aesthetic tastes." In other words, it was mostly a European commodity, a taste that sophisticated diners may have enjoyed over in France, England, or Italy, and then brought back to the United States.

As well as being awkward to eat, artichokes were also very expensive. *The National Cook Book* (1896), coauthored by the famous cookbook writer Marion Harland, noted that large, fine specimens of artichoke might fetch 50 cents in the New York markets. This was at a time when fresh salmon was running around 25 cents per pound. This was because most artichokes in the East were imported from France. However, this was not for lack of trying on the part of American farmers. They were grown in California and Louisiana as early as the eighteenth century, but initially were not a successful crop. According to *The Oxford Encyclopedia of Food and Drink in America*, "In the 1890s, Italian farmers in northern California's Half Moon Bay planted the crop, and beginning in 1904 boxcar loads of artichokes were sent east from California to supply the needs of artichoke

lovers on the East Coast—at that point, mainly Italian immigrants." By 1896, specimens from California could be had in the East late in the season.

The Green Laon artichoke was the most favored variety of imported artichoke, and was grown in the United States as well. The artichoke was named after the town of Laon, about ninety miles northeast of Paris, at the heart of which was a citadel and fortress. Its residents were noted gardeners, also producing asparagus from the sixteenth century on. In the latter part of the twentieth century, however, growers from southern Europe took over a good deal of the artichoke production.

By 1899, the artichoke was receiving renewed culinary attention and respect. Fannie's recipe started with boiled artichokes, which were then cut in quarters, sprinkled with salt, pepper, and parsley; dipped into a batter of bread flour, milk, and eggs; then deep-fried in fat and drained. But because of the heavy batter, the artichokes were heavy and pedestrian. We fiddled with the batter, making it leaner, but the finished coating was still thick and the artichokes tasted flat. The best solution was to soak the cooked artichoke halves in buttermilk and then make a light coating of flour, baking powder, and salt. Getting as much of the flour mixture in between the leaves also helped to provide a more interesting, crispier result. The last refinement was to score the leaves so that they would open up like petals of a flower.

FRIED BABY ARTICHOKES

The secret to this recipe is forcing the artichokes open so that they produce a fan of crisply breaded leaves. When done just right, you get a nice pairing of great crunch followed by the moister stem of the choke.

> 6 lemons, halved, plus 2 whole lemons for wedges
>
> 18 baby artichokes
>
> 4 teaspoons salt, plus more for seasoning fried artichokes
>
> 3 quarts peanut oil
>
> 2 cups flour
>
> 1 teaspoon baking powder
>
> 1 teaspoon salt, plus more for seasoning
>
> 2 cups buttermilk
>
> 2 tablespoons chopped parsley

1. Squeeze juice from 3 halved lemons into large bowl of water and add halves to water as well (reserve the remaining 3 halved lemons for step 2). Cut off the top quarter and snap off the fibrous outer leaves of the artichokes until you reach the yellow leaves. With a paring knife, trim dark green exterior from base of artichokes as well as the exterior of stems. Trim a thin slice from the end of stems, and peel stems. Drop trimmed artichokes into bowl of acidulated water until ready to cook.

2. Drain artichokes and transfer to large Dutch oven of boiling seasoned water (4 quarts water, juice of 3 halved lemons, 4 teaspoons salt). Cook until tender, 7 to 12 minutes. Remove and place cut-side down on paper towel–lined plate to drain. Once cool, cut each artichoke in half length-wise.

3. In large, heavy-bottomed Dutch oven fitted with clip-on-the-pot candy thermometer, heat oil over high heat to 375 degrees. While oil heats, whisk flour, baking powder, and 1 teaspoon salt together in large bowl. Whisk

buttermilk and parsley together in second large bowl. Working in batches, submerge artichoke halves in buttermilk mixture, making sure that buttermilk gets in between leaves. Working one at a time, transfer soaked artichoke halves to flour mixture and gently coat and open leaves to ensure that flour mixture coats all leaves; transfer to tray. Repeat with remaining artichokes. Note: artichokes can be breaded up to 1 hour before frying.

4. Working one at a time, hold each artichoke by the stem with tongs upside down, slowly submerge leaves into hot oil, and hold for about 5 seconds so that the leaves are forced open. Release into oil to continue frying, stirring occasionally until golden brown, about 1 to 3 minutes. Working quickly, repeat process with remaining artichokes, frying in batches of 8 to 12. As they are ready, using slotted spoon, remove from oil and transfer to paper towel–lined plate, then transfer to wire rack set in rimmed baking sheet in warm oven to hold while frying remaining artichokes. When ready to serve, sprinkle evenly with kosher salt. Serve with lemon wedge.

Serves 12 (3 halves each).

Canton Punch

Everyday American Food, 1896:
Try the Roast and Beans but Skip the Fish

I f you lived in Boston during the 1890s, what would you be cooking at home and how would you cook it? For starters, home cooking in 1896 was vastly different from what the typical household was preparing a century before.

Let's take Thanksgiving. In the eighteenth century, the Thanksgiving feast would have been made entirely from local ingredients, and would have appeared provincial to an 1896 Bostonian. The baking would have been done in a brick oven by the fireplace. Wild partridge might have been substituted for the turkey. Pie crusts were made from a fine rye and "adorned with all sorts of fanciful flutings and architectural strips laid across the great cranberry tarts." Egg flip, considered old-fashioned and almost never served by the late Victorian era, was a popular holiday drink around 1800. (Egg yolks were beaten with sugar, hot milk, and brandy, then beaten egg whites were folded in and grated nutmeg sprinkled on top.)

Thanksgiving itself was considered a semireligious day in the early 1800s, with a special service at the meeting house, which, by the way, was not heated. ("A good mug of hot cider before leaving home in the morning had fortified us against the bitter cold of the first service.") Women brought their foot warmers (cast-iron footrests that contained hot coals and had a handle for carrying), people stood in the "sheep pens" (squared-off sections for the congregation), and the congregants stood for the first hour and then sat for the second hour, which was devoted to the sermon. This was also a day to help out the minister with gifts. He would have been paid roughly $300 per year and given twenty cords of wood. But on Thanksgiving, he would receive all sorts of beef and pork, butter, a bushel or two of beets, candles, geese, and brandy.

By contrast, Fannie's "Menu for Thanksgiving Dinner" seems rather modern. It began with oyster soup with crisp crackers, celery and salted almonds, and then roast turkey with cranberry jelly, mashed potatoes, onions in cream and squash, then a course of chicken pie, followed by fruit pudding with sterling sauce. Three dessert pies were next—mince, apple, and squash—and then Neapolitan ice cream and fancy cakes (small, individual cakes or cookies), fruit, nuts, and raisins, bonbons, and a final course of café noir with cheese and crackers. Variations on this theme would have included creamed oysters instead of the soup, green peppers stuffed with shrimp, and cooked artichoke hearts served with a white sauce. Some sort of sponge cake might have been added for dessert, since it was popular and could be easily dressed up with colored whipped cream.

Victorian cooks pot-roasted, fricasséed, roasted, fried, panfried, braised, stewed, and boiled. Roasting first meant cooking over an open fire and then, when wood and coal cookstoves came into use, cooking over "fierce heat." Braising was originally done in a braising pan with a cover that would accommodate coals, so there was no need for an oven. This method was good for "large pieces of tough, lean meat." A stew might also be referred to as a haricot, a ragout, or a salmi. Salmon or other oily fish was started in cold water and brought almost to the boiling point quickly for best texture and flavor.

Broiling was translated as "to burn." A one-inch steak would have been broiled for about four minutes, and an inch-and-a-half steak for six minutes or so. They also turned it every ten seconds because they were concerned about overcooking. How did they know when a steak was done? The meat should "spring up instantly when pressed with a knife"—otherwise, it was overcooked. (Late Victorian cooks did understand the benefits of rare to medium-rare meat, so the penchant for overcooked steak that is common among many Americans today did not come from this earlier era.) Chickens were also broiled, and, as stated earlier, often a buttered glazed paper was used to protect them. White letter paper was buttered, folded over, and then pinched together to seal. This was, in effect, a clever *en papillote* technique that they felt would help the chicken to baste in its own juices. The chicken was done when it was well browned.

A fricassée was a common approach to many dishes, defined as "frying" although it was also a form of stewing. Chicken, veal, or some small game was cut into pieces and fried either before or after stewing, and then served with a rich white or brown sauce, without vegetables. They often dipped tougher pieces of meat in vinegar to "soften the fiber." Panfrying was done with a pan that was heated up "to blue heat" and then rubbed with a bit of beef fat. The meat was seared on both sides and cooked for about four minutes. They also used just about every part of an animal, including the heart. Here is a less than promising recipe from 1896 entitled Stuffed Beef Heart: "Thoroughly cleanse in salt water, fill all cavities with veal stuffing, two ounces beef suet, chopped fine, four ounces bread crumbs, one tablespoon chopped parsley, half teaspoon each of thyme and marjoram, juice of half a lemon, half teaspoon salt, a pinch of pepper and dust of nutmeg. Skewer a few slices of fat pork over the heart, flour, bake one and one-half hours, make gravy, serve hot."

In terms of cooking times, beef was cooked eight to ten minutes per pound for rare (the desired end state). A thick five-pound halibut would take an hour to cook, whereas a small fish would take twenty to thirty minutes (they either loved overcooked fish or were using extremely low temperatures). Asparagus and hard-boiled eggs were cooked fifteen to twenty minutes (so much for *al dente* vegetables), and they often boiled certain fish such as cubed salmon, cod, haddock, and bass.

When roasting, the Victorians always salted and floured the outside of their meat, which they felt helped retain the juices. (The theory was that salt would draw out juices, which would mix with the flour to help form a coating. Both Lincoln and Farmer went in for this approach.) We tested this method when roasting a chicken and found, oddly enough, that there was some merit to the method, although not for retaining juiciness. Fannie's recipe suggested rubbing a chicken with salt, then spreading the breast and legs with three tablespoons of softened butter that had been mixed with two tablespoons of flour. The chicken was roasted in a hot oven and, once the flour in the bottom of the roasting pan had browned (some was thrown in as an aid in measuring oven temperature), the bird was basted every ten minutes until cooked.

Following in Fannie's footsteps, we salted and then floured (no butter paste) a chicken only on one side, and left it sitting on a cooling rack over a baking sheet in the refrigerator overnight. We then roasted it at 425 degrees for twenty minutes, then reduced the temperature to 350 degrees, and roasted it another twenty minutes, basting it just once. Then we roasted the bird a final thirty minutes until just cooked through. The result? The half that had no flour had a tough skin, but the side with the flour was perfectly crisp and delicious. The meat on both sides—that is, with or without the flour coating—was juicy and tender. Turns out that this method does provide crisper skin on a roasted chicken. So the Victorians did have a few tricks up their sleeve.

FANNIE FARMER'S ROAST CHICKEN
WITH CRISPY FLOUR COATING

The secret is to use flour, not a butter-flour paste, and to baste the bird only once. Air-drying the bird overnight is a time-tested method for producing a thin, crispy skin during roasting. This air-drying method also works for your Thanksgiving turkey.

> 1 whole chicken, 3½ to 4½ pounds, giblets removed and discarded
> 1 tablespoon kosher salt
> ½ teaspoon ground black pepper
> ¼ cup flour
> 2 tablespoons butter
> ⅓ cup water

1. Pat chicken dry with paper towels and sprinkle all over with salt and pepper; rub with hands to coat entire surface evenly. Coat chicken evenly with flour and pat to knock off excess. Set chicken, breast side up, in a V rack set on a rimmed baking sheet and refrigerate, uncovered, for 12 to 24 hours.

2. In small saucepan (or in microwave), heat butter and water until butter melts. Adjust oven rack to lowest position and heat oven to 425 degrees. Flip chicken so breast side faces down. Roast chicken for 20 minutes. Reduce oven temperature to 350 degrees; continue roasting for 20 minutes. Baste with butter mixture, flip chicken breast side up, and baste again. Continue roasting until skin is golden brown and crisp and thermometer registers 160 degrees when inserted in thickest part of breast, and 175 degrees in the thickest part of thigh, about 40 to 50 minutes.

3. Transfer chicken to cutting board and let rest, uncovered, for 20 minutes. Carve and serve immediately.

TO CLARIFY FAT FOR FRYING AND BAKING, UNCOOKED FAT FROM chickens, lard, and beef suet were cut into small pieces, covered with cold water, and cooked over a slow fire until the fat had melted and the water nearly all evaporated. Then this mixture was strained and pressed. The fat was placed in a pan over the fire; when it melted, a small raw potato, cut into thin slices was added. This stood on the stove until the fat stopped bubbling and the scraps were brown and crisp and had risen to the top. The fat was then strained and kept in a cool place where it lasted for weeks. This clarified fat could also be used for bread, plain pastry, and ginger-bread.

Larding, daubing, and barding were common techniques, rarely used today. Larding started with strips of salt pork, two inches wide and four inches long, cut into lardoons, a quarter of an inch both wide and long. Then, the cook was instructed to "with the point of the needle take up a stitch half an inch deep and one inch wide in the surface of the meat." The ends of the salt pork would then stick out of the surface of the meat, making it look a bit like a porcupine. Daubing was used with a broad, thick piece of beef or veal—the notion was to insert fat all the way through a piece of meat, not just on the surface, as was done with larding. Salt pork was cut into strips a third of an inch both wide and thick. A hole was punched clear through the meat with a steel larding needle and then the strips of pork were inserted with a large larding needle or with the fingers. Another technique was to simply cover a roast with wide strips of salt pork before cooking. (This latter technique, referred to as barding, was offered up in *James Beard's American Cookery* and tried in our test kitchen with a roast turkey. With a few modifications, it works admirably.)

So what would a Victorian Boston family have to eat during a typical day in 1896? This is easily determined by looking at the menus printed in the back of Fannie's cookbook. But I also spent time reading two columns from the *Boston Globe:* "Our Cooking School" and the "Housekeeper's Column." First, a word about the column. By this time, recipes were no longer rough notes, but very precise, with specific ingredient amounts. The preamble to each day's column was as follows: "It is also suggested that directions for mixing ingredients should be very explicit, and quantities should be definitely indicated. Only favorite, true and tried recipes should be sent in. Mere skeletonized recipes, such as some cook books give, are not desired." I also noted that not all of the correspondents to the "House-keeper's Column" were female. One such writer referred to himself as "Male Cook" and offered a recipe for broiled veal.

Let's start with breakfast. One almost always had meat at breakfast: lamb chops, chopped beefsteak (cooked rare), broiled steak, ham, bacon, cold meat, or broiled rump steak were popular. A hearty breakfast was not out of place for a population that was doing a lot of hard manual labor: 38 percent of workers labored on farms; 31 percent were in mining, manufacturing, or construction; and the remainder, 31 percent, were in service businesses. (Today, 78 percent of American labor is in the service sector.) Eggs were served occasionally, but were not a central part of the breakfast table. Fruit was usually included, whether it be prunes, oranges, canned pears, stewed apricots, or stewed apples. For bread, rolls, muffins, or toast was served.

Buckwheat or potato cakes were not uncommon, and maple syrup was often served, even when one did not have griddle cakes on the menu. Pancakes had various names, including fritters, flapjacks, slapjacks, butter cakes, griddle cakes, and slappers. Pancakes were originally a muffin batter mixture, stiffer than a drop batter but not stiff enough to roll out. The batter was dropped from a spoon into hot fat and fried like doughnuts. More recently, Mrs. Lincoln noted in her 1883 cookbook, the name had been applied to a thin batter usually made without soda, cooked one cake at a time on a small well-buttered frying pan and turned like a griddle cake. She described griddle cakes as "any kind of small, thin batter-cakes cooked on a griddle." Pancakes were "larger, thin batter-cakes made without soda and cooked in a small frying-pan." Griddle cakes could be made out of many things, including stale bread crumbs, boiled rice, fine hominy, cornmeal mixed with buckwheat flour, dried peas that were boiled, sifted squash, and flour. Potatoes, cornmeal mush, or hominy were on almost every breakfast menu, whether browned, mashed, baked, or lyonnaise. Oatmeal was not as common as one might expect, and coffee, not tea, was the hot beverage of choice.

Dinner, the large meal served in the middle of the day, was not that different from what one might expect in modern times except for the Victorians' use of pickled foods, love of jelly, and devotion to cheese. Occasionally, dinner would start with a soup such as tomato, turkey, or consommé, but more often than not, there was no first course. The main offering might be veal stew, chicken pie, fricasséed oysters, a leg of pork (fresh pork, I assume, not a ham), roast beef, steamed chicken, stewed beef, roast leg of lamb, or roast turkey. For starch, they served sweet potatoes, rice, potatoes (steamed, mashed, or boiled), and some pasta or "macaroni" as a side dish. The vegetables were most often tomatoes (baked, stewed), turnips, cabbage, canned string beans, or canned corn.

Pickling was popular since it was a preservative, and they served spiced grape pickles, pear sweet pickles, and just regular "pickles." For jams, marmalades, and jellies, served at most dinners, they used apples, lemons, raspberries, quince, and grapes (for marmalade), cranberries (more for sauce), currants, and peaches. Breads included white bread (often store-bought), cornbread, or just "bread and butter." For dessert they were fond of ginger cakes, apple and squash pies, floating islands, puddings, turnovers, chocolate cake, canned fruits, sherbet, and gingerbread, although a meal could have been finished with just fresh fruit. Dinner usually ended with cheese and crackers, but not always.

Supper was the evening meal, and it was modest. It could be as simple as crackers and milk, bread and butter, fruit, oatmeal wafers, and tea. Or they might have tucked into Boston baked beans, bread, prunes, cookies, and tea. Cold meats (leftover from dinner) were quite common, although one might see an oyster stew or perhaps dried beef in cream gravy on the table as well. The rest of the menus were fruit (baked apples were popular, although canned fruits were readily available by this time as well), cookies or cake, bread and butter (brown bread was popular for supper), and tea, not coffee. Compared to the current playbook used by the average home cook, the Victorians were a cauldron of culinary enthusiasm and technique.

A useful way to look at the changes in cookery from 1800 to 1900 is to consider that ingredients were scarcer and more expensive at the beginning of the century, and therefore earlier recipes were designed to use every scrap. Take bread, for example. Fresh crumbs could be dried in an oven, then pounded in a mortar and pestle and sifted through a coarse sieve. They were then used as a coating for fried foods, but never for bread puddings or scalloped potatoes, since they would absorb too much liquid. Stale bread was simply coarsely grated and used for stuffing, bread puddings, griddle cakes, or scalloped fish. The crumbs had to be used quickly before they became musty. Stale bread was also steamed without becoming soggy or wet, and then spread with butter and served on a hot platter. Stale bread could be used for toast, employing either a toasting fork or a wire broiler. Or a simple bread pudding could be made by immersing "two 5-cent loaves of baker's bread into 2 quarts of sweet milk and soak[ing] over night." The mush was beaten the next day with eggs, molasses, butter, sugar, spices, raisins, currants, and citron, and then baked in a six-quart pan in a slow oven for six hours.

Key ingredients, such as corn, also provide a good snapshot of the changes in cooking during the nineteenth century. Take an ingredient you have probably never heard of, *samp* (the term probably derived from a local term, *newsamp*). Samp is dried corn that is ground or pounded into a powder, coarser than meal but finer than grits. Two common ways of cooking it included boiling it into a mush (this was eaten with milk or cream and sugar) or allowing the mush to cool, then slicing and frying it. Before mills were common, samp was pounded in mortars. Charles Ranhofer in *The Epicurean* (1894) suggested cutting cooked, cooled samp into squares, dipping it in egg and bread crumbs, and then frying it as a side dish to be served with canvasback ducks. This was a far cry from pioneer porridge.

Macaroni (a general term for pasta) was an ingredient that became increasingly popular during the nineteenth century, although it was often cooked to death and often in milk. By the Civil War, macaroni was generally available, and whatever snob appeal this new food may have had earlier in the century had disappeared. According to Corby Kummer in an article in *The Atlantic*, the first American pasta maker may have been Louis Fresnaye, a French immigrant operating out of Philadelphia. By 1873, the *Boston Directory* contained a listing for Richard Pfeiffer as a macaroni manufacturer, the earliest such listing that I could find. However, Italian immigrants tended to prefer imported pasta, since it was made from durum wheat, a commodity that was well suited to the soil of Sicily and Campania. Regardless of his business acumen, Fresnaye was probably the first American to offer a recipe for macaroni and cheese. One pound of vermicelli was broken into one-inch pieces, boiled in three quarts of salted water until al dente, drained, placed into a shallow baking dish, spread with grated Parmesan, then drizzled with melted butter. The dish was then placed into a preheated 375-degree oven for ten to fifteen minutes or until the cheese was toasted.

Fannie recognized three types of pasta—macaroni, spaghetti, and vermicelli—and notes that although macaroni was produced in the United States, the best pasta came from Italy. Her basic preparation was to boil macaroni in salted water for twenty minutes (why did they overcook almost everything except meat?), drain, and then pour cold water over it to prevent sticking. She then added cream, reheated it, and served it with salt. She also served macaroni with a basic béchamel and often baked it with sauce and buttered bread crumbs. She did offer a recipe for baked macaroni and cheese: a layer of pasta, one of grated cheese, more pasta, white sauce, and then buttered crumbs on top. She also offered a few ersatz Italian recipes, including a Milanese version that called for mushrooms and smoked beef tongue. Her standard recipe for tomato sauce was particularly vile, combining a cup of brown stock, a very thick roux, and canned tomatoes.

One ingredient I would bet no modern epicure has enjoyed is pickled limes. Limes that were soaked in a brine so they would be preserved during the long voyage from the West Indies were all the rage among schoolgirls in the nineteenth century. Here is an excerpt from *Little Women*, which was published in 1868: Amy comments, "It's nothing but limes now, for every one is sucking them in their desks in school-time, and trading them off for pencils, bead-rings, paper dolls, or something else, at recess. If one girl likes another, she gives her a lime; if she's mad with her, she eats one before her face, and don't offer even a suck." In addition to sucking on them like candy, pickled limes were used as a garnish, in a relish or conserve, and to make lime squash, a drink that was traditionally made with lemons.

Since molasses was such a common ingredient in Boston (huge quantities were imported for use in making rum), local cooks would often use it instead of sugar. One such recipe used one cup molasses in an apple pie, and there was a lively discussion of how to keep it from leaking out. The answer was to wet the bottom crust so it adhered well to the top crust, to use cassia (this is what tapioca is made from) as a thickener, and to employ a slow oven, baking for an hour and a half.

To get a better sense of what everyday cooking was like in Boston in 1896, we chose a handful of representative recipes and went into the kitchen to test and improve them, if possible. Additional recipes—Baked Rosewater and Cardamom Custards with Pistachio, as well as Ginger Cream—are available at www.fannieslastsupper.com.

BAKED TOASTED COCONUT
AND VANILLA CUSTARD

This Victorian-era custard is made without egg yolks, an unusual approach that makes the custard a bit lighter, more like an Italian panna cotta. The coconut can be toasted on a baking sheet in a 350-degree oven for a few minutes—check it frequently, as it can burn. The egg whites should be about half-beaten—foamy and white on top and still a bit liquid on the bottom.

    4 ounces sugar
    1 cup heavy cream
    1 cup milk
    ½ vanilla bean, halved lengthwise
    Pinch salt
    1 teaspoon vanilla extract
    ½ cup sweetened coconut, toasted for 10 minutes in a 350-degree oven
    4 egg whites, beaten until well frothed throughout, but *not* soft-peaked

1. Adjust oven rack to lower-middle position and heat oven to 350 degrees. Place kitchen towel in bottom of large baking dish and arrange six 4-to 5-ounce ramekins on towel. Bring kettle or large saucepan of water to boil over high heat.

2. Whisk gently to combine sugar, cream, milk, seeds from vanilla bean, salt, vanilla extract, and coconut; whisk until sugar has almost completely dissolved. Add coconut and frothed whites to cream mixture and gently whisk to combine. Pour or ladle mixture into ramekins, dividing evenly among them.

3. Carefully place baking dish with ramekins on oven rack; pour boiling water into dish, taking care not to splash water into ramekins, until water reaches two-thirds height of ramekins. Cover loosely with foil. Bake until centers of custards are just barely set but no longer sloshy, and digital

instant-read thermometer inserted in centers registers 175 degrees, about 25 to 35 minutes.

4. Transfer ramekins to wire rack. Cool to room temperature, about 2 hours. Refrigerate until cold, at least 4 hours or up to 2 days.

 ## MUNROE BAKED BEANS

Baked beans from the nineteenth century used a whole lot more pork than we do today. For one quart of beans, Fannie would use a pound of "mixed pork" (this is a great recipe to use up odd bits and pieces). Everything was simply thrown together in a pot, including molasses (half a teacup), a bit of mustard, salt, and hot water, and then baked all day. Half an onion and salt pork were other common ingredients. If you have not soaked the beans overnight, they can be quick-soaked by placing them in a pot, covering them with an inch of water, and boiling them for one minute. Drain and proceed with the recipe. However, we prefer the overnight soak.

> 6 ounces salt pork
> 1 pound navy beans, rinsed and picked over, and soaked overnight
> 1 medium onion, peeled and cut into quarters
> ¼ cup molasses
> ¼ cup light brown sugar
> 1 teaspoon Dijon mustard
> ¾ teaspoon salt

1. Place salt pork in a small saucepan of boiling water. Allow to return to a simmer and cook for two minutes. Remove from pan, rinse, and cut into three or four large chunks. Meanwhile, heat oven to 250 degrees and adjust a rack to the center position.

2. Drain beans and place in a Dutch oven. Arrange salt pork and onion

wedges in the center of the pot. Add molasses, sugar, mustard, and salt and cover with 8 cups water. Place over high heat and bring to a boil. Transfer to oven and cook 4 hours. Stir, check for seasoning, and cook until very soft and creamy and the beans and liquid have turned a uniform color, about 2 hours longer.

 TAPIOCA PUDDING

Yet another recipe that intrigued us—mostly because of the use of large pearl tapioca—was a peach and tapioca pudding, which was nothing more than canned peaches topped with soaked pearl tapioca and then baked for an hour, served with cream and sugar. We baked up a batch and it was—and I am not holding back here—truly horrible. It turned into a gelatinous paste over mushy canned peaches.

Thinking that perhaps we were to add some milk and sugar along with the soaked tapioca, we included a cup of milk and one-third cup sugar. This time the paste was slightly looser, whiter in color, and a bit sweeter, but still, well, disgusting. We should also note that canned peaches are not agreeable to a modern palate. They have a soft mushy texture, a strange uniform color, and artificial flavor. So we headed back to the drawing board, taking the underlying concept of this recipe but starting completely from scratch. The recipe below is wonderful when topped with fresh berries or thinly sliced stone fruit. The pudding is best served on the day it is made, and is equally good whether cold, at room temperature, or warm.

(CONTINUED)

½ cup small pearl tapioca

2 cups whole milk

⅓ cup granulated sugar

½ teaspoon salt

2 large egg yolks

1½ teaspoons vanilla extract

1. Soak the tapioca in enough cold water to cover by 1 inch for at least 4 hours and no more than 12 hours. Drain. Place in a medium-sized sauce-pan with the milk, sugar, and salt and bring to a gentle simmer, with small bubbles around the perimeter of the pan. Simmer gently, stirring often, until the pearls are translucent and almost tender, about 40 minutes.

2. Meanwhile, lightly beat the egg yolks. Add them to the pot and stir well to combine. Continue to cook until the pudding is very thick, about 10 minutes longer. Remove from heat and add the vanilla. Transfer to a serving bowl or individual serving dishes. Serve (with fresh fruit as a topping if you like) warm or cooled to room temperature. If you choose to chill the pudding, do not refrigerate until it has reached room temperature.

Serves 4 to 6.

JULY 2009. ALTHOUGH BOSTON SOCIETY WAS AN INSULAR world, it was also America's busiest port in the nineteenth century, so, over time, the world of the Cabots and the Lodges changed forever, mainly because of modern transportation. The first true transatlantic steamer, the *Curaçao*, made the first crossing of the Atlantic in 1827, from Rotterdam to the West Indies. By the 1880s, virtually all transatlantic voyages were made by steam, reducing the crossing time from six weeks to just one. In 1896, 343,267 immigrants arrived on our shores, including 68,060 from Italy, 45,137 from Russia, 39,908 from Ireland, 31,885 from Germany, and 31,496 from Austria.

Steamboats also meant that the markets between Europe and the United States were more closely joined, leading to the widespread availability of items far beyond the usual list of tea, spices, and fortified wines: olive oil, real Italian Parmesan, French Brie, durum wheat pasta, Spanish olives, jarred French peas, plus domestic items, including oranges from Florida, peaches from California, and Hubbard squash from Michigan. In addition, the culinary practices of modern-day Paris were no longer a world away, nor were modern techniques of European food production, including, for example, compressed yeast. Although the first edition of *The Boston Cooking-School Cook Book* did not fully reflect this groundswell of social change, I wondered if later editions, still edited by Fannie Farmer, might reflect the times. So I found a 1913 edition and compared it to the original.

The most obvious change was the extensive use of illustrations, about 150 black-and-white photos in all, emphasizing presentation more than basic cooking methods. Puréed spinach is garnished with the yolk of a hard-boiled egg with radiating strips of white and toast points. We are offered a long list of stuffed foods, from eggplant to peppers. French recipe names, from Macedoine of Vegetables à la Poulette to Charlotte Russe, abound. We are taken on a world tour, from Mexican jelly to Russian cutlets to Dresden patties. Foods are presented in baskets (cucumbers, fruit); recipes are given honorariums, as in "à la Newburg" or "à la Lucullus"; and cakes are dressed to the nines, as is a Valentine's Day cake sprouting giant lilies, and an Ornamental Frosted Cake, decorated with mistletoe and a half-dozen sturdy candles. Toward the end of the book, we find a series of formal table settings, from Table for Formal Luncheon to Centerpiece of Thanksgiving Table, all of which include floral sprays, bunches, arrangements, and sprouts.

Sweetbreads, since they lend themselves to myriad preparations, also made a good comparison. The later edition included exactly the same introduction plus all the recipes from the 1896 edition. However, by 1913, Fannie had added three recipes that say a lot about how American cookery, and her style of teaching, had changed since the 1890s. The Sweetbreads, Country Style are simple enough, baked with a slice of salt pork. However, both the

Sweetbreads à la Napoli and the Braised Sweetbreads Eugenie are a bold attempt to tart up the cooking, make it more continental, and appeal to a class of women who were trying hard to impress their guests. The Napoli recipe involves rounds of bread, a layer of Parmesan cheese, a slice of sweetbread, and then a large cap of mushroom all baked in domed glass–covered dishes. The Eugenie version is similar, but substitutes sherry for cheese and adds multiple mushroom caps, also baked in a covered glass dish. It is the domed glass dish that Fannie is after—the presentation itself—rather than the underlying culinary approach. (I also noted that the original 1896 edition had only two chocolate cakes, yet by 1913, chocolate had come on strong, Fannie offering a total of seven cakes in this category, plus a series of frostings.)

The ads in the back of the 1913 edition tell us how quickly home cooking was changing. One could still purchase coal-fired Hub ranges, but Chambers "fireless" cooking gas ranges were now being advertised and, believe it or not, electric ranges were also available. One would also recognize many of the brands advertising in 1913, including Ivory soap, Crisco, Welch's grape drink, Karo corn syrup, Bell's seasoning, Wheatena, White Mountain freezer, King Arthur flour, Fleischmann yeast, Chase & Sanborn coffee, Royal baking powder, and Baker's chocolate.

Two things that had not changed at all were the first line of the first chapter—"Food is anything which nourishes the body"—and the dedication to Mrs. William B. Sewall, in which Fannie thanks her for her work in promoting scientific cookery, "which means the elevation of the human race." On one hand, Fannie was working hard to make her food appeal to the nouveaux riche. On the other, she still defined cooking as a means of elevating the human race through better nutrition. Perhaps investing cooking instruction with a higher, nobler purpose while, in effect, playing with her food was the perfect formula for success. After all, Fannie always described herself as a businesswoman, and anyone good at business knows the fine art of selling totally contradictory messages: it's fun, but it's also good for you.

One of the more modern culinary notions of Fannie's time was the palate-cleansing sorbet course, which, today, appears old-fashioned and often tastes more like dessert than a change of pace served between savory courses. Many cooks served this course almost—not completely—frozen in glasses and then sipped as a liquid. We tested this notion and found that, unfortunately, this almost frozen drink had a very short window of perfection—it would quickly melt and become rather unpleasant. So we decided to stick with a frozen sorbet and noted that Fannie did the same with her Victoria, Cardinal, Roman, and even—gulp—hollandaise punches. (The latter, thankfully, is based on grated pineapple, brandy, and gin.)

The earliest version of a frozen punch that we could find was a recipe entitled Punch Water Ice that was published in *The Complete Confectioner* in 1807 in London. The Victoria punch recipe in the 1896 edition of *The Boston Cooking-School Cook Book* is nothing like the drink; it is a frozen alcoholic ice. Fannie calls for water, sugar, lemon and orange juices, orange rind, angelica wine (a sweet fortified white wine), cider, and gin. The mixture is then frozen. We made a batch and found that it was too sweet and on the syrupy side (the angelica wine made it boozy); it had too little lemon flavor and the gin was pretty much lost.

Boston being the epicenter of trade with the Far East, new ingredients were constantly showing up on store shelves, and one of these was Canton ginger, an item that Fannie used in her recipe for Canton punch. Boston's fortunes were built on shipping. It all started with salt cod, which was shipped to the West Indies and sold for a cargo of sugar, molasses, and tobacco, which were loaded and then transported to England. Finished goods were then taken onboard for the trip back to Boston. Later, Boston distilled rum that was shipped to Africa, where it was traded for ivory, gold dust, mahogany, and slaves. The ships then sailed for the West Indies, where molasses was taken on and the slaves were off-loaded, and then made the return trip to Boston, where the molasses was used to make rum, the cycle starting afresh.

In 1748, a total of 540 ships left and 430 entered the port of Boston. A century later, in one single day, a whopping 70 ships sailed out of Boston. No other American city had command of the international trade in the 1840s—not New York, Philadelphia, or Baltimore. This was due in part to Boston's natural deep-water harbor, which, by 1700, had forty wharves (Long Wharf was built in 1710 and extended two thousand feet from the foot of King Street out into the deeper waters of the harbor). But also Boston's fleet of tall ships opened up trade with the Far East, where tea, opium, spices, and silk became dominant players in foreign commerce in the colonies. Huge fortunes were made, mansions built, and families catapulted into the highest ranks of Boston's social circles.

Looking at maps from the early nineteenth century, one can see why. The city was not much more than a port with a maximum amount of waterfront and a minimum amount of city. Lewis Wharf was perhaps the greatest wharf in mid-nineteenth-century Boston, the peak years being 1840 to 1860, with ships arriving from Liverpool as well as great clipper ships from San Francisco. However, by the 1860s, Atlantic Avenue was built; this signaled the beginning of the end, reducing the footprint of Boston's wharves and marking the decline of the great sailing ships. (So much of Boston was on the waterfront and so little of it is now that a modern resident of Boston would be shocked to learn that British ships anchored in Copley Square during the siege in the Revolution. Copley is located in the middle of town, sandwiched between Back Bay and the South End, in the heart of Boston's upscale shopping district. This would be like ships docking at Times Square in New York.)

Going back to the recipe for Canton punch, we researched Canton ginger to get a better understanding of what this recipe might have been like in 1896. Just using fresh ginger did not seem the right way to go because it would be much too strong. It turns out that there are two different meanings to "Canton" ginger: it referred to "true ginger," or *Zingiber officinale*, but it also described preserved ginger that was packed in a sugar syrup in

Canton and then shipped in stone jars, a common gourmet item in the United States by 1900.

The process for making preserved ginger was very similar to the process of making candied or "dry" ginger. Both were boiled in water after washing, and then the preserved ginger was boiled again in equal parts water and sugar. The candied or crystallized ginger would also get a second boiling, but with very little water added, contributing to its dry texture.

After much testing, we decided to use galangal, a very mild form of Asian ginger that gave the sorbet a subtle flavor. This was probably not what Fannie had in mind, although she probably did not mean fresh ginger of any kind. The good news is that Fannie's Canton Sorbet recipe was virtually perfect, a frozen palate cleanser that was light, refreshing, and perfect between courses.

 ## CANTON SHERBET

Although this recipe is listed as a sherbet, it is really nothing more than an ice, since sherbets usually have either milk or egg whites added. Do not use traditional ginger for this recipe—you need to purchase galangal or a similar ginger that is much milder. This is the ginger served with sushi: it tastes like ginger, but has much less bite. This recipe will serve 12 as a palate cleanser between courses.

    4 cups water
    1 cup sugar
    5 ounces peeled and trimmed galangal, cut into ¼-inch pieces
    ½ cup freshly squeezed orange juice
    ⅓ cup freshly squeezed lemon juice

Heat water, sugar, and galangal in medium saucepan over high heat until it reaches a boil. Cook for 13 to 15 minutes until reduced to 3 cups (including galangal). Cool to room temperature. Add fruit juice, strain mixture through fine mesh strainer, refrigerate until it reaches 40 degrees. Start ice-cream machine and add juice mixture to canister. Churn until sherbet has texture of soft-serve ice cream, 25 to 30 minutes.

Serves 12 as a small palate cleanser.

Roast Stuffed Goose

The Transformation of the Victorian Kitchen:
The Lady of the House Rolls Up Her Sleeves

The original kitchen of our house on Worcester Square was located at the rear of the first floor, but since that floor had been converted into a rental unit, we did not have access to it. Our own kitchen, of more recent vintage, with cheap chipboard cabinets and Formica countertops, had been shoehorned into what used to be the music room off the parlor-floor dining room. Since we needed the income from the rental unit, we had to make do, but we were planning for the day that we could return the kitchen to its original location, once again using the 1859 hearth, which was, remarkably, still intact.

Ours was a modest affair compared to a true Victorian kitchen in a wealthy household in England. In the English countryside, kitchens were positioned so they faced either north or east to keep them cool. In an architectural approach, which also found favor here in the States, the Victorians did not like built-in cabinetry, since it encouraged mice and vermin. The center of the kitchen contained one very long worktable. There was often tile on the walls, or, in less wealthy households, the plaster walls were simply whitewashed. And if there was room, there was also a separate scullery for cleaning as well as a larder for food storage. Oilcloth was used as an early floor covering if one could not afford tile. (Take cloth, cover it with a thin coat of rye paste, then add paint and let it hang for two months.)

Linoleum was invented in 1863 by a British subject named Frederick Walton. In the 1870s, he founded the American Linoleum Manufacturing Company in New York City. Made from linseed oil, fillers, and ground cork on a burlap backing, linoleum was stronger and more durable than oilcloth and less expensive than tile, so it was favored primarily by the middle class. And for tin ceilings, far from being a luxury, they were nothing more than a cheap imitation of the carved plaster ceilings found elsewhere in the more public portions of the house.

Coal was stored in a separate area, in a shed attached to the back of the kitchen (one large home on Beacon Street in Boston still has its attached coal bin) or emptied into the a stone-walled chamber under the outside stairs leading up to the parlor floor. A coal chute was built into the sidewalk just in front of the stairs. It was covered by a piece of stone, which was lifted off for deliveries. Our coal bin was still intact, and we now use it as a wine cellar, the perfect spot given the constant below-grade temperature throughout the year. (One Newport mansion stored its coal underground on the other side of the main road; the coal was brought to the kitchen by an underground railroad.) Shelving was simple, the wood to make it was nothing more than pine (expensive materials were reserved for the upstairs living spaces used by the owners), and the kitchen was not much more than a room, sparsely furnished, with a stove, worktable, and wall storage. It was easy to clean, easy to move around in for the staff, and very, very hot all year round. Hoosiers, the one-piece minikitchens with storage, an expandable shelf, and a built-in flour dispenser, were not introduced until the turn of the twentieth century, although our kitchen still uses one, to hold spices, jams, extracts, oils, and baking chocolate.

Coal was dirty, and the Victorians were extremely keen on cleanliness. To wash glasses and silverware, they employed two pans, one with hot soapy water and the other just hot water, with ammonia added. A half cup of milk was often added to hard dishwater to keep hands soft and promote sparkling dishes. By the late nineteenth century, however, lots of prepackaged cleaning supplies were also popular, including Armour's white soap. In the 1890s, there were outbreaks of smallpox and cholera, so sanitary measures became even more important in the kitchen. In this war against germs, householders used carbolic acid and water, chloride of lime, chloride of zinc, corrosive sublimate, sulfate of iron, sulfate of zinc, and chloride of lead, the latter employed for sinks and drains.

The Victorians were substantially different from modern epicures—the whole notion of an open kitchen with savory smells wafting out into the dining area would appall them. Under no circumstances did they want to smell the food as it was cooking, and that is one reason the kitchens were usually located in the basement or in the rear of the first floor. (Another Newport mansion has an entire wall of glass windows between the kitchen and the hallway. These windows were kept closed during cooking, and only opened when dinner was served.) In addition, the kitchen had rules about reducing odors: grease was not to fall onto the oven floor (if it did, hay or straw was immediately burned in the oven); a crust of bread was put into water used for boiling green vegetables and when discarded, either poured into a corner of the garden or, if in the sink, followed by carbolic acid. In very large English Victorian houses, the kitchen was as far away as possible from the dining room, sometimes connected by long passageways that had air ducts to keep them smelling fresh. If you have ever wondered about covered serving dishes, this is why they were invented: to keep the food hot on the sometimes long journey from kitchen to dining room. Plates and serving dishes had to be preheated, and many dishes sat over hot water as they traveled up to be served.

However, by Fannie's time, the kitchen was no longer the culinary equivalent of a boiler room, the engine of the house, occupied only by the poorly paid lower classes. Domestic help, once cheap and plentiful, had become a rare commodity for most households. As a result, the lady of the house was now spending a lot more time in the kitchen. This was to change the culinary arts and American cooking forever.

The American kitchen depended on domestic help of one sort or another from the very beginning. The early-seventeenth-century colonists at Jamestown and Plymouth had brought servants with them, and black slaves were used by the Hudson Valley Dutch. Other families relied on the practice of indentured servitude—many who came to the New World paid for their passage through long work contracts—as well as apprenticeships. However, by the early part of the nineteenth century, many immigrants were paying cash for their voyage, so this source of cheap labor started to dry up. (Tickets were becoming cheaper and existing communities of immigrants here in the United States were providing economic assistance for the passage.) By the mid-nineteenth century, indentured labor had pretty much disappeared, but the ranks of young women available for paid domestic work were growing as urban centers started to prosper with the Industrial Revolution. Prior to this period, a woman might employ the daughters of neighbors (and therefore of the same social class) for short-term paid help, but these women usually went on to start their own families and were not career domestics. In fact, Fannie herself was a family helper for a short time before attending the Boston Cooking School.

The rapid growth of the middle class in the latter half of the nineteenth century brought with it the opportunity to work in either a factory or a domestic job. Yet many young women preferred to take factory work, even though it often paid considerably less than domestic work. One reason, not usually mentioned in history books, is that the public workplace was an excellent opportunity to meet men, whereas a domestic servant had little chance to socialize and start her own family, since she worked twelve-hour days and had but one half-day off per week. One example is cited in *Family Life in 19th-Century America*. The husband of a household in New York had advertised for a female copyist at $7 per week, while his wife was advertising for a cook at $10. Nevertheless, there was "one applicant for the cook's place, while 456 ladies were anxious to secure the post of copyist."

In addition, women now had a wider range of job options beyond factory work. By the last quarter of the nineteenth century, women could choose from a variety of (admittedly mostly uninspired) professions, including attendants in asylums, bookbinding and folding, bookkeeping, china painting, Christmas card making, clerkships, embroidery, feather making, glove making, hairdressing, indexing, laundry work, literary work, lithographing, medical drawings, and nursing. Some women became entrepreneurs, offering their services as spiritualists, helping the living speak to the dead. One such spiritualist was headquartered right across from our Boston home in the late nineteenth century.

This huge demand for domestic help coincided with the immigration of large numbers of Irish women, many of whom came to America alone or with small groups of other unmarried females. They were available; they were similar in culture to the families that hired them (black servants were often considered socially awkward, especially after the Civil War); they spoke English, unlike many other immigrants, and they had been sent to America in order to earn money to send it to starving relatives back home, so they had plenty of incentive to get a steady, well-paying job.

However, life as a domestic servant or cook was hard. Accommodations were basic, if not outright prisonlike, a small, barely furnished room in an attic or basement. Working conditions were also poor, since the lady of the house spent little or no time in the kitchen and therefore cared little for its convenience, health, or decoration. Cleaning was an ongoing, difficult activity, given the messy coal stove and the reliance on plenty of elbow grease and caustic ingredients such as lye. In addition, the cook had to manage all of the suppliers, and the foodstuffs, such as large cuts of meat, often had to be broken down and preserved in various fashions—this in an environment that had only one small icebox, an appliance that was only invented in 1827. Especially in the earlier part of the nineteenth century, cooking focused, in large part, on time-consuming preservation cooking methods that would extend the shelf life of perishables.

As the 1896 World's Fair indicated, cooking at home had changed dramatically from the midcentury. A middle-class American family prior to the Civil War might have had two or three servants, but by the end of the century, it would be lucky to have just one. In 1870, one out of eight families had a domestic servant; by 1900, it was just one in fifteen. So the woman who headed up the household was now likely to be involved in the shopping and perhaps also helping with the cooking, even among the upper classes. As for the middle class, well, they were much less likely to be able to afford a cook.

Foods were no longer sourced locally—the railroads and steamships were bringing in ingredients from California and Europe. Convenience foods—canned and jarred fruits and vegetables, pancake mix, self-rising flours—were already in the market. Time-saving gadgets were making domestic labor less about drudgery and more about the joy of cooking and entertaining. By the turn of the twentieth century, convenience was key and industry was stepping up to the plate. The front door had been opened and American industry had stepped right in.

One reason for this explosion goes back to a simple invention in 1851: the Brown and Sharpe sliding caliper. It revolutionized tooling work, making manufacturing much more precise. This led to the building of steam engines, which, in turn, made the construction of kitchen appliances and tools that much easier—everything was made from water power prior to this. For example, the total of manufactured goods in the United States was just $199 million in 1810; by 1860, it had exploded to $1,885 million. The problem was that mass production of cookware and kitchen tools also meant that manufacturers were loath to invest in expensive dies or time-consuming processes. Simply put, many of these goods were poorly made and had little in the way of decorative features; why use two rivets when one would do? The result? A handle on a pot might fall off more readily, but the marketplace was soon packed with time-saving devices.

One of the early kitchen appliances was Johnson's Patent Ice Cream Freezer, invented by William Young around 1848. The Dover eggbeater (there were also Miller's, Earle's, and Munroe's Patent eggbeaters) was nothing more than a hand-cranked beater that replaced the common whisk for beating eggs or egg whites. (I used one as a kid in Vermont.) The well-respected cookbook author Marion Harland sang the praises of this device in her 1875 volume, *Breakfast, Lunch and Tea*: "But if I could not get another, I would not sell mine for fifty dollars—nor a hundred. Egg-whipping ceased to be a bugbear to me from the day I speak of . . . with it, I turn out a meringue in five minutes . . . with no after tremulousness of nerve or tendon." One could also purchase the Zeppelin Potato Baker, an egg-shaped device that opened to accept just one potato at a time; or pick up the Novel Egg Boiler, which had a whistle attached to the boiler to let you know when the eggs were done.

Many manufacturers wrapped their products in a thick skin of pseudo-scientific jargon, such as the "anti-Burning or iron Clad salamander bottom for sheet Metal kitchen utensils," which was nothing more than a metal ring to be used between pot and burner. American industry was turning out so many new kitchen devices that in an 1894 article in the *New England Kitchen Magazine*, Mrs. Lincoln offered a list of 373 kitchen tools that the well-equipped home ought to have. One utensil store in Boston offered a catalog with over one thousand pictures showing "useful and ornamental goods for the parlor, dining room, kitchen and laundry."

Many kitchens had been moved from the basement to the first floor, owing to the arrival of indoor plumbing. This meant that the kitchen could now be considered a room, not just a workspace, and the mistress of the house might actually care about its decoration. Paint colors such as tan, light gold, or soft green, rather than whitewash, started to come into use. In 1891, in *Manners, Culture, and Dress of the Best American Society*, Richard Wells pointed out that the kitchen should have fresh air, windows, plants on the window sill, an easy chair, and woodwork grained instead of painted. In fact, the home itself had become the focus of social status, given the rapid growth of the middle class. As a result, women started returning to their kitchens. The lady of the house might have started by helping her domestic workers with the lighter chores: washing glass and china, sweeping floors, ironing, opening the front door to receive visitors (something only done by domestic help just a generation before), and helping with the preparation for baking day, which was often on Wednesday.

AUGUST 2009. AFTER THE VAST MAJORITY OF FANNIE FARMER recipes we had tested turned out close to inedible or a country mile from being enjoyable, I was getting the feeling that Americans had almost no discerning palates whatsoever in the nineteenth century and that food was, for the most part, fuel rather than pleasure. Sure, Fannie was on solid ground when dealing with simple roasts, chops, puddings, and the like, but once she tried to tart up a dish or had to cook more delicate items such as vegetables or fish—well, the modern cook would find the food more compost than compelling. (To be generous, there is often something lost in translation, as when we made Fannie's plum pudding which calls for "½ pound chopped suet." It was inedible. Of course, we soon realized that the suet had to be rendered first, which improved the dish considerably, although it was still second-rate.)

I am not, however, throwing out the baby with the bath water. The nineteenth century did have some great food, including much of the food at Delmonico's in New York, and a whole range of fruit desserts, including pies, cobblers, pandowdies, betties, and grunts. Plus, Fannie did know how to roast a chicken and make Canton sorbet. A few of her more unusual desserts—orange snow, for example—were actually rather good. But taken as a whole, the recipes in *The Boston Cooking-School Cook Book* were a mediocre, middle-class lot at best. So here was the obvious question that I was going to have to answer by the end of this project: what had I learned about American cookery by cooking through dozens of Fannie Farmer recipes, reading through an entire year of *Boston Globe* food columns, and thumbing through dozens of nineteenth-century cookbooks?

For starters, we live in a country that always thought of food as necessity rather than art: it was fuel, it was medicine, or it was a social affectation like a new ball gown. In fact, I would state unabashedly that American cooks had little common sense in the kitchen compared to most of their European brethren when it came to good taste and good technique. They simply made the best of whatever was on hand. Cooking for Americans was more a matter of life and death, an issue of taking expensive local ingredients and putting them up for future meals, like squirrels storing nuts. And don't forget that prior to 1850, the United States was still a rather primitive place, especially in the kitchen, and certainly compared to France or Italy.

Then, as soon as food manufacturers offered easier, quicker solutions to putting food on the table, we rushed to buy what they were selling— from good ideas such as powdered gelatin and compressed yeast, to really bad ideas such as Jell-O ice-cream powder, margarine, and canned vegetables. The Industrial Revolution did two things simultaneously: it deprived home kitchens of inexpensive labor, thus making the preparation of meals more onerous for the woman of the household; and it offered time-saving solutions that were wholeheartedly accepted by this same oppressed mother/ cook/household manager. It was a winning combination.

Rather than look at our past as a halcyon culinary age, I conclude that it is simply a matter of different choices. Prior to 1850, the American home cook had no options; everything was local and natural, and therefore the food was probably reasonably healthy, albeit heavy. By the end of the century, American industry had completely changed the culinary landscape and increased the possibilities, from an expanded range of sources (California, Italy, France, Florida), to preparation method (fresh, canned, bottled), to natural versus ersatz (ice-cream powder versus homemade ice cream), to high quality versus adulterated (manufacturers using food coloring, some of it outright poisonous, to make bad food look inviting). The current culinary scene is merely an extension, albeit an exponentially more complex one, of what began in the era of Fannie Farmer. I am quite certain that we are no different from our Victorian ancestors, who would have been standing in line right next to us at McDonald's. Convenience sells.

Although my admiration for all things Victorian is virtually boundless, I would choose to live in modern times as a food lover. Many of our choices seem to be going in the right direction, toward local, toward quality, toward an appreciation of well-prepared, healthy food. Maybe for the patient to get better, he first had to get sick. The Victorians had no sense of what they were about to lose; we do. Like a second marriage, we now know how good it can be—and how much worse it can get.

Our last savory course was to be game. Goose was our first choice because it is worthy of a fancy dinner party and because it is hard to cook well. I had developed a recipe years ago that involved simmering the goose in water for forty-five minutes and then letting it air-dry in the refrigerator overnight, uncovered, before roasting the next day. This seemed to render much of the excess fat under the skin, but the results were still lackluster. The big problem with goose is that the dark meat and the breast meat need to be cooked quite differently, as we were soon to discover. This meant deconstructing the bird and coming up with a whole new way to cook it.

GEESE WERE POPULAR IN ROME AFTER CAESAR CONQUERED Gaul, but in this country it wasn't until the mid-nineteenth century that they were bred in quantity because wild ducks and geese were so plentiful. However, geese were extremely valuable, not just for the meat, but also for down for comforters, feathers for mattresses and pillows, quills for pens, along with their fat and oil, which were used in cooking as well as in medicine. In fact, early on in American history, the feathers were more prized than the meat. The average goose produces about a pound of feathers per year, so feathers were often picked from live geese, a practice that was considered inhumane and therefore pretty much abandoned by the mid-1900s. Early farmers, mostly because their options were limited, had a more ecologically sound approach to most things, and used geese to control weeds in cotton fields, a major reason why the goose population in the South was much higher than in the North. By 1890, there were 8.5 million geese on American farms, which was only slightly less than the number of turkeys. Yet today, geese are rare and expensive, running up to $100 for a good-sized bird (about $7 a pound). Probably because their meat is less desired by consumers, ducks and geese have not been as refined genetically.

The poor turkey has gone from large legs and small breasts to just the opposite—consumers love white meat—and they fatten up quickly and live only eighteen weeks; a "heritage breed" takes thirty weeks to bring to market. Geese are more like heirloom turkeys—they have not been turbocharged and redesigned to meet the needs of the marketplace.

In the nineteenth century, there were a few common approaches to preparing and roasting a goose. First off, a goose was never to be killed and eaten on the same day. It would hang for at least twenty-four hours, but in cold weather it could be hung for up to a week. Onion and sage were two common ingredients for the dressing, but many cooks mixed in mashed potatoes or bread crumbs as well. One particularly interesting recipe called for using sliced fingerling potatoes tossed in goose fat.

Fannie's recipe from 1896 is as follows: "Stuff, truss, sprinkle with salt and pepper, and lay six thin strips fat salt pork over breast. Place on rack in dripping-pan, put in hot oven and bake two hours. Baste every fifteen minutes with fat in pan. Remove pork last half-hour of cooking. Place on platter, cut string, and remove string and skewers. Garnish with watercress and bright red cranberries, and place Potato Apples between pieces of watercress. Serve with Apple Sauce."

Having roasted a number of geese over the years, we knew that the large amount of fat under the skin was going to be a problem. We also guessed that since modern birds are fed a fattier diet and are larger than their Victorian brethren, simmering the bird in water first might be a good idea, since it would melt a good deal of the fat and help to render the skin crisper. We tried steaming, air-drying, roasting, and parboiling, but the breast meat was still tough. The more it was cooked, the more it had an unpleasant gamy flavor, as well as being tough and chewy, similar to the taste of a cheap cut of beef from the round. Separating the cooking of the breast meat from the legs worked well; the dark meat, when thoroughly roasted, was tender, moist, almost shredded, while the breast meat was sautéed in a skillet and then finished to medium-rare in the oven. We thought that salting or brining might help, and indeed, we achieved crisp skin, juicy tender meat, and no livery flavor. Overnight salting instead of brining was clearly an improvement.

As for the stuffing, we started with a mashed-potato recipe used by Fannie and many other nineteenth-century cooks, but it was poorly rated by our tasters—too soft and boring. Next, we moved on to bread crumbs (we tested both dried and fresh) and mushrooms and ended up with a damp, mediocre result. Chestnuts were suggested by many nineteenth-century authors, so we included them as well. At first we boiled them in the shell, and then we found that roasting was actually easier and produced a better flavor.

ROAST GOOSE WITH
CHESTNUT STUFFING AND JUS

If, once stuffing comes out of oven, the legs and breasts have cooled too much, simply put them on a tray in the oven for 5 minutes to quickly reheat. (*Note:* Legs can stay in longer if necessary, but to keep breasts from overcooking, don't heat for more than 5 minutes.) We bard the goose, which simply means laying strips of salt pork on top of the legs as they roast. This adds flavor and also helps to protect the meat during the early portion of roasting. Our recipe for Goose Gravy and Goose Stock can be found at www.fannieslastsupper.com.

1 goose (12 to 15 pounds), neck and gizzards reserved for stock,
 liver reserved for stuffing (recipe follows)
Kosher salt
Ground black pepper
12 ounces salt pork, fatty, partially frozen, sliced into ⅛-inch slices
1 teaspoon vegetable oil
1 recipe Goose Gravy

1. *To prep the goose:* Remove wing tips; reserve for stock. Remove breasts, trim excess fat and silverskin, and score skin every quarter inch, being careful not to cut into flesh. Sprinkle each breast evenly on both sides with 1 teaspoon kosher salt per pound of meat; wrap tightly and refrigerate overnight. Crack backbone in half; with chef's knife, cut through backbone at split and cut to remove leg section from remaining carcass; reserve for later use. Trim excess fat from legs, and score entire surface of skin with ¼-inch crosshatch, being careful not to cut into flesh. Wrap and refrigerate leg section and remaining carcass until ready to use.

2. Once goose is broken down, trim carcass of all skin and fat; save along with skin and fat trimmings from leg and breast for rendering. Cut into 2-inch pieces, place in medium saucepan, add ½ cup water, cook slowly

over medium-low heat until skin has rendered, become crisp, and turned a light golden brown, 1 to 1½ hours. Strain through fine mesh strainer; discard cracklings and reserve fat for use in gravy and stuffing. Remaining fat can be frozen. One bird can yield up to 3 cups of rendered fat.

3. *To cook the goose:* Set oven rack at lower-middle position. Preheat oven to 325 degrees. Unwrap leg section and carcass and pat dry. Place carcass on wire rack set in rimmed baking sheet. Pour ½ cup water into pan. Season leg section with 1½ teaspoons kosher salt and ¼ teaspoon freshly ground black pepper, then place over carcass. Lay salt pork over surface to cover. Roast for 1½ hours until salt pork is stiff, crisp, and just beginning to brown. Remove salt pork and discard and continue to roast for another 1½ to 2 hours until skin is rendered, crisp, and golden brown and thickest part of thigh reaches 190 degrees, turning pan halfway through. Reduce oven temperature to 250 degrees. Remove legs from oven and let rest 20 to 30 minutes.

4. While legs are resting, pat breasts dry, season with pepper. Heat oil in heavy-bottomed 10-inch ovenproof skillet over medium-high heat until beginning to smoke, about 3 minutes; swirl skillet to coat evenly with oil. Place each goose breast skin side down and cook until skin is fully rendered and golden brown, about 6 to 8 minutes. Flip and brown second side, about 2 to 3 minutes. Transfer skillet to oven and cook until thickest part of breast registers about 125 degrees on instant-read thermometer, about 15 to 25 minutes. Transfer breasts to wire rack and let rest 10 minutes. Slice breasts into ⅛-inch slices; carve legs and thighs and serve with stuffing and gravy.

Serves 12 (small servings).

CHESTNUT STUFFING

Don't even think about using jarred chestnuts—they tasted moldy and made the stuffing inedible. The only commercial chestnuts we liked were from D'Artagnan.

1 goose liver, patted dry

Kosher salt

Fresh ground black pepper

2 tablespoonfuls rendered goose fat or butter

2 shallots, chopped fine (½ cup)

8 ounces sausage meat

36 chestnuts, roasted, shelled, and peeled; 24 of them chopped into
  ¼-inch pieces and the remaining 12 pounded in a mortar
  (Do not use jarred chestnuts)

10 ounces mushrooms, chopped finely

3 tablespoons finely chopped sage

2 tablespoons finely chopped parsley

2 tablespoons brandy

1 ounce fresh bread crumbs, fine

¼ cup goose broth

1 tablespoon rendered goose fat

4 to 5 drops lemon juice

1. Season liver with salt and pepper. Heat fat in 10-inch skillet over medium-high heat until shimmering. Add liver and cook until well browned on both sides, but not cooked through, about 1 to 2 minutes per side; transfer to plate and refrigerate immediately. Add shallots to skillet and cook, stirring constantly, until just softened, about 1 minute. Add sausage and cook, breaking it up into small pieces (the largest, the size of a large pea), 4 to 5 minutes, until browned and just cooked through. Add chopped

chestnuts, stirring constantly until heated through, about 1 to 2 minutes; transfer mixture to bowl.

2. Add mushrooms, ½ teaspoon kosher salt, and ¼ teaspoon black pepper to skillet and cook, stirring occasionally for about 2 minutes until pan begins to deglaze. Add mashed chestnuts and cook, stirring occasionally, until the mixture comes to boil; cook down until mixture is almost dry, about 6 minutes. Add sage and parsley; stir to combine. Add brandy and cook until dry, about 30 to 60 seconds. Transfer to bowl with sausage mixture. Chop liver into ¼-inch pieces. Add liver, bread crumbs, broth, and goose fat to sausage mixture and mix thoroughly to combine. Season with salt, pepper, and lemon juice. Transfer to an 8-inch Pyrex pan, cover with foil, bake in 375-degree oven for 15 minutes, remove foil, and bake until heated through and top begins to dry out and darken, another 10 minutes.

Applesauce

Our farm in Vermont includes an orchard that we planted over fifteen years ago: mostly apple varieties, but also plum, cherry, and pears, as well as raspberry, currant, and blueberry bushes. Here's the deal. Apples are incredibly difficult to grow unless one is willing to dump a fair amount of poison on the trees (and, in turn, your backyard) to prevent apple maggots, powdery mildew, apple rust, coddling moth, aphids, mites, plum circulio beetle, scab—the list just goes on and on. It is, indeed, much like trying to control terrorists—they just keep reappearing in different forms.

The basic drill is as follows: start with a spray of dormant oil in the early spring to control insects that have overwintered in the bark of the trees. Then, once the leaves have appeared, spray a copper sulfate mixture in an effort to control fungi. After the blossoms have dropped and the bees are done with their work, the trees are supposed to be sprayed regularly, every two weeks or so, with a poison, usually something with foul-smelling malathion in it.

Given that many of our trees are next door to the farmhouse, we use only dormant oil and copper sulfate, which are nontoxic or pretty close. Then we discovered a product called Surround, a white powder made from kaolin clay that is dissolved in water and sprayed on the trees weekly, turning them white and providing protective covering, both from insects and sun damage. So, how did we do?

Are you kidding me? With about forty fruit trees, we produced no more than a few bushels of mostly scarred, misshapen fruit. If we had not wrapped the bottom of the trees with tape, animals would have eaten the bark, ringed the trees, and killed them. If we did not prune properly, the inside of the canopy would be too dark, the fruit wouldn't grow well, and the trees would spend all their energy growing more shoots, not producing fruit. Then, unless the young trees were properly fenced, the deer would show, acting like greedy New Yorkers at the annual James Beard gala buffet, pushing each other aside to snag yet another handful of Michel Richard's fried shrimp.

Finally, we got rid of all toxic sprays, simply using dormant oil and the Surround, which, truth be told, did not seem to be helping all that much. Oh, and did I mention the $4,000 irrigation system we had to install? Every time we weed-whacked around the trees, the hoses would get split and the water would simply shoot up into the air. And then, to top it off, we pressed most of the apples for cider, froze the containers, and promptly forgot about them until next year. And the bushel or two of apples that we placed in the root cellar? Well, they lasted about a month or so before turning black and soft. So, to complete the great circle of apple production, we dumped them outside for the deer.

As a result of this experience, I have great respect for anyone who grows apples, especially if they go down the organic road. Until the mid-nineteenth century, farmers were 100 percent organic, used plowing, washed the growing fruit with soap or ashes, or coated the trees with tar in an effort to combat pests. By the 1870s, farmers were experimenting with arsenic, pyrethrum (organic insecticide made from dried, ground chrysanthemum flowers), carbolic acid, hellebore (made from hellebore plants), petroleum, kerosene, whale oil, soap, hydrocyanic acid gas (extremely deadly), and lead arsenate. Gas engine–powered spray pumps came along in the 1890s, and by 1908, things had gotten so out of hand that a bill was introduced into Congress to supervise the use and sale of agricultural poisons.

Hand in hand with the development of insecticides came commercial fruit operations, and farms near large populations began selling excess fruit in local markets. The particular problem with apples, however, was that most of these varieties did not lend themselves to shipping or storage, so growers started to focus on varieties that made commercial sense, but not much culinary sense. In addition, apples grown without modern herbicides were often scarred, bug-infested, or otherwise unsuitable for sale. This meant that the bulk of an apple crop was destined to be pressed and turned into cider, this noncommercial fruit being referred to as "cider apples."

The two leading commercial apple varieties of Fannie's era were the Ben Davis and the Baldwin. Over time, of course, the demands of the marketplace reduced the diversity of apple varieties from thousands to a few dozen. By the late twentieth century, fewer than a dozen varieties were generally distributed and available at supermarkets. As one wag supermarket employee once told me, "We offer three apple varieties: red, green, and yellow."

FANNIE'S APPLESAUCE
TO ACCOMPANY ROASTED GOOSE

This recipe is a bit unusual since it begins by making a sugar syrup that is flavored with ginger and lemon rind. Then the cored, quartered apples are added to the pot and cooked quickly, about 6 minutes. This is a relatively small recipe designed for our dinner party. You can increase it easily, although you will want to use the widest possible pot so that the apples can be cooked in one layer if possible. If not, stir them a bit during cooking. To double this recipe, cook the first batch of apples, remove them with a slotted spoon, and then cook a second batch in the same syrup. To quadruple the recipe, double the sugar syrup, use four times the amount of apples, and cook them in two batches. If you cannot find Rhode Island Greenings or Northern Spy, simply use one pound of crisp, tart apples.

1 cup granulated sugar

1 piece lemon rind, ½ inch by 2 inches

2 slices ginger, each about the size of a nickel and ⅛-inch thick

1 pound McIntosh

8 ounces Rhode Island Greening

8 ounces Northern Spy

1. Place the sugar, lemon rind, ginger, and 2½ cups water in a large saucepan over medium-high heat. Bring to a lively simmer, stirring occasionally until the sugar is dissolved, about 3 minutes. Cover and simmer for an additional 3 minutes to allow ginger to flavor the sugar syrup.

2. Meanwhile, wash the apples, cut them into quarters, and remove the seeds and cores. When the sugar syrup is ready, add the apple quarters, cover, and cook until tender, about 6 minutes.

3. Using a slotted spoon, remove apple pieces and place into a food mill set over a medium-sized bowl. Remove and discard ginger and lemon pieces. Pass apples through food mill until only skins remain. Add cooking liquid to applesauce in small increments until desired consistency is achieved.

Makes about 1½ cups.

Wine Jelly

The Science of Cooking, According to Fannie

Today, food science has traveled all the way from the laboratory to popular television. One might easily make the mistake of thinking that this is a purely modern phenomenon—that the Victorians were cooks, not scientists, and were not particularly interested in or knowledgeable about the whys of their profession. Of course, this is nonsense. Fannie Farmer and Mary Lincoln both wrote cookbooks full of food science, some of it wildly inaccurate, but some was right on the money. They were curious, and it was an age when scientific principles were being applied to everything, including the domestic arts.

The field of culinary science got its start with food preservation. In 1809, a Frenchman named Nicolas Appert was the first person to seal foods (cooked meat, vegetables, and milk) in glass bottles and heat them to preserve the food in response to a request from Napoleon. Breakable bottles were replaced by cans in 1812 by Brian Donkin in England. Most of this technology was developed without a knowledge of the science of food, although in 1860 Louis Pasteur did pioneer the discovery that bacteria caused the spoilage of wine and milk. The first studies of the science of food preservation were published by Samuel Cate Prescott at MIT in 1896. His work ultimately led to the establishment of one of the first food science departments in the the United States. Others followed at the University of Wisconsin and the University of California (1913). Prior to the establishment of these departments, there was little real study of the science of food. Ella Eaton Kellogg did publish *Science in the Kitchen* in 1893. Her approach to cooking was very precise, but not truly scientific. (Her husband founded the Kellogg Cereal Company in Battle Creek, Michigan.)

There was a broader cultural backdrop to the movement of science into the culinary arts. Simply put, many women found their lives boring, tedious, and thoroughly unfulfilling. This, combined with the Industrial Revolution and the emergence of a wealthy middle class, meant that women were desperately seeking a new role for themselves in society. Science and technology would be the tools to free them from their bondage and provide new opportunities to express themselves in more creative and compelling ways. In the best-selling 1888 utopian novel, *Looking Backward: From 2000 to 1887*, Edward Bellamy predicts a desirable future for housework: "Our washing is all done at public laundries at excessively cheap rates, and our cooking at public shops. Electricity, of course, takes the place of all fires and lighting. We choose houses no larger than we need, and furnish them so as to involve the minimum of trouble to keep them in order. We have no use for domestic servants. 'What a paradise for womankind the world must be now!' [the fictitious heroine] exclaimed." This sentiment was just one of many movements in the late nineteenth century to remove the vast burden of home cooking and cleaning off the backs of women.

As a result, in Victorian times the kitchen was often viewed as a laboratory. A good example was to be had at the World's Columbian Exposition in Chicago in 1893. At the Massachusetts Pavilion, two home economists, Mary Abel and Ellen Richards (the latter the first woman to graduate from MIT and join the faculty) displayed a kitchen as scientific laboratory in order to "extract the maximum amount of nutrition from food substances and the maximum heat from fuel." Yet another example was the New England Kitchen, which was built in Boston in 1890. It was promoted as a public kitchen to teach American workers to cook more scientifically.

So it is no wonder that the cooking process itself was subject to scientific principle, with the goal to provide better and more nourishing foods. These principles are easily found in many books of the era, two of the best examples being those of Lincoln and Farmer. Having investigated the scientific principles of the Victorians and compared them to modern kitchen science, we found that their understanding of how foods cooked was about half right. Their most common mistake was to think that rapid boiling of foods would quickly harden the exterior, thus keeping the juices trapped inside. Fannie Farmer was correct about the effects of cooking in hard versus soft water: the former is more likely to keep vegetables firm and bright-colored, whereas the latter is best for extracting flavors, in tea or coffee, for example.

Fannie believed that frying was healthier than sautéing and that bacon fat was easier to digest than butter or cream. She also suggested adding cold water halfway through boiling potatoes (to prevent overcooking the outer layers), but this had no effect when tested. Victorian cooks finished baking bread at a lower temperature than the one they started with, a technique that did not seem to matter when tested in our kitchens. They did know how to extract the maximum flavor and nourishment when making stocks (cut the meat into small pieces and cook gently), but when it came to making tea, their advice about never using "twice-boiled" water turned out to be demonstrably true when we did a blind taste test. And, as we have also found, it is best to add the sugar to cream before whipping so that it dissolves properly. All in all, not a bad showing, considering that food science was still a nascent discipline.

SEPTEMBER 2009. IN 1898, THE TOWLE COMPANY'S GEORGIAN pattern had 131 different pieces for one setting, 1,572 pieces for twelve settings—which would have cost a small fortune. This excess, which implied as well a rigorous ritual surrounding the serving of food, grew out of rather humble beginnings. Most homes did not have formal dining rooms until after 1850; people ate in the kitchen, especially if they lived on a farm. In the city, only the rich actually owned an entire house; most city dwellers were living in boardinghouses of one sort or another. (Half of Americans, even in the late nineteenth century, did not own property.)

As the Industrial Revolution elevated the upper middle class in terms of wealth, the dining room became the domestic showcase. It was a semi-public room, one that could be displayed to one's peers. This was quite different from the period prior to 1880, when the dining room's primary purpose was to reinforce the sanctity of family life. Some dining rooms featured stained glass and an organ: it was a place for a Christian family to reassert its bonds and its faith.

In fact, the notion of allowing the public—one's friends—into the family dining room was debated vigorously for some time, and was not common in midcentury. It was the existence of new money, of created wealth, that turned the dining room from a refuge from the world into a place of self-expression and creativity. Women, in particular, were interested in being perceived as artists, not just housewives, and thus the home became a blank canvas on which to paint their sensibilities and notions of personal artistry. Of course, architects and designers wanted the dining room to reflect modernity and practicality, hence the pass-through pantry and the sideboard for convenient storage and buffets. In terms of decoration, ferns and trailing ivy were often used in the bay window, paintings of hunting dogs on the walls, fruit on the sideboard, and partially closed blinds on a south-facing window. Many classical motifs were incorporated as well, whether in the wallpaper or through the use of pedestal urns.

Flatware also changed with the times, and so did its use. Forks originally had but two very sharp tines. The food was speared, elevated, and then pushed into the mouth with the aid of the flat side of a knife. Forks slowly added more tines, and the convention of cutting food—switching the fork from the left to the right hand, putting down the knife, and then using the fork to lift a piece of food to the mouth—came into vogue. Silver-plated tableware, which became available in the 1840s, was the first step in bringing the Victorian notion of elegant dining to the middle classes. It started in and around Sheffield, England, but electroplating was being done in the United States by that time as well.

In addition, the Comstock silver lode was discovered in Nevada in

1859, and this provided much of the materials for the silverware industry. At first, mass-produced flatware was rather crude, but eventually shaped dies and better machinery created deeper impressions, so handles became elaborately decorated, even to the point of reproducing actual figures. Tea sets were quite popular, including a coffeepot, teapot, and a hot-water pot, as well as a sugar bowl, a creamer, and a waste bowl. By the late nineteenth century, these sets came in myriad styles, including neoclassical, Persian, Elizabethan, Jacobean, Japanese, Etruscan, and even Moorish. Things soon got out of hand. Castors containing condiments and seasonings made sense, but then these sets started to include egg cups, bells, and bouquet holders.

Once commercially produced butter was available (until the mid-1800s most butter was made at home), then one could purchase silver butter dishes, many of them quite elaborate, as well as cake baskets that held cakes or cookies for tea and desserts. Napkins in the Middle Ages used to be quite large and were frequently washed, since food was eaten with the fingers. They were soon downsized, and then, of course, the napkin ring became popular. Reed & Barton had 129 styles of napkin rings by 1885, 43 of them figural, including animals, playing children, and so on. Ornate ice-water pitchers were being sold with two walls for insulation (some of them were constructed on hinged stands so they could be tilted forward for pouring), although refrigeration made these items less popular after 1900.

An important part of our dinner party would be authentic Victorian table settings. The first item on our shopping list was a silver punch bowl. After months of searching, Adrienne found a stunning example dated November 21, 1894, and made by the firm of Hennegan, Bates of Baltimore. It was pure sterling silver and decorated using repoussé, a form of relief decoration produced by hammering on one side so that the decoration appears on the other. The pattern was elaborate, in high Victorian style, and the motif was floral, including leaves, tendrils, and blossoms. It was completely over the top and perfect for the occasion.

Adrienne also purchased sterling silver placecard holders shaped like upright flower blossoms, which held a small flower for each guest. We assembled a vast army of bowls, main-course plates, and chargers, made or sold by a variety of firms, including Higgins & Seiter of New York, and many Limoges items from William Guerin & Co., Theo. Haviland, and M. Redon, among others. Dessert plates, also used for the salmon course, were made by Adderley's of England, and I had inherited a mother-of-pearl fish fork and knife set from my mother's side of the family. We purchased gold-rimmed glass bowls for the sorbet.

We were also on the lookout for a few key kitchen and dining room accessories, including jelly molds, in particular one with a pineapple design on the bottom. After scanning eBay and similar sites, we discovered that antique jelly molds were generally small. The reason for this soon became apparent during testing. Larger molds required excessive amounts of gelatin to maintain the proper shape during and after unmolding. A series of taste tests made it clear that the less gelatin used, the better the flavor. So we were going to have to make a series of jellies, each of them of modest size, instead of one large centerpiece.

We very quickly fell in love with this course. It turned out that the jellies were highly elaborate, multicolored, multiflavored, and often filled with Bavarian cream, fruit, and other items. The simpler recipes had vertical layers of colors, all based on a simple lemon jelly. Others used special molds to produce layers within layers. One recipe instructed the cook to cut strips of different jellies and then line a mold with alternating colors, binding these strips with a fresh batch of warm jelly. This was edible sculpture; sadly, Jell-O had replaced one of the most creative and interesting features of the Victorian table. The first step, however, was to go back in time and make gelatin using calf's feet. First, we had to find them.

SO HOW, EXACTLY, DOES ONE CALL UP THE LOCAL MEAT MARKET and order a box of calf's feet? Well, we did just that, although we had a lot of trouble locating them. Watching the pointy pink feet sticking up out of a tall stockpot, busily simmering away for hours, did make one think that a modern culinary education is a bit lacking in terms of breadth. Now we were really getting into the meat of it, heading back into time like the good culinary pioneers that we thought we were. And, thankfully, the result was pretty good—a clear, strong, bouncy gelatin that would be much too firm to eat as it was, but would make a good base for a flavored gelatin. In the end, the flavor was sweet and lemony, with a texture reminiscent of Jell-O, just firm enough to hold its shape. So, yes, one can make one's own home-made gelatin. Like all things Victorian, it's just a matter of time.

Speaking of time in the kitchen, cooking prior to 1850 required a prodigious amount of labor because food was not just being cooked, it was also being preserved. Some of it—for example, gelatin—was transformed into basic cooking ingredients used for a myriad of recipes. They also had to make their own vinegar, soaps, sugar syrups, stocks, jams, jellies, potted meats, pickled vegetables, and corned beef. All this, however, had changed radically by 1900.

Gelatin is probably the best example of the time-saving trend offered by commercial food producers. After homemade calf's-foot gelatin went out of style, home cooks could turn to either isinglass or Irish moss. Lower-quality isinglass was often dyed and sold in various colors, including red, green, and blue. The term *sheet gelatin* came from the process of extracting gelatin from animal skins; it was dried on nets into thin sheets. *Leaf gelatin* was made from sturgeon bladders; it was an accurate description of what was left once the outer and inner membranes of the swim bladders were scraped away. Irish moss was made from a form of seaweed called carageen, making it more economical, and was so named because it was harvested off Ireland's southern and western shores. By the 1860s, Irish moss was produced locally—a half-million pounds of Irish moss was pulled annually off of Scituate, Massachusetts.

By the late 1890s, calf's-foot gelatin was hopelessly outdated, as a tongue-in-cheek recipe published by the *Boston Daily Globe* on May 4, 1890, demonstrated: "Get [a Chicago] calf, cut off the calf, which can be used for making hash or chicken salad; wash the feet, having first removed all chillblains, thicken with glue, add a few molasses, strain through a cane-seated chair, pour into a blue bowl with red pictures on it, set in the shade to get tough. Then send it to a sick friend." So when commercial manufacturers of instant gelatin (including Plymouth Rock, Junket, Crystal, Cox, and Knox) offered a simple, economical solution to setting up jellies and similar desserts, consumers immediately made the shift. In addition, home cooks no longer had to make their own natural food colorings for jellies; the food industry was doing the job for them. In 1856, Sir William Henry Perkin discovered the first synthetic organic dye, mauve, and the synthetic food coloring industry was born. Cheap food substitutes were coming on the market, and food coloring made these items appear either more natural, as in the case of margarine, which is pure white, not yellow; or more appealing, as in the case of soft drinks. Ordinary oranges were injected with red dye to make them look like the more expensive blood oranges. Old meat was dyed to make it appear fresh. Jams and jellies were tinted to make them look like they had more fruit than they actually did. This practice became so common that dye manufacturers offered their colorants with the following descriptions, "egg substitute," "mustard color," "beer," "pie filling," and "raspberry color."

To make matters worse, some of these artificial colors were poisonous. According to Daniel Marmion in the *Handbook of U.S. Colorants*, "In 1820, Frederick Accum reported the demise of a woman who frequently ate pickles while at her hairdresser—pickles that had been colored green with copper sulfate. A survey taken in Boston in 1880 showed that 46% of all candy examined contained one or more mineral pigments, chiefly lead chromate. Perhaps the classic horror story of the time is that of the druggist who in 1860 gave a caterer copper arsenite to use for making a green pudding for a public dinner. Two people died as a result." A headline in an 1884 edition of the *New York Times* cried out, "Poison in Every Cup of Coffee," the reporter detailing two coffee mills in Brooklyn that had been using coloring agents containing arsenic and lead to make their beans look like Java.

It was Pearle Wait who thought up the notion of adding colors and flavors—raspberry, lemon, orange, and strawberry—to the granulated gelatins currently on the market. Jell-O was born. Sales reached $250,000 in 1902 and continued to climb quickly over the next decades, thanks in part to the printed color recipe booklets. So when food writers lament the decrease in quality cooking time spent in American kitchens, don't forget our friends the Victorian cooks, who were more than happy to never have to look at another calf's foot, piece of seaweed, or powdered, dried sturgeon bladder again.

Finally released from the drudgery of unwieldy thickeners, jellies and custards of all kinds, both wine and fruit, were now easy to make and therefore these recipes were printed in almost every cookbook. Orange pudding was made from segmented, seeded oranges covered with cold custard and topped with beaten egg whites. Snow pudding, for which there are endless recipes and flavors, is a molded dessert made from fruit juice, gelatin, and beaten egg whites. It was often served with a sauce that is similar to a crème anglaise. Here is a recipe from Fannie that we adjusted slightly to give you a good idea of the range of gelatin desserts enjoyed in her time.

ORANGE SNOW

Snow was a very popular dessert and had many variations. The *Boston Globe* was full of similar recipes throughout the 1890s. I prefer to make it with fresh-squeezed orange juice for a very light, refreshing dessert. Note that the egg whites will lose their shape and structure as they are gently whisked into the fruit juice. This is not a mistake.

2¾ cups fresh-squeezed chilled orange juice, plus 2 teaspoons zest

¼ cup lemon juice, plus ½ teaspoon zest

1 cup sugar, plus 1 teaspoon (for whipping egg whites)

½ ounce powdered gelatin (2 envelopes)

3 cups boiling water

2 egg whites, whipped to soft peaks

Pinch salt

8 to 10 wineglasses for serving

1. Combine citrus juice and zest with 1 cup sugar and whisk until sugar is almost completely dissolved. Sprinkle gelatin on top. Let stand 5 minutes. Add 3 cups boiling water and stir. Strain and chill to 45 degrees; mixture should just begin to set up.

2. Beat egg whites and salt until very soft peaks start to form (peaks should slowly lose shape when whisk is removed). Add 1 teaspoon sugar and continue to beat until soft peaks have formed (and hold their shape). Add egg white mixture to gelatin mixture and fold whites in gently with whisk until incorporated. Transfer to mold or wineglasses and chill.

Serves 8 to 10.

An updated recipe for prune pudding can be found at www.fannieslast supper.com.

✻

TO MAKE FANCY JELLIES FOR THE PARTY, WE HAD TO START WITH molds, and these were originally made by the English out of tin-lined copper. Molds were made in the shape of royalty, pets, and even famous locations in London, including the Belgrave, the Savoy, and the Carlton. By the late 1800s, the Victorians had over a thousand mold designs to choose from. Here in the States, molds were made from steel, which was easy to bend and less expensive than copper. However, steel tended to rust over time and was a poor heat conductor—not a good thing when trying to produce a chilled dessert. These molds also tended to be simpler and plainer in design, mostly oval and round (the ubiquitous melon mold comes to mind), since odd shapes and projections were difficult to manufacture.

Layered Lemon Jelly

This gelatin mold is based on a basic lemon jelly which is then colored using natural ingredients to create multicolored layers. You can mix and match as you like, use a small mold or a large one, and play with the color combinations any number of ways. The design of the mold will determine how many colors you wish to use and how to use them. For example, the mold we used for the dinner party had a pineapple design on the bottom (the top when served), and therefore we used yellow colored jelly for the pineapple, green for the leaves, etc. I have also provided two versions of this recipe. One uses homemade calf's-foot gelatin; the other, easier version simply calls for powdered gelatin.

HOW TO MAKE
NATURAL FOOD COLORINGS

Green: Process 1 bag baby spinach in food processor. Sieve liquid, then pass through jelly bag.

Yellow: Simmer ½ teaspoon of saffron in 2 cups water until liquid is reduced to about 1 ounce (2 tablespoons) and is vibrant in color. Pass through fine sieve.

Red: Peel and grate three small beets. Place in medium saucepan and cover with cold water, about 3 cups. Bring to simmer over medium heat and simmer for 40 minutes. Drain beets, reserving liquid and discarding beets. Reduce liquid to ½ cup. Pass through jelly bag.

White: Add 2 tablespoons heavy cream per pint of jelly.

HOMEMADE GELATIN
FROM CALF'S FEET

This was a much less smelly and easier proposition than we had originally thought it would be. Yes, you do need to purchase split calf's feet, but the good news is that this gelatin base can be used to thicken a great many jellies or puddings. We decided to use this gelatin in our lemon jelly but used regular powdered gelatin in the other two jelly molds. We did detect a slight aftertaste to the calf's-foot gelatin, and did not want the flavor of the Spatlese or rhubarb jellies to be affected.

    4 calf's feet, split in two
    1 tablespoon sugar
    ¼ cup lemon juice, from 2 lemons
    1 cup white wine
    Water

1. Soak split calf's feet in cold water for 1 hour; drain. Transfer soaked feet to 17-quart stockpot, cover with water, and bring to boil for 10 minutes; drain. Return feet to stockpot, and add sugar, lemon juice, wine, and 6 quarts of water to cover. Bring to boil and reduce heat to maintain gentle simmer; simmer for 4 hours. Remove and discard feet, skim fat, and strain liquid through fine mesh strainer. Let cool to room temperature. Transfer to refrigerator and chill overnight.

2. When it firms up, remove any fat from the top and wash the surface with warm water to remove all traces of grease. Lift out the jelly without disturbing the sediment at the bottom. Use per recipe for Lemon Jelly Mold.

Yields about 3 quarts

LEMON JELLY USING POWDERED GELATIN

Lemon-flavored jellies were the most common base flavor for Victorian jellies. Using powdered gelatin, they are also very easy to make.

4½ cups water

7½ teaspoons powdered gelatin

¾ cup lemon juice

1¼ cups sugar

1. Measure ½ cup water into a small bowl. Sprinkle powdered gelatin on the surface of the water and set aside for 5 minutes to soften.

2. Meanwhile, combine lemon juice, 1 cup water, and sugar in a small saucepan and warm over medium heat, stirring occasionally, until sugar is melted. Remove from heat. Stir in softened gelatin until dissolved. Slowly add remaining 3 cups water, stirring constantly. Pass through jelly bag or fine sieve until mixture is clear.

3. Divide the gelatin into separate bowls and color as desired, adding ¼ teaspoon of coloring at a time. (See page 190 for natural colors.) Pour into chilled jelly mold. Let each layer set completely before adding the next.

For additional jelly recipes, including Lemon Jelly Made with Calf's-Foot Gelatin, Spatlese Jelly with Black Corinth Grapes, and Rhubarb Jelly with Strawberry Bavarian Filling, go to, www.fannieslastsupper.com.

Cake

Technology Transforms the Victorian Pantry

T he late-nineteenth-century American cook was at the epicenter of changes so profound in terms of ingredients that it was much like the music aficionado in the late 1990s, who used a turntable for his LP collection while relying on a large group of CDs, and then a smattering of digital downloads from iTunes for his MP3 player. The old sat next to the new; the from-scratch traditions were taken for granted, while the newer convenience foods were adopted with the enthusiasm only the long-suffering can muster for life-changing technology. In terms of baking, the first area that was revolutionized by science was leaveners, a shift away from yeast to natural forms of baking soda and chemical leaveners such as baking powder.

Yeast has been the leavener (this term comes from the Latin word *levare*, which means "to raise") of record for over four thousand years, and many home cooks, at least until the mid-1800s, still followed the old method of creating their own starter for bread baking: making a thin batter with flour and water and then letting it stand in a warm place until it fermented. This worked reasonably well in kitchens that were already full of yeast spores, but it was by no means a sure thing. No wild yeast spores might be attracted, or the starter might go "off" and sour. Other methods included making starters with potatoes or grapes. Flour, salt, boiling hop water, potatoes, sugar, and a little ginger was one recipe. Old potatoes were best, since they have more sugar; the hops and ginger prevented the yeast from souring.

The starter mixture would have to be kept warm, stirred several times while rising, and then put away in glass—not metal—containers the next day. (Metal would cause the yeast to turn dark.) And, of course, starters had to be fed and maintained properly, something that was not a problem in a household with a full-time cook who was constantly making bread. However, when bread could be purchased at a store and when the woman of the household now had to do her own cooking, this old-fashioned starter method was hardly convenient.

Other than making one's own starter at home, the cook had three choices by Fannie's time. Brewer's yeast was nothing more than the skimmings from fermenting beer vats. Dry yeast cakes were brewer's yeast combined with cornmeal, cut into small biscuits, and dried. These were relatively low in potency, since they had a smaller percentage of yeast. (Cornmeal was used here; starch or flour would have been used in England.) Finally, there was compressed yeast, small moist cakes enclosed in tinfoil. It contained a very high percentage of yeast, making it more potent; thus it became the preferred yeast among both home and professional bakers. It did not last long, however—just a few days—and had to be kept cold in the ice chest. Brewer's yeast was all that was available in the United States until the mid-1800s. However, it spoiled easily and it had to be kept cold and used within a short time after preparation.

Baking powder, a mixture of baking soda and cream of tartar, was invented by a chemist named Hoagland who founded the Royal Baking Powder Company in 1866. The problem with these early mixtures was that the chemical reaction took place rather quickly, and much of the leavening power was dispersed during the mixing of the batter. Chemists needed to find alternatives to cream of tartar, which they did as early as 1864—the substance was referred to as MCP (monocalcium phosphate) and also as ACP (acid calcium phosphate). Additional refinements led to SAS (sodium aluminum sulfate) in the early 1890s, then SAPP (sodium acid pyrophosphate) in the early 1900s, and, finally, SALP (sodium aluminum phosphate) in 1960.

The other ingredient that came a long way in the twentieth century and therefore affected home baking was sugar. Cane existed a long time before the refining process that turned it into the white crystalline sugar that we know today. The stalk was simply chewed, and the sweet juices were released and enjoyed. The next step was to use vertical wooden rollers to crush the cane stalks, extracting about 25 percent of the available juice. This primitive method was eventually supplanted by a series of cast-iron rollers that boosted production to 40 percent. Eventually, steam-powered rollers came into vogue, and processors were capturing 65 percent of the total cane juice. To produce sugar, the cane syrup was simply boiled in a series of large kettles; lime juice was added to bring about the coagulation of undesirable albuminous ingredients, which rose as a scum to the top of the boiling sap that was removed. The boiled and clarified syrup eventually ran into granulation tanks, where it cooled, and a crust of crystals formed on top. The mixture was stirred, scattering the crystals throughout the syrup. The final operation was called *potting*, in which the mixture was placed into hogsheads (these were casks containing roughly sixty gallons) that had holes in the bottom, allowing molasses to drain out from the sugar mixture into a cistern below. This last phase of the initial process might take up to six weeks to ensure proper drainage.

At this point, the sugar had to be refined. One old method used lime water, bull's blood, and heat. Animal charcoal (made from bones) was introduced in the 1830s from France and was the principal purifying agent in the United States. Sugar then had to be dried, either on floors or in heated drums, and it was also stirred so that the crystals broke up—this was referred to as the granulation stage. However, granulated sugar as we know it today was not invented until 1860, at the Boston Sugar refinery. Before this, loaf sugar was commonly sold in cones. It had to be grated at home before use—a difficult and time-consuming process.

There were yellow sugars as well as white sugars, the former being cruder and having a lower percentage of sucrose, sometimes as low as 80 percent and up to 92 percent. (The best white sugars were 99.8 percent pure.) The whiter the sugar, the more expensive it was. The goal in producing white sugars was to remove all traces of molasses or other impurities to provide a hard, clean, granular sugar. Yellow sugars started with less pure syrup and were boiled in a manner that caused the sugar and molasses to bind together, producing a softer and yellower product. (One can still buy a cone of yellow sugar in some Hispanic grocery stores.) Cube sugar was a later invention that was usually made through the use of molds, centrifugal force, and baking to finish, although sometimes it was simply sawed into cubes. Powdered and bar sugars were passed through fine silk cloths, and starch was added to prevent caking. Red frosting sugar was a Boston specialty used for decorating; it was nothing more than granulated sugar dyed red.

Fully refined, pure, granulated sugar was at the heart of the Victorian love of confections. Brightly colored penny candies, ice-cream parlors, confectionary stores selling sugar sculptures for table decorations, and even birthday cakes, a craze that originated in the 1890s, all got a boost or a start from the availability of refined white sugar. How popular was sugar? Total consumption rose 150 percent from 1879 to 1900, from 2,097 million pounds to 4,488 million pounds. No doubt that Americans had a sweet tooth.

Although Fannie Farmer recognizes the following types of sugar in her first chapter—brown sugar, loaf, cut, granulated, powdered, and confectioner's—her recipes rely almost solely on fine granulated sugar, with special applications requiring powdered or confectioner's sugar. Brown, loaf, and cut sugar really had no place in home cooking by 1896.

Perhaps the biggest result of the sugar and chemical leavener industries was the explosion in variety and number of cakes. The list was virtually endless: tea cake, snow cake, caramel prize cake, Empire State cake, sea foam cake, Dolly Varden cake (Dolly Varden is a character in Dickens's *Barnaby Rudge,* and the term was often used to refer to a dress of sheer muslin worn over a brightly colored petticoat; this notion of something sheer over something colorful was applied to fish as well as to cakes, as in the Dolly Varden trout), poor man's cake, one egg cake, white perfection cake, cheap cream cake, walnut cake, orange cake, sour milk cake, lemon cake, and gold cake. One could also find pound cakes, an earlier form of

LEFT: This sterling silver punch bowl was decorated using repoussé and was made in 1884 by the firm of Hennegan Bates & Company, Baltimore.

BELOW: Oysters, a common first course, were provided by the Island Creek Oyster Company in Duxbury, Massachusetts.

The Mock Turtle Soup was garnished with fried brainballs, shredded meat from the calf's head, and a julienne of carrot and leek.

Rissoles with three fillings: duxelle and chicken, chicken liver, and cherry chutney and onion with blue cheese.

Lobster à l'Américaine.

Roast Saddle of Lamb with Currant Jelly Sauce, Potatoes Lyonnaise, and Glazed Beets.

Photographs on pages 2–3 copyright © Stephen Hussar.

Wood-Grilled Salmon with Caper Vinaigrette.

Fried Baby Artichokes.

Roast Goose with Chestnut Stuffing and Applesauce.

Canton Sorbet made from galangal, a mild ginger.

ABOVE, LEFT: The Spatlese Jelly with Port Jelly Cubes.

ABOVE, CENTER: Rhubarb Jelly with Strawberry Bavarian Cream.

ABOVE, RIGHT: Layered Lemon Jelly made with homemade colors and calf's foot gelatin.

Trio of Victorian Jellies.

LEFT: Mandarin Cake with Fresh Clementine Sherbet, Grand Marnier Pastry Cream, and Jellied Clementine Segments.

BELOW: The plated Mandarin Cake.

Photographs on pages 4–8 copyright © Kate Kelley.

GRUYÈRE VIEUX

MONTGOMERY FARMHOUSE CHEDDAR

Coffee, cheese, crackers, and liqueurs served in the front parlor.

Renee Montagne (NPR's *Morning Edition*) and Harry Smith (*CBS Early Show*).

The author decked out in a Victorian tailcoat with vest.

From left to right: Harry Smith, Brian Jones, Amy Dickinson, Gordon Hamersley, and Adrienne.

Left to right: Mark and Kelly Bittman, both from the *New York Times*.

ABOVE: An after-dinner toast with sous-chef, Keith, and chef, Erin, standing in the background.

BELOW: The kitchen crew. Front row left to right: Ryan Delgado (Maria's son) and chef, Erin McMurrer. Back row, left to right: Andrea Geary (jellies), Keith Dresser (sous-chef), Maria Eleana Delgado (scullery), Dan Souza (brown bread), Yvonne Ruperti (Mandarin Cake), and Maria Silva (scullery).

cake including a wedding cake, which used a pound each of butter, sugar, and flour, plus ten eggs and lots of dried fruit, including raisins, currants, citron, almonds, brandy, wine, and spices. Angel cake, similar to the modern angel food cake, was also popular. Yes, they did have fruit cake, made two or three weeks ahead of time from a cup of pork fat, hot coffee, brown sugar, molasses, spices, flour, baking soda, cream of tartar, raisins, currants, and chopped dried figs; it "will keep all winter if you lock it up." The one major exception, a cake that was almost never made, was a chocolate cake. It was, however, becoming a more popular ingredient (chocolate was rare earlier in the century), and one could make chocolate (hot cocoa), Vienna chocolate (this version has beaten egg whites added at the last minute), chocolate Bavarian cream, chocolate blanc mange (milk, gelatine, grated chocolate, sugar, and vanilla), chocolate tartlets, chocolate caramels, and chocolate creams.

The sponge cake was the ultimate all-purpose recipe of the era. It was the basis for Boston cream pie, invented at the Parker House in Boston (two layers of sponge cake filled with pastry cream and drizzled with chocolate ganache). It was often made into an endless series of two-layer cakes with a simple filling, jam for example, with nothing more than confectioner's sugar as a topping.

VICTORIAN SPONGE CAKE

Although I have developed my own recipe for a modern sponge cake, this recipe is an authentic sponge from the Boston Cooking School and gives you a good idea of what one of its workhorse recipes was really like. I have updated the recipe to reflect modern appliances and mixing methods.

4 eggs, separated
½ teaspoon cream of tartar
8 ounces sugar
4 ounces cake flour
2 teaspoons lemon rind
2 tablespoons lemon juice
⅛ teaspoon salt

Beat egg whites with cream of tartar and 2 tablespoons of the sugar (reserve the rest) until it holds 2-inch peaks. Whites should still be moist and slightly soft. Remove to a separate bowl. Using the same mixing bowl as for the whites, beat the yolks with the remaining sugar until light and ribbony, 4 to 5 minutes in an electric mixer. Add flour and mix on low speed for 10 seconds. Remove bowl from mixer, add whites, lemon rind, juice, and salt and fold together by hand with a large rubber spatula. Bake in a 375-degree oven for about 30 minutes.

ANOTHER COMMON RECIPE, ONE FOUND ON MANY FANNIE menus, was the French cream cake, similar to Boston cream pie. The earliest recipe we came across was from 1870 in *The Godey's Lady's Book Receipts and Household Hints*. The cake was a standard cold-water sponge cake, baked in a pie pan, split when warm, and filled with the cream. The cookbook suggests, as is the case with a genoise, that the cakes stand for a day or two before serving. We made the Royal Baking Powder Company version of this recipe and discovered something interesting. Since the cream used over one hundred years ago was so much thicker and better, our custard filling came out thin and runny, making slicing difficult. This turned out to be a common problem in all of our testing—matching modern ingredients to Victorian recipes. Other recipes for French cream cake—and this was Fannie's approach—were based on classic *choux* paste, the type of pastry used to make éclairs, *gougères*, and Paris-Brest. This may be the origin of the term "French" cream cake, since *choux* paste is very French indeed, made by boiling water and butter, stirring in flour, and then beating in eggs one at a time, usually after the mixture has cooled a bit.

The following recipe uses my own slightly adapted recipe for sponge cake filled with pastry cream. The cake needs to sit for twenty-four hours before serving.

FRENCH CREAM CAKE

Although Fannie's recipe uses a *choux* paste for the cake, we decided to develop this recipe using the lighter and more appealing sponge cake. It is crucial to beat the egg-and-sugar mixture a very long time until it is very pale and light. This may take five minutes, which will seem almost forever. You will be tempted to stop beating at three minutes or so. If using an 8-inch round cake pan, be sure that it is at least two inches high, otherwise the batter will rise above the sides of the pan. This is one cake you do *not* want to underbake because it will collapse on you. Make sure that the middle of the cake springs back when lightly touched with your finger or a fork.

For the cake:

½ cup cake flour

6 tablespoons all-purpose flour

½ teaspoon baking powder

¼ teaspoon salt

3 tablespoons milk

2 tablespoons unsalted butter

½ teaspoon vanilla extract

5 eggs, room temperature

¾ cup sugar

For the cream:

2 cups milk

3 tablespoons cornstarch

¾ cup sugar

Pinch salt

4 egg yolks

4 tablespoons cold butter, cut into 4 pieces

1 teaspoon vanilla extract

1. *For the cake:* Adjust oven rack to lower-middle position and heat oven to 350 degrees. Grease two 8- or 9-inch round cake pans and cover pan bottom with a round of parchment paper. (If using an 8-inch pan, it must be at least 2 inches high.) Whisk flours, baking powder, and salt in a medium bowl (or sift onto waxed paper). Heat milk and butter in a small saucepan over low heat until butter melts. Off heat, add vanilla; cover and keep warm.

2. Separate 3 eggs, placing whites in the bowl of a standing mixer fitted with the whisk attachment (or large mixing bowl if using hand mixer or whisk). Reserve the 3 yolks plus the 2 whole eggs in another mixing bowl. Beat the whites on high speed (or whisk) until whites are foamy. Gradually add 6 tablespoons of the sugar and continue to beat whites to soft, moist peaks. (Do not overbeat as stiff, dry egg whites will be difficult to incorporate into the batter.) If using a standing mixer, transfer egg whites to a large bowl and add yolk–whole egg mixture to mixing bowl.

3. Beat yolk–whole egg mixture with remaining 6 tablespoons sugar at medium-high speed (setting 8 on a KitchenAid) until eggs are very thick and a pale lemon color, about 5 minutes (or 12 minutes by hand). Add the beaten whites to the mixing bowl and then sprinkle the flour mixture over beaten eggs and whites. Mix on the lowest speed for 10 seconds. Remove bowl from mixer, make a well in one side of the batter, and pour melted butter mixture into bowl. Fold mixture with a large rubber spatula until batter is evenly mixed, about 8 additional strokes.

4. Immediately pour batter into prepared baking pans; bake until cake tops are light brown and feel firm and spring back when touched, about 16 minutes for 9-inch cake pans and 20 minutes for 8-inch cake pans.

5. Place one cake pan, bottom side down, on a kitchen towel; run a knife around pan perimeter to loosen cake, cover pan with a large plate. Invert pan and remove it. Remove parchment paper and then invert cake onto cooling rack. Repeat with remaining cake.

6. *For the cream:* Heat 1¾ cups milk; combine cornstarch, sugar, salt, yolks, and remaining milk; slowly whisk hot milk into egg mixture; return mixture

to pot. Heat mixture over medium-high heat, about 3 minutes, stirring constantly until boiling. Boil 20 to 30 seconds, until thick enough to drop from the spoon without running; remove from heat; whisk in butter in 4 pieces; cool over an ice bath. Add vanilla extract.

7. Split cooled cakes into four layers and fill with cream. Chill for 24 hours. Let sit at room temperature for about 2 hours before serving.

For the recipe for Portsmouth cake, a sponge cake with a sliced orange filling and orange frosting, go to www.fannieslastsupper.com.

OCTOBER 2009. IN VICTORIAN AMERICA, TABLE MANNERS WERE rapidly becoming the supreme test of refinement and character, and any misstep would instantly betray one's poor upbringing. Clearly, society has taken a serious turn for the worse. In fact, the "Meal of the Century" that I was re-creating was not just about the food; it was also about an event, about dining, about the ritual of sitting around the table with a group of interesting people and bringing the entire experience up to a new (or, I guess, old) level. Could we re-create a formal fin-de-siècle dinner party, or would we simply look like a bunch of starved chimps in monkey suits?

A high Victorian dinner party—now we are talking about the wealthy, not just the aspiring middle classes—was formal, so it was tails for the gentlemen and full dress costume for the ladies. One was not to arrive early, and fifteen minutes was the outer limit of being tardy. Cocktails were not served (I intended to break that rule by serving punch before dinner), so nothing was consumed before the butler announced dinner (which might have been nothing more than a slight nod to the mistress of the household). At that point, a procession would form, the host leading the way into the dining room, escorting the most honored lady of the evening, elders preceding young invitees, and the gentlemen escorting their assigned dinner partners. One had to take one's seat properly, at the proper distance from the table, and the napkin was intended for the lap, not the shirtfront "like an Alderman." Even with a large number of courses, up to twelve or so, the meal was to be served within two hours or less: it was a briskly paced event. At the end, the ladies would adjourn to the drawing room, leaving the men at the table with their cigars and brandy. After a bit, the gentlemen joined the ladies, and demitasse and candies were served.

Dining in a formal setting involved a complex series of rules and regulations. Rules in the dining room were nothing new: they existed as far back as the Middle Ages, when diners were hardly sophisticated, drinking from common goblets, sharing the same board (plate) with another guest, and eating with one's fingers. By the Victorian era, the thirst for etiquette guides was on the rise in the United States, with five or six books being published each year on the topic, double the rate earlier in the century.

The essence of table etiquette in Victorian times derived from the disturbing relationship between eating and animal behavior. One manual said, "Eating is so entirely a sensual, animal gratification, that unless it is conducted with much delicacy, it becomes unpleasant to others." These dinner parties were, in effect, a test of one's control over bodily appetites. One was never to appear greedy, draining the last drop from a wineglass or scraping the last morsel from the plate, and one was never to eat hurriedly, implying uncontrolled hunger. Since meal preparation was not shown in public, all the plates were prepared out of the view of the diners and then simply served, the servants being careful never to touch a plate, avoiding doing so by using a napkin, or small silver trays for passing.

Eating with one's fingers was a no-no, even for fruit, which was to be handled with utensils. Teeth marks were also viewed with horror as an "unmistakable imprint of bodily processes." Eating noisily was also abhorrent, and it was supposed that those who were well-bred instinctively understood the nature of this offense and would therefore avoid it. Hands were to be kept below the table unless occupied, but never so with scratching one's head or picking one's teeth. Coughing or sneezing was also not allowed; the diner so afflicted was to leave the room to perform these functions. Conversation was to be lively, but never heated or moody. A calm, orderly table was the goal, even in the event of a spilled wineglass. No apology or fuss was to be made in those circumstances; it would interrupt the calm flow of the perfect evening.

The social context for all of this was the notion that the United States was a democracy, governed not by a higher power but by the individual's ability to control him- or herself. In Europe, where the lower classes were separated from the aristocracy, this mattered less. The peasants could eat with their fingers all they liked. Here, the various classes were constantly interacting and etiquette was important to keep the peace—and, I would guess, also to reassure ourselves that a democratic society was a workable notion, an improvement over the European culture that we had so recently left behind.

The Victorians are to be applauded for their emphasis on good manners, but there existed a fundamental conflict in their approach, one that is still at the center of American life today. On one hand, our society was more communal than Europe's, so an emphasis on personal self-control was a means of making the melting pot a workable reality in lieu of a more formal hierarchy. (The promise of America was that the middle class could purchase a book on etiquette and learn to behave like those at a higher station in life—this was the dream of upward mobility.) At the same time, this rather rigid display of rules and manners did the opposite; it made the rich and powerful even more distinct from those below. In effect, wealthy Americans wanted to be an aristocracy, but they wanted to feel good about it at the same time.

As we moved to the last course before coffee, we were sadly disappointed with Fannie's offerings. There were two dessert courses, the first of which might be a molded jelly, a mont blanc (cooked, puréed, and sweetened chestnuts decorated with a cream sauce), a pudding, or frozen pudding (ice cream). The cakes on her menus were, however, rather uninspired, the choices including sultana (raisin) roll with claret sauce, sponge drops, almond crescents (I tested these and they were awful), and then French cream cake with a filled baked *choux* paste. (See above for our final version of this recipe, which uses sponge cake, not *choux* paste.) It was time to look across the Atlantic to find something more elegant, the sort of dessert that might indeed have made it to Boston or New York in the late nineteenth century.

The most comprehensive and best illustrated reference book on the subject is *The Victorian Book of Cakes*, which was reprinted in a new edition in 1991. The desserts in this book were at the top of their class at the time, winning prizes or included in major confectionary exhibitions. It should also be noted that this was an English, not an American, work, and Fannie's repertoire was a great deal more down-to-earth. That being said, *The Victorian Book of Cakes* provides a good overview of baking around 1900. The basic items in the book included shortbread, gingerbread, sponge cake, meringues, cookies, and pound cake. There were special-occasion cakes, including birthday, wedding, and christening cakes. Charlottes and trifles were their own category, and then there were the savoy molds— cakes baked in fancy molds, decorated, and sometimes filled.

We soon discovered that savoy cake had become a standard cake of the time. A recipe in the 1846 edition of *The Modern Cook* by Charles Francatelli calls for a pound of sugar, fourteen eggs, and four and a half ounces each of all-purpose and potato flour. The cake is baked in a fluted savoy mold, which is well coated with fat and sugar, in a moderate oven. The savoy molds were tall, fluted molds that looked a bit like the Chrysler Building in New York or vertical thrusts of ladyfingers. Usually there was a simple round base, and then one or two upper layers of decreasing diameter. American cakes quickly became standardized into simple round layers by the twentieth century, although we did find examples of these molds in an 1899 cookbook, *Warne's Model Cookery*.

The ultimate French cake book is *Cuisine Artistique* by Urbain Dubois (Paris, 1888), which contains page after page of fantastic creations, including Pêches à l'Andalouse, Fruits à la Madeleine, Gâteau Meringue à la Polonaise, and Gâteau Princesse de Galles. The one that piqued our interest the most was Gâteau Mandarin, which is a high dome of sponge cake decorated with candy roses, with their leaves, and then brushed with an orange syrup much like a typical genoise. This cake was simply a variation on the basic savoy cake, which was popularized by the famous chef Antonin Carême. Dubois added his own touch: tangerines that were filled with ribboned or striped orange and crème jellies (layered jellies were, of course, nothing new), and then used as decorations around the base of the cake. This recipe was also known as Savoy Cake with Oranges. A few weeks later, we came across a recipe in *The Epicurean* that was similar to the Dubois creation, called Mandarin Cake.

Mandarin Cake

This cake is best made over the course of two days. On the first day, make the clementine sherbet, marzipan, almond butter cake, simple syrup, and lemon leaves. On the second day, make the clementine segments and Grand Marnier pastry cream and cover the cake with marzipan. Finish the cake by filling the decorative cake mold with pastry cream and then decorating the cake with the lemon leaves, orange segments, and orange sherbet halves.

The recipes for Clementine Sherbet, Almond Blanc Mange, Clementine Jelly, and Sugared Lemon Leaves (these decorative elements are optional) can be found at www.fannieslastsupper.com.

EASY MARZIPAN

This is an easy and foolproof version of marzipan because it incorporates corn syrup, cornstarch, and confectioner's sugar instead of a fondant, which can be fussy since it uses a sugar syrup. It rolls out well and is easily modeled into fruit shapes. It can be prepared one day ahead and stored at room temperature, wrapped tightly in an airtight container.

> 9 ounces almond paste
>
> 1 ounce sliced almonds, unblanched
>
> 4 ounces cornstarch
>
> 4 ounces confectioner's sugar
>
> 6 to 8 tablespoons corn syrup

1. In food processor, process almond paste, almonds, cornstarch, and confectioner's sugar until mixture is sandy in texture, about 1 minute.

2. Add 6 tablespoons corn syrup and pulse (about 15 one-second pulses) until mixture just comes together. If mixture seems dry, stop processor, remove top, and press mixture together with fingers. If it doesn't hold together, add more corn syrup, 1 tablespoon at a time, until mixture will just hold together.

3. On work surface, gently knead marzipan until smooth, about 1 minute. Wrap tightly and let rest for at least an hour before using.

ALMOND BUTTER CAKE

Moist and buttery, with a hint of clementine essence, this cake forms the base of the mandarin cake and is also used to make the fluted savoy cake that sits on top. The key to making the batter is to smoothly incorporate the almond paste with the sugar and butter so that there are no remaining lumps of almond paste. Because of the volume of cake batter, you need a 6-quart-capacity mixer for this recipe; the alternative is to halve the recipe and make two separate batches.

Coating for savoy mold:

4 tablespoons granulated sugar

2 tablespoons cornstarch

1 tablespoon Wondra flour

4 tablespoons vegetable shortening

For the two cakes:

3 cups (12 ounces) cake flour

1½ teaspoons baking powder

1½ teaspoons table salt

15 ounces almond paste, room temperature, cut into ½-inch pieces

4½ tablespoons zest from 6 to 8 clementines

3¾ cups plus 2 tablespoons granulated sugar

24 ounces unsalted butter, cut into ½-inch pieces, softened slightly

18 large eggs, room temperature

13½ ounces blanched slivered almonds, finely ground

4 large egg whites

½ cup apple jelly

1. *To coat the pans:* Preheat oven to 350 degrees and adjust oven rack to middle position. Line 12-inch cake pan with parchment and spray with nonstick cooking spray. In small bowl, stir together the sugar, cornstarch,

and Wondra flour. Heat 6-cup decorative cake mold in oven for 15 minutes. (We used a tall fluted mold, the typical shape used in French patisserie of the period.) Meanwhile, in small saucepan, heat vegetable shortening over low heat until melted. Remove mold from oven and immediately pour melted shortening in mold. Turn mold to coat evenly and pour out excess shortening. Sprinkle sugar mixture into mold and, holding mold on its side, turn so that sugar mixture coats the mold evenly. Gently knock out excess. Set mold aside.

2. *To make the cakes:* Sift flour, baking powder, and salt together in large bowl; set aside. In standing mixer fitted with paddle attachment, mix almond paste, clementine zest, and just 1 cup of the sugar on low speed, until almond paste is softened, about 2 minutes. Increase speed to medium low and slowly add 2¾ cups sugar (reserving 2 tablespoons), alternating with butter, until mixture is smooth, with no remaining lumps of almond paste. Increase speed to medium high and beat until light and fluffy, about 2 minutes. Reduce speed to medium and slowly add eggs, scraping down sides and bottom of mixer and paddle as necessary, about 2 more minutes. Add ground almonds and mix to combine. On low speed, mix in flour mixture until just combined. Remove bowl from mixer and fold batter once or twice with rubber spatula to incorporate any remaining flour.

3. Reserve 5 cups batter and set aside. Spoon remaining batter into prepared cake pan and smooth top with offset spatula. Bake until top is golden and skewer inserted into cake shows moist crumbs, about 40 to 50 minutes. Cool cake in pan on wire rack for 1 hour. Invert onto wire rack to cool completely, about 2 hours. Wrap tightly until ready to cover with marzipan.

4. While first cake is cooling, adjust oven rack to lower-middle position. In standing mixer fitted with whisk attachment, whip whites until frothy using medium speed. Slowly add remaining 2 tablespoons sugar and whip on medium high until whites hold soft peaks. Briefly stir reserved cake batter and then using rubber spatula, fold ⅓ whites into reserved cake batter

to lighten. Fold remaining whites into batter until just combined. Fill prepared biscuit mold with batter within ½-inch from top rim. (You may have a little leftover batter.) Place mold on sheet pan and bake until toothpick inserted into center of cake is clean, about 75 to 85 minutes. Let cool on wire rack for 20 minutes, and then carefully invert cake onto wire rack to cool completely, about 3 hours. When cool, carefully hollow out cake to no less than ½ inch from exterior of cake. Allow to dry at room temperature overnight. (Drying out is important so that it is structurally sound when filling with pastry cream.) Reserve a few thin pieces of removed cake (preferably from the bottom of the cake) to use later to seal up hollowed cake after it has been filled with cream.

5. *To cover the bottom cake layer with marzipan (best done on the second day):* Place 12-inch cake on serving platter, bottom side up. Using offset spatula, spread a thin layer of apple jelly over top and sides of cake. Lightly dust work surface with confectioner's sugar. Using rolling pin, roll out marzipan to 16-inch diameter (about ⅛-inch thick). Using rolling pin, carefully roll up marzipan and then unroll onto cake. Smooth marzipan onto top and sides of cake. With paring knife, trim excess marzipan.

Yield: Enough for one 12-inch cake and one 6-cup molded cake.

GRAND MARNIER PASTRY CREAM

This cream is used to fill the fluted cake that sits on top of the base layer.

½ vanilla bean

1½ cups half-and-half cream

⅓ cup plus 1 tablespoon granulated sugar

Pinch table salt

5 yolks

2 tablespoons cornstarch

3 tablespoons Grand Marnier

½ cup heavy cream

1. With paring knife, slice vanilla bean in half lengthwise and scrape out seeds; reserve seeds. Heat half-and-half cream, ⅓ cup sugar, vanilla bean seeds, and salt in medium heavy-bottomed saucepan over medium heat until simmering, stirring occasionally to dissolve sugar.

2. Meanwhile, whisk egg yolks and remaining 1 tablespoon sugar in medium bowl until thoroughly combined. Whisk in cornstarch until combined and mixture is pale yellow and thick, about 30 seconds.

3. When half-and-half mixture reaches full simmer, gradually whisk into yolk mixture to temper. (It is important to add hot mixture to yolks slowly to prevent yolks from curdling.) Return mixture to saucepan; return to simmer over medium heat, whisking constantly, until 5 or 6 bubbles burst on surface and mixture is thickened and glossy, about 30 to 60 seconds. Remove from heat and whisk in Grand Marnier. Press wax paper or plastic wrap directly on surface, and refrigerate until cold and set, at least 3 hours, or up to 48 hours until ready to use.

4. Gently stir chilled pastry cream to loosen. In chilled medium bowl, whisk heavy cream to soft peaks, about 2 minutes. Fold whipped cream

into pastry cream (this mixture can be make up to 3 hours in advance) and fill hollowed biscuit mold just before serving.

Yield: about 3 cups.

 ## ASSEMBLING THE CAKE

Just before serving, you have to assemble the various components of the cake. We used an ornate silver cake stand—you will want something rather fancy, given all the work you went through to prepare it. Note that recipes for the lemon leaves and the filled tangerines, both the sherbets, and the two jellies, can be found at www.fannieslast supper.com.

1. Arrange optional lemon leaves around 12-inch Almond Butter Cake base (that has been covered in marzipan), which is positioned on a serving stand.

2. Gently hold hollowed-out cake mold upside down, and carefully fill with lightened pastry cream mixture to about ½-inch from bottom. Seal with reserved pieces of cake. Once cake is filled and sealed, place sealed side down over center of marzipan-covered cake.

3. Slice optional jelly-filled clementines pole to pole into quarters and arrange over lemon leaves, around marzipan-covered cake.

4. Place optional clementine sherbet halves around the molded pastry cream–filled cake and on top of the marzipan base cake.

5. When ready to plate, take a photo first! Then, use serrated knife to slice 1 inch off top of cake to reveal pastry cream filling. Serve slice of marzipan-covered cake with 1 sherbet half, 1 jelly segment, and a dollop of pastry cream. Garnish plate with sugared lemon leaf.

Coffee, Cheese, and Cordials

The Coffee Industry Awakens America

Coffee drinking was not unknown in America, but it wasn't until the War of 1812, when both the supply of tea was cut off and French culture became popular, that the French custom of drinking coffee really came into its own. Brazilian coffee was cheaper than tea and geographically closer than the Far East, so Americans increased their daily intake. By 1850, coffee was already a key part of chuck wagon fare, and beans were carried out west by frontiersmen. Many Native Americans also got hooked, among them the Sioux, and in one particular case it was said that a cup of coffee was exchanged for a buffalo robe. Until the mid-nineteenth century, most coffee was purchased as green beans and then roasted at home, usually in a cast-iron skillet; home roasters were also available, although reportedly not very effective. By the 1840s, commercial coffee roasting had come into vogue; James W. Carter of Boston had invented the Carter pull-out roaster, which had huge perforated cylinders placed into brick ovens. These coffee-roasting houses were smoky places indeed—it was hard, dirty work and many of the beans burned. Eventually, a better coffee roaster was invented by a Jabez Burns that was self-emptying and moved the beans around an inner chamber as the cylinder turned, making for a more even roast. Oddly enough, the invention that did the most to promote the sale of roasted coffee beans and spur the drinking of coffee was the paper bag that was invented in 1862 for selling peanuts.

The paper bag? John Arbuckle was a partner in a grocery store in Pittsburgh at the outset of the Civil War. He began to sell roasted coffee beans, with an egg and sugar glaze to "prevent staling," in one-pound paper bags under the brand-name Ariosa. He was also a successful and aggressive marketer, whose advertising campaign featured a frustrated housewife lamenting, "Oh, I have Burnt my Coffee again!" The tagline for his ads was, "You cannot roast Coffee properly yourself," and he claimed that every grain of his coffee was evenly roasted. Boston also had its hand in the promotion of coffee drinking through the firm of Chase & Sanborn, founded in 1878. Its marketing gimmick was the sale of roasted coffee beans in specially designed sealed tin cans. The factory was on Broad Street, and by 1882, the company was selling one hundred thousand pounds per month. It also used a mammoth sales force—it claimed twenty-five thousand agents, who had exclusive sales territories around the country. This firm was also brilliant at publicity, forgiving debts in 1927 from those involved with the Vermont flood and handing out free materials with its coffee, including cards, blotters, booklets, and store displays. It also sent holiday greeting cards to every one of its customers and even accepted noncash payments from time to time, cotton being one such commodity bartered in the South.

Coffee was perhaps the ultimate consumer item for which marketing and sales techniques made a big difference—after all, few consumers could tell the difference between high and low quality. In fact, a great deal of coffee on the market was either adulterated or not coffee at all. There were ersatz beans made from rye flour, glucose, and water. Other dubious ingredients included baked horse liver, brick dust, burnt rags, coal ashes, dirt, dog biscuits, mesquite, monkey nuts, sawdust, vetch, and wood chips. During the Civil War, Confederate soldiers could not obtain real coffee and were therefore reduced to using substitutes, including acorns, dandelion roots, sugarcane, parched rice, cotton seed, peanuts, wheat, beans, sweet potatoes, corn, rye, okra, and chicory. (Chicory continued as a legitimate additive and was often advertised openly.) Meanwhile, the Union government was levying a 4-cent duty per pound of coffee while, at the same time, purchasing 40 million pounds of green beans in 1864 alone. The price of coffee almost tripled during the Civil War, although it collapsed by 1865.

This feast-and-famine cycle continued for decades as the industry would buy up beans during periods of oversupply in an effort to prop up prices. The most serious such collapse occurred in 1880 after the death of a key coffee baron; as a result, in 1881, the New York Coffee Exchange was founded in order to regulate and stabilize the industry.

Hot chocolate was another popular drink of the day, and when made with cocoa shells, it was often referred to as "little coffee." The shells, which are the thin outer covering of the beans, cost just 7 to 12 cents per pound in 1896, whereas cocoa cost almost ten times that much. Here in the States, the most common method of making little coffee was to boil a few ounces of roasted shells in three pints of water for half an hour, allow it to settle, strain, and then add cream or boiled milk and sugar. Since cocoa shells have less chocolate flavor than the beans themselves, the key was to extract as much flavor as possible without turning the liquid bitter through overextraction. Other home cooks reduced the roasted shells to a fine paste and then used it much like cocoa, dissolving it in hot water, boiling it for twenty minutes, and adding milk or cream and sugar.

OCTOBER 23, 2009. IT WAS LATE OCTOBER; WE WERE JUST TWO weeks away from the Dinner Party of the Century. A cooking practice session was scheduled for Saturday, October 24, and we ran into a wall of problems starting the previous Monday. We had unexpected puff pastry issues—the butter kept pushing its way out of the rectangle of dough as we rolled it out, even though the air conditioner was on high and we were using the same brands of butter and flour we had used during recipe development. The galangal used for the Canton sorbet was poor quality and provided too little flavor and bite. We tested frozen galangal, which turned the sorbet bitter. We finally increased the amount from 4 to 5 ounces to approximate the original result when galangal was of higher quality.

At the last minute, the supply of Champagne grapes gave out; they were to be used in the Spatlese jelly. After numerous phone calls, Erin found a purveyor in New Market Square who said that he had "a couple" left. After confirming that he meant bunches rather than single grapes, Erin rushed over in the pouring rain only to discover that he had Concord, not Champagne, grapes. We eventually turned to a port jelly, which we cut into small cubes and then layered into a spiral pattern in the Spatlese gelatin.

We also had a long discussion about the tangerine wedges, filled with almond blanc mange and tangerine jelly, for the mandarin cake. Would any of the guests think that the whole thing was edible, rind and all? "No," I shouted. "Impossible!" A few minutes later, Mike, who was handling the service, popped an entire wedge into his mouth and noted, "The bitterness of the rind complements the sweetness of the jellies!" Well, we would leave this decision to our guests.

Baby artichokes for the fried artichokes course were also a problem— they were just too small. But a few days before the rehearsal dinner, we stumbled upon a good supply of larger specimens. (If the artichokes are too small, the leaves are not big enough to fan out, coat, and fry, so each one has a distinctive crunch.) Geese were also hard to source, since we were cooking before the Thanksgiving holiday, but we did manage to find a high-end supplier (D'Artagnan) who came through at the last minute. Finally, we decided to try three different rums for the punch, a cheap liquor-store variety, a twelve-year-old rum, and then a twenty-year-old rum. The winner, of course, was the older, more expensive brand.

On Friday, we did a dry run grilling the salmon and found that the fire was not hot enough. Someone had added a couple of split logs to the fire just before grilling, thereby insulating the fish from the heat of the coals. We would have to remember to bank the coals, leaving off fresh additions of wood.

By midafternoon on Saturday, things were heating up, literally. The fire alarm, a heat sensor, went off—we had to cover the offending sensor with foil. This resulted in a rather embarrassing visit by the fire department, during which I had to explain that we were attempting to cook a twelve-course dinner on a wood cookstove. They seemed rather confused, as if they had stepped onto the wrong movie set, but after a quick check of the premises, they took off.

In fact, the heat was so terrific in the main kitchen that we had to create a separate staging area for the oysters, the gelatin desserts, and the mandarin cake. It quickly became clear that we needed two full sets of dessert courses: three finished Victorian jellies for display at the table, and two mandarin cakes: one for display, and the other for serving the pastry cream tucked inside the central savoy cake. (Each cake took an entire day to bake and assemble.) In addition, we realized that the sorbet filling in the tangerine halves of the cake would melt quickly while sitting on a sideboard in the dining room; therefore, Yvonne Ruperti, our pastry chef, would have to come up with a fake sorbet, one that was heat-resistant.

We also realized that the rissoles could not be mass-produced, since each one required constant basting in hot oil, limiting the production to a few at a time. Since we would be serving twelve guests, each consuming three rissoles, that was at least a dozen batches. We would have to set up a production line of two, perhaps three Dutch ovens filled with oil, so that we could fry six rissoles at a time. We would also have to find the best way to hold the rissoles so that they would maintain their crispness.

The final test would be the service. With a dozen guests, we would need six servers so that the hot courses could be brought up from the kitchen in just one trip and the plates cleared in the same efficient manner. As the evening progressed, each course was photographed with the proper plate and wineglass, and a rotating scullery system had to be devised so that we could recycle the same plate, bowl, or piece of glassware through multiple courses. As for the cookstove, we used it for roasting the goose and venison, preparing the stocks, and cooking the lobster à l'Américaine (simultaneously, in three separate skillets); the salmon would be grilled directly over the wood fire, and the cooktop would be used to keep sauces and other items warm. The frying would also be done on the wood cookstove, but the mandarin cake would be baked in a conventional oven. Of course the Canton punch would be made in a hand-cranked ice-cream machine, which would take twenty-five to thirty minutes. (I knew this firsthand, since I had been assigned this recipe a half dozen times during the recipe development process.)

TODAY, ALMOST EVERYONE MAKES ELECTRIC DRIP COFFEE AT home. In 1896, there were a variety of methods and, seemingly, no consensus on the best way to brew it. First off, Americans were still boiling their coffee, although in Europe, the two-tier drip pot, a method that was vastly superior to boiling, was in use as far back as the French Revolution. It was improved in 1809 by an American expatriate living in England, Benjamin Thompson, and a partial vacuum system for making coffee was already in use in France and England by 1850. Once again, the United States was lagging behind Europe in the culinary arts. Prepackaged roasted beans were the most common method of purchasing coffee. Most contemporary cookbooks still contained coffee-roasting instructions, since freshly roasted coffee was still considered to provide the tastiest cup.

So, following our test kitchen methodology, we tested all the recipes we could find using an enamel-covered iron pot, which would have been similar to the graniteware of the late Victorian period. For the coffee, we used Starbucks Verona coffee, a medium blend.

How did Fannie do? Well, she won the competition hands down. The coffee was a bit strong but very clear and clean-tasting. To test whether the egg was truly necessary, we made one recipe without it; the resulting coffee tasted stronger, was not as clear, and was slightly bitter.

FANNIE FARMER'S BOILED COFFEE

We did test this recipe without the egg, and it was indeed helpful in making the coffee clearer and less bitter. Fannie even opined on the right time to add sugar and cream to coffee. She claims that it should be put into the cup before the hot coffee for best flavor, although we could not tell any difference.

1 egg
1 cup cold water
1 cup coffee
6 cups boiling water

Whisk egg with one half cup cold water. Add crushed egg shell and stir in the coffee. Transfer mixture to a coffeepot, add the boiling water, and stir thoroughly. Boil for 3 minutes, stuffing the spout with paper towels to prevent aroma from escaping. Remove towel and pour out a small amount of coffee in order to clean spout; return this coffee to the pot. Add half cup of cold water to the pot "to clarify the coffee." Place pot back on stove on the lowest possible heat level for 10 minutes. Serve at once.

THIS LAST COURSE ALSO INCLUDED CHEESE AND CRACKERS. In the late 1800s, cheese would have been sold through retail establishments called creameries, which offered a fairly broad selection. Up until midcentury, cheese, like most other foodstuffs, was produced on local farms and not widely distributed. Around the time of the Civil War, however, cheese factories came into vogue; New York was an important producer (124 million pounds annually) and so was Wisconsin. These two states produced two-thirds of the total national output, mostly Cheddar, which was sold in sixty-pound wheels a foot or more in diameter. U.S. producers were also imitating Edam from Holland, creating a less than successful Gruyère in Wisconsin, and a Stilton from Maine that did well in a tasting contest (most Stilton, however, was still imported). Brie was being produced in New York and Pennsylvania, although most customers did not enjoy it "runny," as well as Limburger (American-made Limburger was more popular than the import, since it was aged less and had a much milder flavor) and Neufchâtel, otherwise known as cream cheese. Parmesan was strictly from Italy, making up roughly one-quarter of total cheese imports, and Camembert was also imported.

In general, Americans had no taste for strong, aged cheeses and therefore American varieties of European imports were aged for only brief periods, the Brie only being aged for two to four weeks, thus producing a cheese quite different from, and much inferior to, the real thing.

Today, of course, American cheese production has come a long way. In fact, unlike in Europe, where a particular type of cheese tends to be produced in a uniform style throughout a region, American cheeses tend to be more individual and eclectic; one producer may do something quite different from another producer in the farm down the road. This doesn't guarantee better cheese, but it does offer more variety and more serendipitous tastings. Here is the list of cheeses that we served after dinner, based in large part on the sorts of cheeses available in the United States in the late 1800s.

GRUYÈRE VIEUX: Fribourg, Switzerland

Slightly spicy flavor with a few stray crystalline bits. It's on the sweet side, with a nice bit of earthiness and a finish that is dusky and complex; not overly sharp or rich.

MONTGOMERY FARMHOUSE CHEDDAR: Manor Farm, North Cadbury, Somerset, England

A classic Cheddar with strong overtones of green pepper; even an undercurrent of unripe vegetable.

PARMIGIANO-REGGIANO CRAVERO: Emilia-Romagna, Italy

This Parmesan has a sweetness to it. We could taste an undercurrent of pineapple, and it shows a good balance of salt. Unlike lesser Parmesans, the flavors almost explode in the mouth and the texture is neither too dry nor too soft.

ROQUEFORT GABRIEL COULET: Mayran, Midi-Pyrénées, France

Rich and particularly soft and creamy, not harsh or overpowering, with lots of limestone minerality and nice spice, good salt, and an up-front citrusy quality, an oystery brininess, then a great satiny finish.

FROMAGE DE MEAUX: Meaux, Ile-de-France, France

Very buttery and light, not strong-flavored in any way; must be served at room temperature—any colder and it loses much of its subtle qualities. It has a bit of lactic tang, a hint of olive, and then a slight bitterness at the finish.

TARENTAISE, SPRING BROOK FARM: North Pomfret, Vermont

A bit milder and more buttery than the equivalent French version, this cheese hints at green olives, a slight undercurrent of anchovies, and also mushrooms.

Wine

In the early days of our country, America was not in love with wine, unlike the French and other Europeans. Beer and ale were much more common, and when Americans did drink wines, they were usually fortified wines such as sherry, port, or Madeira. Madeira was the most sought after; it was collected in private cellars, some bottles costing the absurd amount of $40 each, a month's wages for the average blue-collar worker. This was the state of affairs in the first half of the nineteenth century, but by Fannie Farmer's time, a great deal of wine was being imported and also grown in this country.

By the 1890s, S. S. Pierce in Boston was selling a wide assortment of wines, purchased either in bottles or in barrels, including selections from the great châteaux of the period, some slightly lower-quality wines, fortified wines, and a few American sparkling and still wines. In 1896, one could purchase the following: champagnes, clarets, sauternes, sherries, hock, sweet wines, Madeira, Tokay, Beaune, Pommard, Beaujolais, Macon, Volnay, and American wines.

Local American wines were also produced with some success in North Carolina, Virginia, Ohio, New York, and Missouri, from native grapes such as the Scuppernong, Delaware, and Catawba. Wine from native grapes was generally considered too "foxy" and not of good quality, with few exceptions.

Sparkling wines and champagnes were very popular in the late 1800s, almost always served with oysters and as a palate cleanser between courses. American sparkling wines were available in Fannie's era, one such producer being the Pleasant Valley Wine Company, located in the Finger Lakes region of New York and founded in 1860. Occasional homegrown attempts were made to produce a local American champagne from ingredients such as cider or "a mixture of turnip juice, brandy, and honey," which was referred to as "Newark's champagne."

Claret was a generic term used to describe red wines from the Bordeaux region. The term *claret* came from a medieval French practice of short fermentation, which produced pale, rosé-colored wines that were known in export as *vinum clarum, vin clar,* or *clairet.* By the late seventeenth century, however, these clarets were much improved, and considerably deeper and richer, and were referred to as New French Clarets.

Sweeter wines, sauternes for example, were preferred over the drier whites of the time—white Bordeaux and Chablis—probably because fortified wines, port and sherry, had been consumed for generations with dinner. The generic term for these sweeter wines was *hock,* named after the town of Hochheim on the river Main in Germany.

Sherry is a fortified wine, a practice that was begun to protect wines shipped over long distances, where heat and motion would ruin a regular burgundy, for example. The additional alcohol—some sherries were over 20 percent alcohol by volume—killed off remaining yeast cells, thus providing stability during transportation.

Based on our historical research (and many, many happy tastings), here is the final list of wines for the dinner. A complete annotated description of the wines and after-dinner liqueurs may be found at www.fannies lastsupper.com.

THE WINE LIST

OYSTERS: 1990 Veuve Clicquot La Grande Dame

MOCK TURTLE SOUP: Lustau Rare Amontillado Escuadrilla Sherry

RISSOLES: 1996 Heimbourg Pinot Gris, Domaine Zind Humbrecht

LOBSTER À L'AMÉRICAINE: 2005 Saint Joseph Blanc Lyseras, Yves Cuilleron

SADDLE OF VENISON: 1986 Château la Mission Haut Brion

WOOD-GRILLED SALMON AND FRIED ARTICHOKES: Reichsrat von Buhl Riesling Spätlese Trocken Pfalz Forster Ungeheuer

ROAST STUFFED GOOSE: 2002 Domaine Comte Georges de Vogüé, Chambolle-Musigny

MANDARIN CAKE: 1988 Château Guiraud 1er Grand Cru Classé

AFTER-DINNER LIQUEURS

Absinthe Superiéure, Lucid

Bénédictine

Belle de Brillet

Crème de Menthe

Martell XO Supreme (Extra Old)

Trimbach Framboise Grand Reserve

Chartreuse VEP Green

The Dinner Party

Amy Shakes Her Jelly and
José Andrés Falls in Love with a Mermaid

The final attendee list of twelve included Harry Smith (CBS), Renee Montagne (NPR), José Andrés (chef/owner Think Food Group), Mark and Kelly Bittman (*New York Times*), Amy and Bruno Dickinson (*Wait Wait...Don't Tell Me!*), Gordon and Fiona Hamersley (proprietors, Hamersley's Bistro, Boston), Brian Jones (former musical director for Trinity Church in Boston), Adrienne, and myself. Both Peter Gomes and Maggie Rodriguez from CBS had last-minute health problems. Renee was flying in on Friday evening from Los Angeles and spending the weekend. Mark, Kelly, Harry, and José (he was flying in from Spain) were arriving Saturday afternoon and staying at the house.

Cooking started on Tuesday, November 3. This was a day for stocks—a fumet, the calf's-head stock, chicken stock, etc. When preparing the calf's head, we remembered a note from a nineteenth-century recipe that suggested cleaning out the nostrils with a wire brush. We dismissed this as both unnecessary and rather primitive—after all, today's calf's heads were sold perfectly clean and well prepared, right? Well, one of the nostrils was plugged with a dark substance that turned out to be a compacted bit of hay. Hay? So, yes, we had to ream out the nostrils with a baby-bottle brush. This was the ultimate experience in locally sourced foodstuffs. In fact, Kate Kelly, the photographer recording the event, lost her appetite one evening while reviewing her photos of the making of the calf's-head stock—she recalled the toothy grin of the calf's mouth as it bobbed upward in the broth.

We decided to ramp up the oyster display, so we hired a company to carve a four-foot-high ice sculpture of a mermaid, the base of which would hold the Island Creek oysters. I reviewed a number of sketches, but it all came down to a simple choice: bikini-clad top or not? Well, the naked version sported spectacular breasts, somewhere on a continuum between the Little Mermaid and Annie Sprinkle, so I decided to let it all hang out. Of course, bare breasts would have been totally out of place in the Victorian era. They didn't even like topless statues, having banned the nude figure of Bacchante from the Boston Public Library in 1897.

As we got closer to the big evening, we descended deeper and deeper into puff pastry hell. We had by now mastered making the puff pastry, but we were having considerable problems with it when it was rolled out, cut, filled, and fried. Some of the rissoles broke apart at the seams and others would not puff properly, even when we tried freezing them first. By early Saturday morning, we were still having only mixed success. We would fry up four rissoles; three would come out fine and one would fail. Finally, by midafternoon, Erin, our test kitchen director, seemed to have things under control. After hundreds of tests and days of failures, she finally realized that the puff had to be kept very cold—it warms up quickly when rolled and cut, especially in a kitchen with a large wood cookstove. The edges had to be pinched and sealed extremely carefully, then checked once more before frying. This was the ultimate fussy recipe and required a great deal of last-minute attention. José Andrés, who had arrived midday on Saturday, watched the testing process and commented, "What's the problem? They're beautiful! They're delicious!" to which Andrea responded, "But they're not *perfect*," and then stamped her foot for emphasis. Finally, my favorite detail of the preparation: the brains were poached and left in a bowl in the refrigerator marked "Abnormal."

Meanwhile, the kitchen, front parlor, and dining room were lit by Jim Hirsch, whose company High Output also handles Hollywood movies. It took about six hours to install the metal scaffolding from which were hung a series of lights, including two large pillow-shaped soft lights over the dining room table. Jim explained that light levels are expressed in foot-candles, and a small handheld meter was used to check the output. With the cameras wide open at the largest iris setting, we would still need about eight foot-candles, which was a lot more than I wanted. Instead of a dark, romantic room, this was bright Hollywood lighting. So the food and the conversation (not to mention our makeup artist) were going to have to pull us through, not romantic ambiance.

By Thursday, we had a crew of five cooking full-time: Andrea was handling the gelatins, Yvonne was in charge of the mandarin cake, and Erin, Keith, and Dan were prepping most everything else. In another last-minute complication, the calf's-foot jelly was not setting up properly, although it had performed admirably in a dozen previous tries. We tried various strengths, and Andrea rode home at night on her bicycle, a forty-minute trip, with the gelatin packed in saddlebags for further testing. We finally found it necessary to combine three different concentrations of homemade gelatin with the lemon syrup to see which one would hold up while also providing the least rubbery texture. We finally realized that the problem was that all calf's feet are not created equal—younger animals have more gelatin in their feet than older calves. What? We had gone to all the trouble of making homemade gelatin by boiling calf's feet and now we had to worry about how old the feet were? A small packet of Knox was looking rather attractive.

Suddenly it was Saturday morning, the day of the party. I made breakfast for the crew—buttermilk waffles made from a mixture of four flours plus cornmeal, a recipe inspired by the original 1890s Aunt Jemima pancake mix. We were almost out of wood for the stove, so we had a half cord delivered the day before as backup. However, it was not completely dry and therefore did not burn as well. We decided to use this greener oak until late afternoon, when we would have to crank up the cookstove, and then use up the last bit of our well-seasoned wood.

The camera crew showed up in the late morning to set up the control room, install hidden microphones in the flower arrangements on the dining room table, and run the various cables between the cameras and the monitors. Michael, our maitre d', and his crew (his wife, Cindy, Jake, Debbie, Emile, and Melissa) arrived midafternoon and ran through the order of the courses—which menu items had sauce and might be difficult to transport upstairs, for example. They were briefed on the cheese course, the cordials, and the timing; dishes were to be served every twenty minutes.

As the afternoon progressed, the pace started to increase. Renee Montagne and José Andrés were already in-house. Mark Bittman and his wife, Kelly, turned up later in the afternoon, as did Harry Smith. Meanwhile, the kitchen was literally heating up, since meats had to be roasted and a good bed of coals would be necessary for grilling the salmon later in the evening. Brenda Coffey, our makeup artist, set up shop in the library. Showers were taken, suits and dresses donned, and then suddenly, after over two years of research, recipe testing, and intense planning, it was showtime.

The front parlor of our Victorian brownstone is fourteen feet wide by twenty-nine feet long, with a curved front wall featuring two high windows. These overlook a small oval English-style square populated by the few remaining four-story-high chestnut trees and a fountain with a center sculpture featuring dancing children. A fireplace with an ornate carved white marble mantel is on one wall; opposite are two richly varnished nine-foot-high walnut doors leading to the front hall. My great-grandfather, Harper Pennington, was a portrait artist and contemporary of Whistler, and two of his paintings are on the wall flanking the doors—one a standard-issue military portrait and the other, smaller but nicer, of my great-aunt Kid as a child in a white Victorian-style frock. A long, rather primitive landscape adorns the opposite wall, a second-rate painting of an early settler gazing on the Schenectady Stockade and the Mohawk River. The back of the room is framed by two pocket doors with etched glass that open up into the dining room, which itself has a large bay window and a fireplace that used to burn coal (and now burns wood).

The ice mermaid was standing on a well-lit table between the two front windows, replete with oysters. The sculpture was spectacular—her thick hair drifted back as if through water, her tail swooped up and around, and every scale was minutely carved. Champagne bottles stood askew in a large bucket of ice as if slightly tipsy. The silver 1880s punch bowl, resplendent on the center table, was kept chilled by a floating ring of ice. A hint of smoke came from the burning logs in the fireplace, the flue not yet heated sufficiently to stop a curl or two from escaping from the black iron inset in the marble surround.

The room started to fill. Oysters were splashed with mignonette and slurped down. The champagne corks were popped and punch was poured. The conversation grew louder. Newcomers stood and admired the mermaid, while others were deep into the politics of Afghanistan or anecdotes from their professional lives in radio or television. Finally, it was time to move into the dining room and be seated.

The dining table seated twelve, with the fireplace on one end and a shallow butler's pantry with folding doors on the other. There was a grandfather clock on one side of the fireplace, and a small table for staging the food next to it, plus a large mahogany crockery cabinet along one wall. The bay window was filled with a mustard gold upholstered settee, with sprouting ferns as bookends. Hand-inscribed placecards held by silver calla lilly bud–shaped holders were at each setting. Three small arrangements of red roses were set in the middle, surrounded by fern. The chandelier was bedecked with copious greenery. The silver candlesticks rose from a circle of flowers sprouting hand-dipped gold candles; a gold-rimmed charger was set at every place, and the tablecloth, custom-made for the evening, matched the pewter and gold pattern of the wallpaper with an acanthus leaf ribbon pattern and gold trim with tassels around the hanging perimeter. To my left were Renee, Harry, Brian, Amy, and Gordon; Adrienne was seated at the opposite end. To my right were Fiona, José, Bruno, Kelly, and Mark. The candles and fireplace were lit, the parlor doors partially closed, and we were seated.

Ever since college I have had the same dream once a month like clockwork. It is the "I am sitting naked in front of the queen" dream—the one in which my humiliation is so profound that I am frozen into inaction. Well, here I was, with chairs filled with our distinguished guests, some of them having traveled thousands of miles, and now I had to announce that they were about to be served a soup made from a boiled calf's head with garnishes made from the poached brains of said calf. I quickly regained the use of my voice and explained the nature of the first seated course. Amy, our resident humorist, responded cheerfully, "Well, that is good to know." While trying to maintain my share of amiable chatter, I discreetly looked about to see how the brain balls were selling. The clear soup was a winner, but most guests left one or two floaters behind. Had I invited the wrong guests to dinner?

Things picked up when José Andrés got into gear. Proving that he knew something about almost everything, he noted that the Amontillado Sherry served with the soup was made in his wife's hometown in Spain. (Later on, however, when he was singing the praises of a can of fresh clams sold for the princely price of $80, his enthusiasm for all things culinary seemed to lurch out of control.) Then I was rescued by the rissoles, which were served piping hot, salty, crisp, and filled with chicken with three variations: duxelles, blue cheese with dried cherries, and chicken liver with caramelized onion. With the 1996 Heimbourg Pinot Gris, it was a stunner, and everyone was back onboard with the food. Just like a rock band, I thought, never start with your best song. (I discovered later that evening that since we were short on long-handled spoons, Yvonne and Andrea's hands had been frequently splashed with hot oil when frying the rissoles.)

Perhaps the best course was up next, the lobster à l'Américaine. Once again, our Spanish chef opined on the origin of the term *l'Américaine*. His claim was that this was a common dish in the south of France but also in the Mediterranean, including on Minorca, and hence the term *l'Américaine* a long-shot bastardization. Other theories claim that the original dish came from Brittany, which, at one time was called Amorica (hence, *Américaine*).

Regardless of nomenclature, one mouthful of the rich tarragon-scented sauce would be sufficient to convince even Rachael Ray that making homemade fish stock and then combining it with pan-sautéed lobster shells to forge a deeply resonant sauce was worth every second and dollar of expense. "This is why we cook," I thought, "to transform the ordinary ingredients of our trade—fennel, peppercorns, brandy, white wine, and leek—into something extraordinary, a combination that hints at a more perfect state of being."

All of a sudden, the kitchen ran into serious trouble and almost burned down the house. A wood cookstove is not hard to heat up—you add wood, open the vents underneath the firebox, open the flue all the way, and let it crank. Once you get up to temperature, you close the vent and shut the flue until it is just barely open, in an effort to retain the heat instead of allowing it to disappear up the chimney. The venison had been larded with salt pork and required a very hot oven indeed—we were using 600 degrees.

In a burst of enthusiasm, however, Keith, our sous-chef, had cranked the oven so high that the oven thermometer had rotated off the scale, well past 600 degrees—creating, in effect, a pizza oven. (A few days later, it occurred to me that twelve hundred pounds of red-hot iron surrounded by wood, 150-year-old lathing, and plaster was probably a near-miss in terms of spontaneous combustion.) After ten minutes of roasting, Erin discovered that the ends of the salt pork had actually charred. So there they were, snipping off the burned ends of the salt pork and using a pastry brush to wipe them away. Then they had to finish roasting the venison with the oven door open to cool things down.

But, oh, the venison once again reminded me that we live in lackluster times, an era without appreciation for the exalted role of the French sauce. For the saddle of venison, we had turned back the clock and roasted venison bones, made homemade currant jelly, and simmered our own veal stock, all in an effort to transform two thin slices of roasted venison loin with a currant jelly sauce that was sweet yet bracing; a sauce that made one shut one's eyes just for a second in order to appreciate the rich colors of taste.

The overheated oven had transformed the kitchen into the boiler room of the *Titanic*. One of the lightbulbs exploded from the heat, the brass pulls on the drawers in the center worktable could not be touched with bare hands, and the soapstone counters in the scullery in the next room were hot to the touch. An instant-read thermometer sitting on the air conditioner that was blasting cold air read an incredible 93 degrees, although it was probably 30 degrees hotter by the stove. Erin was wearing poly-blend chef pants, which started to melt onto her thighs; Keith, Andrea, Dan, and Yvonne had to crouch down by the stovetop while working in order to avoid singing their eyebrows in the rush of heat, especially when frying the rissoles and artichokes.

For service, Debbie, Cindy, and Melissa were wearing long skirts that made it nearly impossible to climb the stairs to the dining room, so they did what many women have done before them—they hiked them up to midthigh, pinning a few folds of material under one arm. (One wonders if Victorian housemaids did the same when nobody was looking.) Meanwhile, upstairs, there was the usual wine-fueled chatter about the order of the dishes on the menu, the fish course appearing after the venison, and then the goose just before the jellies and dessert. Modern chefs, including Gordon Hamersley, thought this was a bit odd, starting light, going heavy, pulling back to a fish course, and then heading into another full-flavored dish before winding down. I had reviewed dozens of menus from the period, and game was, indeed, served after a sorbet and before the fruit or jellies and then dessert.

Here's the problem: when serving a twelve-course meal, you would not want to start light and then move toward heavier and heavier food in a slow, inexorable march to gastric overload. ("Just one more chocolate, sir?") As with a Beethoven symphony, one needs pacing, a brisk prestissimo followed by a course of adagio, then largo (think funeral march), and then a slightly faster andante, a quick vivace, and a slow lento before moving onto a lively presto jelly course and a crescendo of cake for dessert. The modern notion of light to heavy is just too streamlined, too one-dimensional, for such a puffed-up culinary undertaking. And we were not suffering from the back-and-forth wine service, from Pinot Gris to Bordeaux, from Riesling to Burgundy. I was starting to feel like some rich, useless Victorian fop.

The trick for grilling the salmon indoors was to create a thick bed of fiery coals, since the addition of fresh wood only insulates the fish from the heat of the fire. Since Keith had almost burned down the house an hour before, the good news was that the coals were perfect for grilling, so two of the "burners," the round cast-iron inserts, were removed and the oblong grilling insert was put into place, preheated, and oiled frequently to build up a nonstick surface. The salmon turned out rich and moist with a hint of wood smoke and skin that was near black and perfectly crisp; it balanced perfectly with the caper vinaigrette. The fried artichokes were our salad course—hot, crunchy, and fresh-tasting with a bright splash of lemon. (The cooks found that chopsticks were quite useful in the frying process, a notion that would have been quite foreign to Fannie.)

Meanwhile, Harry Smith was wondering what planet José Andrés was born on, given his optimism about the changing food scene. Harry, a hard-news reporter from the Midwest, felt that José was speaking to an elite audience, the sorts of home cooks who know farci from farfalle—whereas Harry was more familiar with what folks were having for dinner at the Kansas City airport. They were, at once, irreconcilable yet well-paired: José brimmed with vast stores of kinetic energy, while Harry tempered his tremendous intellect and held back his coiled wit just enough to keep the conversation pointed but flowing pleasantly.

The Canton sorbet was up next, a simple frozen ginger palate cleanser, admittedly the bane of third-class French restaurants. (This was not one of my favorite dishes—I prefer the Victorian notion of a small glass of champagne to cleanse the palate rather than a fruited ice—but it was well conceived, not too sweet, and with enough bite to dismiss the notion of dessert.)

As for the roast goose, this was the course that was the diciest of all. Let's face facts: goose is almost impossible to cook well. The breast meat is often tough and livery, and the dark meat is rarely cooked long enough to render it tender. Our final method called for cooking breasts and legs separately, the legs and thighs on top of the bare carcass—using it much like a roasting rack—the breasts sautéed and then finished in the oven. When the oven was opened and the bird was checked, however, it turned out that the legs had slipped to one side, like a tenderfoot off a saddle. This was quickly remedied and the final dish was almost perfect, the breast meat still a tad chewy although the flavor was excellent. However, the dark meat was a triumph, both moist and tender. A gravy based on homemade goose stock worked well, as did the earthy chestnut stuffing and the fresh-tasting, slightly tart applesauce. When cooked properly, it was clear that goose is the epicure's version of turkey—more complex and deeply flavored, but much harder to cook and sauce.

Next, we were on to the three homemade Victorian jellies. Andrea had made two of each jelly—the multilayered lemon jelly with a pineapple design on top, the rhubarb jelly filled with a strawberry Bavarian cream, and then the Spätlese jelly with a spiral of cubed port jelly. If you have never had a homemade jelly, let me offer you this description. The first thing one notices is the flavor—it is not overly sweet or sharp-tasting like a child's notion of lemon or rhubarb, too bright and candylike for the grown-up palate. Instead, the flavors are bright but subtle—they change on the tongue as they melt, a slow process of evolution as the first cool bite of jelly slowly transforms, melting across the tongue and slipping across the pebbled surface down into the mouth, the flavors expanding and becoming less certain, less one-dimensional. Then, if the mold has a secondary flavor, one is introduced to the taste of port or the foamy change of pace offered by strawberry Bavarian, to remind us once again that this is a more complex, adult offering. At the same time, the shape and colors of a perfectly conceived jelly mold are intensely childlike and one finds it hard to stop grinning like a four-year-old at a birthday party. Amy Dickinson, with unabashed enthusiasm, grabbed the platter with the lemon jelly and started shaking it playfully. She evidently couldn't help herself. That started the jellies moving around the table, poked and jiggled, everyone digging in for seconds. The formality of a Victorian meal—a place where any sort of human appetite or uncontrolled behavior was abhorred—was clearly a lost cause.

The final course, the mandarin cake, was the ultimate Victorian fantasy dessert. The center portion, a classic fluted savoy cake, stood almost a foot tall and was filled with pastry cream. The base layer, one large round of almond-orange cake covered with white marzipan, provided the foundation. Around the base of the savoy cake were half-tangerines filled with frozen tangerine sorbet; circling the fluted savoy cake were arranged a series of quartered tangerines filled with alternating layers of tangerine and almond jellies. Sugared lemon leaves were added for decoration. All on one plate, one had a quick tour of the French dessert cart: luxurious warm pastry cream, ice-cold orange sorbet, a perfectly moist almond cake, the intense concentration of almond flavor in the marzipan icing, and then a bright note of clementine jelly and a baseline of almond blanc mange as a partner. The final course—coffee, crackers, cheese, bonbons, and liqueurs—was to be served in the parlor with the rapidly melting ice mermaid. (It was duly and unkindly noted that her figure now resembled that of a naked woman who has had at least two kids.) It was now 11:30 P.M., four and a half hours after we had been seated for dinner.

At midnight, as the guests and the kitchen and waitstaff (who had already been enjoying the leftover punch from the first course) were enjoying the port, Benedictine, Chartreuse, Framboise, etc., the folks from Brookline Ice and Coal showed up to remove the mermaid. The tail had to be removed—hacked off is more like it—so it could be loaded back up on a dolly and stepped down the outside stairs to the street. Then she was summarily tossed into a pile of leaves in the park as José Andrés begged to have this beautiful woman, the woman he "loved," brought up to his bedroom, "Immediately!" (If you ever want a lively dinner party, all you have to do is invite José.)

Finally, around 1:00 A.M. or so, Brian Jones started playing show tunes and Harry, being a fan of *Oklahoma!*, got Amy Dickinson and myself to sing the theme song, "The Surrey with the Fringe on Top," "Oh, What a Beautiful Morning," and then a few favorites from *My Fair Lady*. The upstairs and downstairs were joined, the evening was running down, a few guests started to retire upstairs clutching green bottles of Apollinaris water to head off the inevitable hangover, and it was no longer showtime. The Dinner Party of the Century was over.

Was this just a bunch of overprivileged gourmands enjoying ridiculous overconsumption while the rest of the country was stuck in the worst economic recession since the Great Depression? There is an undeniably frivolous notion to this sort of undertaking, given the nature of the menu and the cost of testing and preparing the food. But as the Cambridge don said, "The best thing about it is that no one can make any use for it for anything . . . this uselessness is the highest kind of use. It is kindling and feeding the ideal spark without which life is not worth living."

One hint that there was, indeed, some deeper meaning in all of this: the kitchen staff, after seventeen hours of cooking over a very hot wood cookstove, said they had loved the experience—the heat, stoking and maintaining the fire, using a large cast-iron work surface to tend stocks, sauté goose breasts and lobster tails, and keep sauces warm. In fact, as I discovered later, they had moved more and more of the preparation from the conventional gas cooktop in the smaller side kitchen to the Victorian cookstove, since they found it both more fun and, oddly enough, more efficient.

The Victorians lived in the most progressive, rapidly changing era in all of human history. In just one generation, they went from local to international, from coal cookstoves to gas, from slow food to fast food, from rural to urban, from family enterprises to factories, from carts to cars, from preservation to refrigeration. The promise was one of change, one of outgrowing the human condition, overcoming our weaknesses—hunger, alcoholism, poverty, poor nutrition—through the application of scientific methods: hence, the creation of domestic science. Technology would help us to outgrow our foibles, move past our baser human instincts, put aside the day-to-day bother and mess of living, including the cooking and the cleaning. Science and improved methods of social organization would allow women to achieve their higher artistic goals, leaving behind the drudgery of daily living. This has always been the promise of science, to alleviate the less desirable aspects of the human condition. The problem, of course, is that technology has taken away too much of what defines humanity, leaving us with little that goes to the heart of being a useful, happy person.

That being said, the notion that advancements in technology may ease the most appalling aspects of the human condition, including disease and hunger, is perfectly sound. But on some level, I suspect that we wish to leave all of the human condition behind because of our modern distaste for what used to be called "daily chores." By returning to an earlier culinary period and employing their methods, we put this proposition to the test. Has the relentless march toward convenience—from roasting meat over a fire to heating frozen meals in a microwave—allowed us the extra time to explore our artistic selves, thus providing happiness? Or, to put it another way, can time be saved so that it can be better spent? Based on the evidence of the last fifty years, the answer is no. Clearly, what modern civilization has done with those additional six hours per day *not* spent cooking and cleaning has been mostly a waste of time, since over five of those hours are spent watching television. And the hundreds, even thousands, of hours spent on this project were well spent indeed, hard work that brought us to the height of the joy of being human. In other words, given lots of free time, most of us have absolutely no idea what to do with it. The myth of leisure is just that—yet another silly misunderstanding about human nature.

Happiness is derived, I propose, from being useful—from putting one's oar in the water and helping move the boat forward. This is an entirely unoriginal notion, but it bears repeating. It is also no surprise that happiness is enhanced when work is shared and appreciated by others.

Excessive leisure, it might be stated, is a recipe for unhappiness. If you doubt this proposition, just spend some time in a retirement community full of folks who have nothing worthwhile to do other than planned activities. (I note that in our small Vermont town, old-timers want nothing more than to be useful. In his early nineties, Russell Baines was strapped to a riding lawn mower with extra seat belts and allowed to mow on Sunday afternoons when he was rescued by neighbors from the old-age home. They even took a picture of him mowing and left it at his bedside so he could enjoy seeing himself at work during the week.)

Life is not about extremes. We consider civilization as a continuum, always moving forward and getting better. Yet history denies that absurd notion—witness the dark ages after the inestimable glories of Rome. As William Manchester so aptly put it, the twelfth century was a "world lit only by fire." Just as a backbreaking schedule of cooking and cleaning is not ideal, neither is its opposite, a life with no responsibilities. Our future lies not in the ultimate life of pleasure after climbing out of the mud and squalor of the dark ages; it lies in finding the point along history's ragged time line that offers the most satisfying life. Much like a pendulum that comes to rest, not at the extremes of the arc but at the center point, as determined by the laws of nature, humans find the greatest happiness when there is still work to be done, when we still have connections to the natural world, when we can balance the joys of physical labor with the pleasures of the mind. Teddy Roosevelt knew this lesson better than anyone: "Far and away the best prize that life has to offer is the chance to work hard at work worth doing."

And speaking of work, cooking over a coal stove that is only twenty-five inches high and blistering hot reinvested the process of cooking with a sense of very hard work indeed. (This made us wonder why the stovetop was so low. Okay, the Victorians were about four inches shorter on average, but even if one was a modest five feet tall, a two-foot-high cookstove is still on the low side. One answer is that if one were used to cooking over a fireplace, any elevated stovetop was a huge improvement. The other, more compelling reason, is that tall stockpots are much easier to look into, and lift up and off, when sitting on a low cooktop. Some stockpots were so large and heavy that it took two people to move them.) It was also bloody hot—so hot that when the ovens were cranked up for roasting meat, the cook could get a nice sunburn just by standing next to the stove and stirring a pot. And burning oneself was a frequent occurrence: when the wood was added, when hot handles were grabbed without a pot holder, when one brushed up against twelve hundred pounds of blistering cast iron or picked up the lid lifter that had been sitting on the warming shelf.

The lesson of the Victorians and the Victorian kitchen is that they were at a midpoint—industrialization was creating wealth and convenience, yet they still had one foot in the day-to-day routines of the past. They were at the very beginning of a period in which refrigerators and gas stoves were coming into use, and Jell-O would make the fabulous Victorian jellies obsolete; yet foods were still mostly local, and the family sat down to dinner each day at noon. It was a bit of this and that, a hands-on life free from the horrors of survival (at least among the wealthier Victorians) and not yet severely diminished by the soul-sucking horrors of industrial food and mass-market entertainment.

There is no tomorrow. Time cannot be saved and spent. There is only today and how we choose to live it. The future is unknowable and unpredictable; it offers no clear path to happiness. Science will not save us. Each of us, then, needs to cobble together a daily routine filled with basic human pleasures, wedded, to be sure, to the best that modernity has to offer. It is a life of compromise rather than extremes. It is a touch of the old and a taste of the new. And cooking, it seems to me, offers the most direct way back into the very heart of the good life. It is useful, it is necessary, it is social, and it offers immediate pleasure and satisfaction. It connects with the past and ensures the future. Standing in front of a hot oven, we remind ourselves of who we are, of what we are capable of and how we might stumble back to the center of happiness. Effort and pleasure go hand in hand.

At the end of the evening, in the wee hours of Sunday morning, there was a warm glow in the kitchen, and not just from the stove. We were hot, tired, and sweat-soaked, our legs drained of energy, having been on them all day, but blissful as well. The kitchen had the forest scent of oak, of wood smoke and hot iron, of roasted larded venison, of rich, all-day veal stock and the lingering taste of grilled salmon and the sharp memory of frosty ginger sorbet, mixed with the almost sexual melting on the tongue of Spätlese jelly freckled with small bursts of sun-ripened port.

Something had happened to us cooks—we became fellow travelers, saddle-sore to be sure, but closely joined as well, like pieces of our massive cookstove. We were in the midst of a long, exhausting journey to a place where the modern kitchen no longer travels. We realized, when we were in for both a penny and a pound, that cooking transcends dinner—it is a thing unto itself, a distant shore that is worth every mile, every bead of sweat. Those who take the journey are transformed along with the pursuit of an idea that has no purpose other than the satisfaction of imagination and a fleeting moment when we share with others our food, our hard work, and our invitation to supper.

Requiem for Fannie

Fannie's Last Word

From 1905 to 1910, Fannie directed the cooking section of the *Women's Home Companion*. She also started to travel more widely, visiting the West Coast, St. Louis, and Texas. Fannie suffered two strokes in later years and was confined to a wheelchair, but she was still lecturing in the last weeks of her life, both at her cooking school and at women's clubs. She even spoke at Harvard, where she focused on the relationship between diet and health (and was also the first woman lecturer at the medical school); she was especially interested in controlling diabetes. Her last book, *Food and Cooking for the Sick and Convalescent*, sold poorly and soon went out of print. She died in January 1915 of Bright's disease, although some said that she died of arteriosclerosis, an ironic coincidence since she was considered an expert on the subject of a healthy diet.

Her ashes are buried in Mount Auburn Cemetery in Cambridge, in very good company with many of the great families of Boston. After her death, Alice Bradley, a cooking-school teacher herself, purchased the school from Fannie's sister Cora and became its principal. She soon added classes for professionals who wanted to open tearooms or restaurants and, in 1916, also became cooking editor for the *Woman's Home Companion*. In 1944, she sold the school to Dr. Dana Wallace and died two years later, in 1946. Fannie's sister Cora took over the editing of the *The Boston Cooking-School Cookbook* until 1929, at which point Wilma Lord Perkins (wife of Fannie's nephew, Dexter Perkins), with "no background in cooking whatsoever," assumed control and went on to revise the cookbook seven more times, as well as authoring *The Fannie Farmer Junior Cookbook* in 1940. The cookbook went on to sell over 4 million copies by the 1960s.

Fannie's estate came to close to $200,000, a vast sum at the time. She had invested in utilities and railroads and also owned real estate, including a parcel of land out in Harvard, where she had started construction on a country home just before her death. It was completed in 1916, and two of her descendants, her nephew Dexter Perkins and his wife Wilma, spent much time there in the summers and later named it Weldon. (The house has nine bedrooms and formal gardens; much of the furniture came from Fannie's home in Boston.)

Much later, Frank Benson, the president of Fanny Farmer Candy Shops, bought the rights to the book and sold the idea of an entirely new revision to Alfred A. Knopf. (Oddly enough, Fanny Farmer candies had nothing to do with Fannie herself. Frank O'Connor, a Canadian candy maker, founded his company in 1919 and named it after Fannie Farmer as a marketing ploy, changing the name slightly, one would assume, to avoid legal troubles. The first Fanny Farmer shop was opened in Rochester, New York, although it soon specialized in mail-order delivery.) James Beard recommended Marion Cunningham, an associate, who spent four years working on a complete revision, which was published in 1979.

Just two months before her death, on November 18, 1914, Fannie demonstrated the cooking of Thanksgiving dinner. An extant copy of the printed lesson from the day, printed with the heading "Miss Farmer's School of Cookery," offered ten recipes in paragraph form, including Thanksgiving Cocktail (parboiled oysters served in the shell with seasoned oyster liquor), Roast Turkey, Giblet Stuffing, Scalloped Salsify, Toasted Crackled Corn Bread, Cranberry Fluff (cooked, sweetened cranberries folded into beaten egg whites and briefly baked), Cider Frappé (a cider jelly), Newport Salad, Plum Pudding, and Brandy Sauce. The margins of the menu are packed with a student's corrections and notations, the printed recipe offering 1½ cups flour rather than the correct ½ cup bread flour penned in the margin. In addition, there are notes filling in information that was not included in the recipe itself, such as how much poultry seasoning to use, the specific recipe for a French dressing, or a small drawing indicating how to assemble a Newport salad. Up until the very end, Fannie Farmer was a dedicated, enthusiastic teacher.

Fannie was not a food lover in the modern sense. Health trumped pleasure; science overrode taste. She admitted that she was first and foremost a businesswoman and a lecturer, rather than an inspired cook. And yet, no other figure from the nineteenth century helped shaped the landscape of American cooking so dramatically in the next. She combined scientific method married to a keen eye for what would sell, for what the public wanted. In other words, Fannie was businesslike both in her approach to recipe development and in her approach to selling herself to the public. This, then, is the enduring legacy of our culinary past: a keen sense of the marketplace, the science of food overriding the passion and pleasure of dining, and the entire package neatly wrapped in a public persona who perfectly captivated the attention of her age. This is the story of America, of our success and also our fatal weakness, seeing the shape of a thing rather than its ephemeral center, ignoring the soul for how the bones fit together, marching forward with our eyes wide open rather than closing them a moment to savor the pure pleasure of a first bite. Fannie always asked about a recipe, "Could it be better?" One wonders if she ever took a spoonful of blanc mange or bisque, sat back, smiled, and said happily, "It just doesn't get any better than this."

NOTES

IF YOU ARE INTERESTED IN THE QUIRKY NATURE OF BOSTONIANS, good gossip, and writing that is light and chatty, I highly recommend George F. Weston's *Boston Ways: High, By and Folk* as well as Cleveland Amory's *The Proper Bostonians*. For anyone interested in the Victorian table, customs, silverware, and decorations, Kathryn Grover's *Dining in America, 1850–1900* is a great read. *The Victorian Book of Cakes* contains drop-dead gorgeous illustrations of high Victorian cakes, although from England. The BBC ran a series entitled *The Victorian Kitchen* and published a companion book. The series is hosted by a cook who grew up working in a large, English Victorian-style kitchen. On our side of the Atlantic, *The American Kitchen* is a terrific resource.

Charles Ranhofer's *The Epicure* is perhaps the most interesting, thorough cookbook ever published. Original copies are quite expensive (and huge) but worth it. I also put my hands on a copy of Urbain-Dubois's *Patisserie d'Aujourd'hui*, which makes modern pastry chefs appear singularly unimaginative.

King's Hand-Book of Boston is one of those odd finds that is packed with useful and fascinating Boston history. It is also well illustrated with detailed drawings of no-longer-extant Boston buildings. I also reviewed the food columns of the *Boston Daily Globe* for 1896, the "Housekeeper's Column" in particular, a treasure trove of information about how Bostonians actually cooked and dined. Earlier columns were also helpful: the "Our Cooking School," which ran from 1894 to 1895 and the "Boston Cooking School" columns, which ran from 1885 to 1889.

Finally, I read *Oystering from New York to Boston* cover to cover, since I could not get enough about oyster boats, oyster sex, and oyster farming. Fascinating stuff.

A Culinary Time Machine

Page 1: Kathryn Grover's *Dining in America, 1850–1900* provides an excellent description of the customs of dining in Victorian America.

Page 4: Descriptions of the Boston Food Fair found in the *Boston Evening Transcript*, Monday, October 5, 1896: "World's Food Fair" and in the *Boston Daily Globe* of October 6, 1896: "Food Fair Opened."

Page 15: Details of the Pie Girl Party are provided in Michael Macdonald Mooney's *Evelyn Nesbit and Stanford White: Love and Death in the Gilded Age*.

Oysters

Page 23: Reporting on the original Boston Cooking School was based on the *First Annual Report, The Boston Cooking School*.

Page 25: Quotes about the Farmer family come from Dexter Perkins's *Yield of the Years*.

Page 35: Information about oystering taken from John Kochiss's *Oystering from New York to Boston*.

Mock Turtle Soup

Page 59: Fannie's revelation regarding inexact measurements was reported in Laura Shapiro's *Perfection Salad*. This epiphany was widely reported in later years and, to my ears, sounds apocryphal.

Lobster à L'Américaine

Page 72: Information about French restaurants in Victorian Boston as well as "cat pies" were found in George F. Weston Jr.'s *Boston Ways: High, By and Folk*.

Page 73: Boston clubs were full of original Boston characters as described in Alexander W. Williams's *A Social History of the Greater Boston Clubs*.

Page 74: The Tavern Club, which still exists, is home to some of the best Boston stories, as described in M. A. DeWolfe Howe's *A Partial (and not impartial) Semi-Centennial History of The Tavern Club*. This book includes two photos of Curtis Guild Jr., who filled in for Dr. Stanley, the explorer, after he had refused an invitation to speak at the club. The first photo shows Guild dressed in white duck, blackface, and carrying both an umbrella and a native shield, and then, in the next frame, he "gravely took off all his clothes and delivered his lecture as a savage, in black tights with a yellow codpiece and a necklace of leaves."

Page 75: The full quote, as found in M. A. DeWolfe Howe's *A Partial (and not impartial) Semi-Centennial History of The Tavern Club*, regarding the Cambridge don is: "An ideal is a principle of conduct carried to its abstract absolute and therefore useless expression, and charm . . . like the Cambridge don who invented an ingenious mathematical theorem and said, 'The best thing about it is that no one can make any use for it for anything . . . ' This uselessness is the highest kind of use. It is kindling and feeding the ideal spark without which life is not worth living."

Saddle of Venison

Page 84: Cleveland Amory's *The Proper Bostonians* pretty much cornered the market on stories regarding the Boston character, including two of my favorites, the one about the investment banker moving to Chicago and the comment about the lack of oatmeal. Amory also provided the quote from Henry Cabot Lodge and the example of social nudism referring to the appearance of a Cabot and a Coolidge in a series of Camel ads. Here is one story that did not make it into the book, and is a good example of the brutal frankness of the Boston character. "Richard Cabot was once asked to dinner and he replied, 'Really I have so many people I should like to dine with but never get around to, I should not pretend that I ever would do it.' "

Page 111: The history of gas ranges and cookery is discussed in Ellen M. Plante's *The American Kitchen*. She was also the source of much of the information regarding American cookware, although newspaper advertisements from the period were also helpful, as were "trade cards," colored handouts that advertised ice cream machines, stoves, appliances, and gadgets.

Fried Artichokes

Page 124: The history of markets in Boston was found in many places but particularly useful was Moses King's *King's Handbook of Boston*. Also of great value was *Quincy's Market* by John Quincy, Jr.

Page 130: The history of S. S. Pierce is covered in many books, but its own publication, *The Epicure*, contained a history in the 1931 anniversary issue by Mary Crawford entitled "One Hundred Years of Boston Hospitality."

Canton Punch

Page 145: A good, if romanticized, description of the old-time Thanksgiving is found in the *Boston Daily Globe*, November 29, 1894, entitled "King of Fall Festivals."

Page 164. Boston's waterfront was covered in William S. Rossiter's *Days and Ways in Old Boston*.

Page 165: The 1912 *Farmer's Cyclopedia* detailed the processing of ginger in China.

Roast Stuffed Goose

Page 167: The history of linoleum and other kitchen history was found in Ellen M. Plante's *The American Kitchen*.

Page 170: Faye E. Dudden's *Serving Women* was the best source of information we found about immigration and household servants. The details of household dos and don'ts were found in Mrs. John M. E. W. Sherwood's *Manners and Social Usages*.

Page 172–173: Kathryn Grover's *Dining in America: 1850–1900* has a chapter entitled "Technology and the Ideal," which describes how American manufacturing changed dramatically as the nineteenth century progressed. The key moment was the introduction of the Brown and Sharpe sliding caliper gauge that went on sale in 1851.

Page 177: The source of the information on raising geese was *Ducks and Geese*, U. S. Department of Agriculture, Standard Varieties of Management, Farmer's Bulletin, Number 64, George Howard.

Wine Jelly

Page 190: Towle Company pattern information was taken from Kathryn Grover's *Dining in America, 1850–1900*.

Page 204–205: Information about how sugar was refined comes from a number of sources, including *The Story of Sugar* by George Thomas Surface; "Sugar: Its History, Production and Manufacture," by Jacob A. Dresser, found in the Massachusetts Institute of Technology's *Abstract of the Proceedings of the Society of Arts for the Nineteenth Year, 1880–1881, Meetings 256 to 270 Inclusive;* and *Something About Sugar* by George Morrison Rolph.

Page 213: Quotes about Victorian dining and eating taken from Kathryn Grover's *Dining in America*, including the fact that the number of etiquette books published in America had risen substantially after the Civil War.

Page 225: The story about the coffee/buffalo robe trade comes from Mark Pendergast's *Uncommon Grounds*, as does most of the other history of coffee, although William H. Ukers's *All About Coffee* was also very helpful.

SELECTED BIBLIOGRAPHY

✵

Alvoud, Henry E. *The Manufacture and Consumption of Cheese*. Yearbook of the United States Department of Agriculture, 1895. Government Printing Office, 1896.

Amory, Cleveland. *The Proper Bostonians*. Parnassus Imprints, 1947.

Ayto, John. *An A to Z of Food and Drink*. Oxford University Press, 2002.

Bailer, Liberty Hyde and Wilhelm Miller. *Cyclopedia of American Horticulture*, Vol. 1. The Macmillan Company, 1900.

Berriedale-Johnson. *The Victorian Cookbook*. Interlink Books, 1989.

Brande, William Thomas. *Chemistry*. Henry C. Lea, 1867.

Bromley, A. G. and T. Percy Lewis. *The Victorian Book of Cakes*. Portland House, 1991.

Davidson, Alan. *Oxford Companion to Food*. Oxford University Press, 1999.

Davies, Jennifer. *The Victorian Kitchen*. BBC Books, 1989.

Delamere, Edmund S. and Ellen J. *Wholesome Fare, or, the Doctor and the Cook*. Lockwood and Co., 1868.

Dubois, Urbain. *La Patisserie D'Aujuord'hui*. Ernest Flammarion, 1894.

Dudden, Faye E. *Serving Women*. Wesleyan University Press, 1983.

Escoffier, A. *The Complete Guide to the Art of Modern Cookery*. John Wiley & Sons, Inc., 1979.

Farmer, Fannie Merritt. *The Boston Cooking-School Cook Book*. Little Brown and Company, 1913.

Farmer, Fannie Merritt. *The 1896 Boston Cooking-School Cook Book*. Gramercy Books, 1997.

Feintuch, Burt and David H. Watters, editors. *Encyclopedia of New England: The Culture and History of an American Region*. Yale University Press, 2005.

Filippini, Alessandro. *The Delmonico Cook Book*. Applewood Books, 1890.

Fitzgerald, Kathleen and Keith Stavely. *America's Founding Food*. The University of North Carolina Press, 2004.

Freeman, Dr. Larry. *Victorian Silver*. Century House, 1967.

Garrett, Theodore Francis. *The Encyclopaedia of Practical Cookery*. L. Upcott Gill, 1895.

Gilbert, B. D. *The Cheese Industry of the State of New York*. Bulletin No. 15 (Dairy No. 6), U.S. Department of Agriculture, Bureau of Animal Industry, Government Printing Office, 1896.

Gillette, Mrs. F. L. and Hugo Ziemann. *The White House Cookbook*. Ottenheimer Publishers, 1887.

Grover, Kathryn. *Dining in America 1850–1900*. The University of Massachusetts Press, 1987.

Gunn, John C. *Gunn's Domestic Medicine*, 1830.

Hall, Mary Elizabeth. *Candy-Making Revolutionized*. Sturgis and Walton Company, 1912.

Hanke, Oscar, John Skinner, and James Florea. *American Poultry History 1823–1973*. American Poultry Historical Society, 1974.

Hooker, Richard J. *A History of Food and Drink in America*. The Bobbs-Merrill Company, Inc. 1981.

Howard, George. *Ducks and Geese, Standard Varieties of Management, Farmer's Bulletin Number 64*. U. S. Department of Agriculture, 1897.

Howe, M. A. DeWolfe. *A Partial (and not impartial) Semi-Centennial History of The Tavern Club*. The Riverside Press, 1934.

Kellogg, Ella Eaton. *Science in The Kitchen*. Modern Medicine Publishing Co. Ltd., 1892.

Kelly, Ian. *Cooking for Kings*. Walker & Company, 2003.

King, John. *King's American Dispensatory*, Vol. 1. The Ohio Valley Company, 1909.

King, Moses. *King's Hand-Book of Boston*, fifth edition. Moses King Publishers, 1878.

Kochiss, John. *Oystering from New York to Boston*. Wesleyan University Press, 1974.

Kummer, Corby. "Pasta." *The Atlantic*, July, 1986.

Kummer, Corby. *The Joy of Coffee*. Houghton Mifflin Company, 1995.

Lincoln, Mrs. D. A. *Mrs. Lincoln's Boston Cook Book*. Roberts Brothers, 1890.

Marmion, Daniel. *Handbook of U.S. Colorants*. Wiley, Interscience, 1991.

Marshall, Mrs. A. B. *Larger Cookery Book of Extra Recipes*. Marshall's School of Cookery, 1891.

Molokhovets, Elena. *Classic Russian Cooking*. Indiana University Press, 1998.

Mooney, Michael Macdonald, *Evelyn Nesbit and Stanford White*. *Love and Death in the Gilded Age*. Morrow, 1976.

Morris, Josephine. *Household Science and Arts*. American Book Company, 1912.

Pendergast, Mark. *Uncommon Grounds*. Basic Books, 1999.

Perkins, Dexter. *Yield of the Years*. Little Brown and Company, 1969.

Pinney, Thomas. *A History of Wine in America*. University of California Press, 2007.

Plante, Ellen M. *The American Kitchen*. Facts on File, 1995.

Quincy, John, Jr. *Quincy's Market*. Northeastern University Press, 2003.

Robinson, Jancis. *Oxford Companion to Wine*. Oxford University Press, 1999.

Rolph, George Morrison. *Something about Sugar*. John J. Newbegin, 1917.

Rosenberg, Chaim M. *The Great Workshop: Boston's Victorian Age*. Arcadia Publishing, 1994.

Rossiter, William S. *Days and Ways in Old Boston*. R. H. Stearns and Company, 1915.

Sammarco, Anthony Mitchell. *Boston's South End*. Arcadia Publishing, 1998.

Scott, Alan and Daniel Wing. *The Bread Builders*. Chelsea Green Publishing, 1999.

Shapiro, Laura. *Perfection Salad: Women and Cooking at the Turn of the Century*. Farrar, Straus, and Giroux, 1986.

Sherwood, Mrs. John M. E. W. *Manners and Social Useages*. Harper & Brothers Publishers, 1884.

Stavely, Keith and Kathleen Fitzgerald. *America's Founding Food*. The University of North Carolina Press, 2004.

Surface, George Thomas. *The Story of Sugar*. D. Appleton & Co., 1916.

Thackeray, William Makepeace. "Of Geese." *The Cornhill Magazine*, July–December, 1863.

Thompson, George. *Venus in Boston*. University of Massachusetts Press, 2002.

Ukers, William H. *All About Coffee*. The Tea & Coffee Trade Journal Company, 1935.

Vrabel, Jim. *When in Boston, A Time Line & Almanac*. Northeastern University Press, 2004.

Volo, James M. and Dorothy Denneen. *Family Life in 19th-Century America*. Greenwood Press, 1947.

Weston, George F., Jr. *Boston Ways: High, By and Folk*. Beacon Press, 1957.

Williams, Alexander W. *A Social History of the Greater Boston Clubs*. Barre Publishers, 1970.

Williams, Jacqueline. *Wagon Wheel Kitchens: Food on the Oregon Trail*. University Press of Kansas, 1993.

Woloson, Wendy. *Refined Tastes*. The Johns Hopkins University Press, 2002.

Zuckerman, Larry. *The Potato*. North Point Press, 1998.

INDEX

❀

Abbott, John, 18–19
Abel, Mary, 180
Accum, Frederick, 186
Alan, Tames, 60
almond butter cake, 208–10
American Kitchen Magazine, 24, 133
American oven, 108
Andrés, José, 225, 226, 228, 229, 230,
    233, 235
Apicius, 63
Appert, Nicolas, 179
apples, 174–76
    Fannie's applesauce to accompany
        roasted goose, 177–78
Arbuckle, John, 213–14
Arktinsal, Emile, 133, 228
artichokes, 132, 133–34
    fried baby, 18, 216
        recipe for, 135–36
Art of Cookery Made Plain and Easy,
    The (Glasse), 44
asparagus, 139
Atlantic, 146

Baines, Russell, 238
bain-marie, 107
baking, 193–97, 205
baking powder, 193, 194
barding, 142
Barrows, Anna, 133
beans, Munroe baked, 149–50

Beard, James, 242
Beaux Arts Club, 15
beef, 56, 139
    heart, stuffed, 139
    steak, 138–39
beets, 98–99
    glazed, 100
Bellamy, Edward, 180
Benson, Frank, 242
Bittman, Kelly, 225, 228, 229
Bittman, Mark, 225, 228, 229
boiling, 181
Borden, Lizzie, 13
Boston:
    clubs in, 70–71
    Kimball home in, 5, 7, 9–10, 13, 159,
        228
    railroads and, 40
    South End of, 7–13, 40
    walking tour of, 39–41
    worldview in, 81–82
Boston, Victorian, 13–14, 39–41, 81–84
    clubs in, 69, 70–71
    commercial establishments in, 39
    food shopping in, 117–27
    homes in, 11–12
    restaurants in, 69–70
    shipping and, 154–55
    tourist attractions in, 14
    transportation and, 14, 82, 151
Boston Cooking School, 2, 12–13, 23–28,
    39, 41, 53, 56

Boston Cooking School Cook Book
    (Lincoln), 24
Boston Cooking-School Cook Book, The
    (*The Fannie Farmer Cookbook*)
    (Farmer), 5, 16, 24, 25, 27,
      28–29, 54, 59, 111, 154, 166, 241
  1913 edition of, 152–53
Boston cream pie, 197
Boston Daily Globe, 185–86
Boston Food Fair, 3–4, 59
Boston Globe, 13, 85, 87, 88, 110, 126,
    142–43, 166
Boston Herald, 27
Boston Public Library, 13
Boston School Kitchen Text-book (Lincoln), 24
bottle jack, 108
Bradley, Alice, 241
brains, 42–43, 47–50, 226
braising, 138
Brandeis, Louis, 13
bread, 109, 145, 181, 193–94
  brown, 36–37
bread crumbs, 109, 145
bread graters, 109
breakfast, 143–44
Breakfast, Lunch and Tea (Harland), 164–65
Brigham, Peter B., 34
broiling, 138
Brooks, Bob, 53
Brooks, Mary, 53–54
Brueggeman, Scott, 42
Buckeye Cookery, 47
Bullfinch, Charles, 120
Burbank, Luther, 95
Burns, Jabez, 213
butter, 85–86, 183

Cabot, Mrs. Powell, 83
cakes, 18, 196–97, 204–6
  French cream, 18, 198–99
    recipe for, 200–202

Mandarin, 18, 206, 216, 217–18, 235
  almond butter cake for, 208–10
  easy marzipan for, 207
  Grand Marnier pastry cream for,
    211–12
  recipe for, 206–12
  savoy, 205, 206
  Victorian sponge, 198
calf's feet, homemade gelatin from, 42,
    184–86, 227
  recipe for, 190–91
calf's heads, 17, 41–43, 46–49
  mock turtle soup, 17, 41–44, 46–49
  recipe for, 50–52
  stock, 225
caliper, sliding, 164
canned goods, 124, 164, 167, 179
Canton ginger, 154, 155–56
Canton sherbet, 18, 218, 233
  recipe for, 156–57
Carème, Antonin, 206
Carter, James W., 213
champagne Mignonette, 36
cheese, 219–20
  served after Fannie Farmer Dinner,
    220–21
chestnut stuffing, 173–74
chicken, 139
  Fannie Farmer's roast, with crispy
    flour coating, 139–40
  recipe for, 141
Child, Julia, 32–33, 72, 75–76
chocolate, 197
  hot, 215
cleaning, 163, 165, 180, 237, 238
  supplies for, 160–61
clothing, 60–61, 62
clubs, 69, 70–71
cockscombs, 84–85
cod, salt, 154
coffee, 186, 213–15, 218
  Fannie Farmer's boiled, 219

Coffey, Brenda, 228
coal, 160
coal cookstoves, 4–5, 83–84, 101–8, 129, 153
Cole, Samuel, 69
Common Ground (Lukas), 12
Complete Confectioner, The, 154
Complete Cook, The (Sanderson), 47
cookbooks, 29
cooking:
    food science and, 179–81, 236–37, 243
    at home, 127–32, 137–40, 142–47, 153, 163–64, 180, 187, 237, 238
Cook Not Mad, The, 49
cooks, Victorian, 59–62
Cook's Illustrated, 96
cookstoves, 101–8
    coal, 4–5, 83–84, 101–8, 129, 153
    gas, 4, 83, 105–6, 111, 129, 153
    height of, 238–39
    wood, 103–6, 111, 129, 231
cookware, 164
    sales of, 132
    Victorian, 107–9
Coolidge, Calvin, 123
Coolidge, Mrs. John Gardner, II, 83
corn, 145
crackers, water, 85
Cuisine Artistique, La (Dubois), 205–6
Cunningham, Marion, 242
currant, red, jelly, 92–94
    recipe for, 94
custard, 187
    baked toasted coconut and vanilla, 148–49

daubing, 142
Davis, Joseph, 105
Dearborn, Carrie, 26
Decker, Peter, 34
deer hunting, 86–88

Delamere, Edmund, 84
Delamere, Ellen, 84
Delmonico's, 17, 30, 166
desserts, 144
Dickinson, Amy, 225, 229, 230, 234, 236
Dickinson, Bruno, 225, 229
dining out, 130
dining rooms, 181–82
dinner, midday, 130, 144, 239
Dinner Party of the Century, *see* Fannie Farmer Dinner
dinners, Victorian, 1–2, 15–17, 32, 110
    table manners and, 202–4
Donkin, Brian, 179
Dresser, Keith, 133, 227, 231, 232, 233
Drowne, Deacon Shem, 120
Dubois, Urbain, 205–6

eggbeaters, 164–65
egg flip, 137
eggs, 139, 165
Ehlenfeldt, Cindy, 133, 228, 232
Ehlenfeldt, Mike, 133, 228
Eleana, Marie, 133
Eleana, Ryan, 133
electricity, 128
Epicurean, The (Ranhofer), 4, 18, 29, 145, 206
Erickson, David, 106, 113
Escoffier, Auguste, 17, 16, 56, 71, 75
Europe, 151–52, 164, 166–67, 204, 218
Expert Maid-Servant, The, 62

Family Life in 19th-Century America, 162
Faneuil, Peter, 119–20
Faneuil Hall, 87, 88, 117, 119–21, 126, 127
Fannie Farmer Dinner, 225–40
    cheeses served after, 220–21
    food preparation methods for, 30–32
    idea for, 2, 4–5

Fannie Farmer Dinner (*continued*)
  kitchen team for, 132–33
  menu for, 17–18
  planning and preparation for, 15,
      17–19, 30–32, 215–18
  recipes for, *see* recipes
  rehearsal for, 133
  service for, 32, 133, 217, 232
  table settings for, 183–84
  wine list for, 223
Fanny Farmer Candy Shops, 242
Farmer, Cora, 25, 26, 241
Farmer, Fannie Merritt, 2, 11, 12–13, 17,
    18, 23–30, 241–43
  birth and childhood of, 25
  Boston Cooking School and, 2, 12–13,
      23, 25–28, 53, 56
  cooking courses offered by, 54–55
  cooking school founded by, 26
  death of, 241
  family of, 13
  home of, 5, 12, 13, 39, 40
  level measurements and, 57, 59
  physical appearance of, 27
  polio of, 26, 39
Farmer, John Franklin, 25
Farmer, Lillian, 25
Farmer, Mary (Fannie's mother), 25–26
Farmer, Mary (Fannie's sister), 25, 26
farmers, 122, 126
fat, clarifying, 142
fireplace, cooking in and around, 102, 108
fish, 111–12, 138, 139
  salmon, 17–18, 112–13, 133, 138, 216,
      217, 233
    grilled, with caper vinaigrette, 114–15
flatware, 182–83
food coloring, 18, 167, 186–87
  natural, how to make, 190
food(s):
  American attitudes toward, 166–67
  canned, 124, 164, 167, 179

commercialized production of, 85–86,
    164, 167
cost of, 129–30
imported, 152, 154, 164
preservation of, 129, 144, 163, 179, 185
science and, 179–81, 236–37, 243
shopping for, 117–27
Francatelli, Charles, 205
Fresnaye, Louis, 146
Friary, Donald, 19
fricassée, 139
fried foods, 57, 181

Gardner, Mrs. Jack, 81
gas cookstoves, 4, 83, 105–6, 111, 129, 153
Geary, Andrea, 133, 226, 227, 230, 232, 234
gelatin, 4, 57, 63–64, 65, 111, 123, 167,
    184–86
  homemade, from calf's feet, 42,
      184–86, 227
    recipe for, 190–91
  Jell-O, 24, 111, 184, 185, 187, 239
  powdered, lemon jelly using, 191–92
  see also jellies
Gillette, Fanny Lemira, 63
ginger, 154, 155–56
  Canton sherbet, 18, 218, 233
    recipe for, 156–57
Glasse, Hannah, 44
*Godey's Lady's Book Receipts and Household
    Hints, The,* 198
Gomes, Peter, 225
Good Housekeeper, The, 49
Goodwin, William W., 105
goose, 168–70, 216, 217
  roast, 18, 233–34
    chestnut stuffing, 173–74
    with chestnut stuffing and jus, 171–72
    Fannie's applesauce to accompany,
        177–78
Grand Marnier pastry cream, 211–12

Green, Steve, 11
griddle cakes, 143
grocery stores, 122–25
Guide Culinaire, Le (Escoffier), 75

Hamersley, Fiona, 225, 229
Hamersley, Gordon, 225, 229, 232
Hamersley's Bistro, 133, 225
happiness, 237–38, 239
Harland, Marion, 133, 164–65
Harper's Bazaar, 61
Harris, William T., 59
heart, 139
Hirsch, Jim, 226–27
Hodgson, Anthony, 120
home cooking, 127–32, 137–40, 142–47,
        153, 163–64, 180, 187, 237, 238
homes, Victorian, 11–12
    dining rooms in, 181–82
    kitchens in, 159–61, 163, 165, 180, 181
Hoosier cabinets, 160
hot closet, 108
Houchin, Jeremy, 118
House Beautiful, 61
How to Mix Drinks (Thomas), 19

iceboxes, 108–9, 127, 163
ice sculpture, 226, 228–29, 235
Industrial Revolution, 60, 162, 167, 180, 182
Irish moss, 185
isinglass, 185
Island Creek Oysters, 17

James Beard's American Cookery, 142
Janjigian, Andrew, 133
jellies, 18, 92–93, 111, 184, 186, 187, 189,
        215–16, 234–35, 239
    lemon, 189
        using powdered gelatin, 191–92

orange snow, 188
red currant jelly, 92–94
    recipe for, 94
    see also gelatin
Jell-O, 24, 111, 184, 185, 187, 239
jelly molds, 184, 189
Jennie June's Cookbook, 47
Jones, Brian, 225, 229, 235–36
Joy of Cooking (Rombauer), 76

Kellogg, Ella Eaton, 179–80
Kelly, Kate, 225
Kimball, Adrienne, 3, 7, 9–11, 12, 13, 92,
        108–9, 183–84, 225, 229
Kimball, Charlie, 11
King's Hand-Book of Boston, 69
kitchens, 159–61, 163, 165, 180, 181
kitchen tools and appliances, 164–65
Klein, Melissa, 133, 228, 232
Kummer, Corby, 146

Ladies' Home Journal, 24
larding, 142
leaveners, 193–94, 196
lemon jelly, 189
    using powdered gelatin, 191–92
limes, pickled, 146–47
Lincoln, Mary, 2, 3, 24, 28, 57–59, 74–75,
        104, 105, 139, 143, 165, 179, 180
linoleum, 159–60
Little Women (Alcott), 147
lobster, 73–75, 76, 111
    à l'Américaine, 17, 72, 75–77, 217, 230–31
    recipe for, 78–80
Lobster at Home (White), 76
Locke, Frank, 69
Lodge, Henry Cabot, 82
Looking Backward: From 2000 to 1887
        (Bellamy), 180
Lowell, John, 82–83

macaroni, 144, 145–46
  and cheese, 146
Manchester, William, 238
*Manners, Culture, and Dress of the Best
    American Society* (Wells), 165
manufactured goods, 164–65
margarine, 85–86, 186
markets, 117–27
marzipan, easy, 207
Massachusetts Horticultural Society, 133
McCarthy, Charlie, 83
McDowell, Debbie, 133, 228, 232
McDowell, Jake, 133, 228
McMurrer, Erin, 17, 72–74, 132–33,
    215–16, 226, 227, 231, 232
measurements, 31, 57–59
meat, 138–39, 143
  roasts, 89, 102–3, 108
Mencken, H. L., 27
Mills, Marjorie, 27
Miss Farmer's School of Cookery, 26
*Miss Parloa's New Cook Book: A Guide to
    Marketing and Cooking* (Parloa),
    24, 99
mock turtle soup, 17, 41–44, 46–49
  recipe for, 50–52
Modern Cook, The (Francatelli), 205
molasses, 147, 154
Montagne, Renee, 225, 228, 229
Morison, Samuel Eliot, 126–27
Mrs. Lincoln's Baking Powder Company,
    24
Mrs. Lincoln's Boston Cook Book, 2, 3, 28,
    57, 58–59, 74–75, 143
Murphy, Maggie, 26–27, 57
Murrey, Thomas Jefferson, 95

napkins, 183
Napoleon I, 179
National Cook Book, The (Harland and
    Herrick), 133

Natural Health, 8
New England Kitchen, 180
New England Kitchen Magazine, 165
New York Times, 15, 110, 131, 186

Ober, Louis, 70
O'Connor, Frank, 242
oilcloth, 159
One Boy's Boston (Morison), 126–27
orange snow, 188
oven thermometers, 105
*Oxford Encyclopedia of Food and Drink in
    America, The* (Smith, ed.),
    133–34
oysters, 17, 32–35
  brown bread for, 36–37
  champagne Mignonette for, 36

pancakes, 143
paper, cooking in, 89, 139
Parker House, 197
Parloa, Maria, 24, 99
pasta, 144, 145–46
Pasteur, Louis, 179
pastry cream, Grand Marnier,
    211–12
Penn, James, 118
Pennington, Harper, 228
Perfection Salad (Shapiro), 56
Perkin, William Henry, 186
Perkins, Dexter, 25, 26, 241, 242
Perkins, Wilma Lord, 27, 241, 242
Pfeiffer, Richard, 146
pickled limes, 146–47
pickling, 144, 186
Pie Girl Party, 16
Pierce, Samuel S., 122–25
pitchers, 183
Pollan, Michael, 131
Pope, Albert A., 41

potatoes, 95–96, 165, 181
    lyonnaise, 96
        recipe for, 97–98
Prescott, Samuel Cate, 179
pudding, 54, 187
    tapioca, 150–51
punch, 19–20, 154, 216
    Victoria, 21

Quincy, Josiah, 121
Quincy Market, 117, 121, 126, 127

Ragland, Meg, 39, 40
railroads, 40, 122
Ramsay, Gordon, 72, 76, 77
Ranhofer, Charles, 4, 18, 29, 145
recipe measurements, 31, 57–59
recipes:
    almond butter cake, 208–10
    baked toasted coconut and vanilla
        custard, 148–49
    brown bread, 36–37
    Canton sherbet, 156–57
    champagne Mignonette, 36
    chestnut stuffing, 173–74
    easy marzipan, 207
    Fannie Farmer's boiled coffee, 219
    Fannie Farmer's roast chicken with
        crispy flour coating, 141
    Fannie's applesauce to accompany
        roasted goose, 177–78
    French cream cake, 200–202
    fried baby artichokes, 135–36
    glazed beets, 100
    Grand Marnier pastry cream,
        211–12
    grilled salmon with caper vinaigrette,
        114–15
    homemade gelatin from calf's feet,
        190–91

lemon jelly using powdered gelatin,
    191–92
lobster à l'Américaine, 78–80
Mandarin cake, 206–12
master recipe for rissoles, 66–67
mock turtle soup, 50–52
Munroe baked beans, 149–50
onion-cherry chutney filling with blue
    cheese, 68
orange snow, 188
potatoes lyonnaise, 97 98
roast goose with chestnut stuffing and
    jus, 171–72
roast saddle of venison, 91–92
red currant jelly, 94
tapioca pudding, 150–51
Victorian sponge cake, 198
Victoria punch, 21
restaurants, 130
    in Victorian Boston, 69–70
Richards, Ellen, 180
Richards, Paul, 20
rissoles, 17, 62–65, 217, 226, 230
    master recipe for, 66–67
    onion-cherry chutney filling with blue
        cheese, 68
Ritz, César, 56
roasting, 138, 139–40
roasts, 89, 102–3, 108
Rodríguez, Maggie, 225
Roosevelt, Samuel M., 15
Roosevelt, Theodore, 238
Ruperti, Yvonne, 133, 217, 227, 230, 232

St. Botolph Club, 19, 84, 101
salad, 57
Salem, Mass., 109, 110
salmon, 17–18, 112–13, 133, 138, 216, 217, 233
    grilled, with caper vinaigrette, 114–15
samp, 145
Samuels, Diane, 45

Sanderson, J. M., 47
Schlesinger, Arthur, 27
Schlesinger, Elizabeth, 27
science, 179–81, 236–37, 243
Science in the Kitchen (Kellogg), 179
servants, 59–62, 161–63, 165, 203
Sewall, Mrs. William B., 153
Shapiro, Laura, 56, 59
Shaw, Mrs. Charles, 26
shopping, 117–27
silverware, 182–83
Smibert, John, 119
Smith, Harry, 225, 228, 229, 233, 236
Somerset Club, 70, 71
sorbet, 154, 217
South End Historical Society, 11
Souza, Dan, 133, 227, 232
S. S. Pierce, 123–25, 126, 222
steak, 138–39
steamboats, 151–52, 164
steam engines, 164
Steele, Zulma, 27
stews, 138
stocks, 181, 225
stoves, *see* cookstoves
Sturgis, John Hubbard, 40
sugar, 4, 194–96
supper, 144–45
sweetbreads, 152–53

table manners, 202–4
table settings, 181–84
tapioca pudding, 150–51
Taste of Home, 128
Tavern Club, 70, 71
tea, 181
tea sets, 183
terrapins, 44–46
Thanksgiving, 137–38, 242
Thomas, Jerry, 19

Thompson, Benjamin, 218
trade, 152, 154–55
turkey, 122, 169
turtle, 44–46
    soup, 41, 44, 49

UnderHill Farms, 90

venison, 17, 87, 88–90, 217, 231
    roast saddle of, 91–92
Victorian Book of Cakes, The (Lewis), 205

Wait, Pearle, 187
Wallace, Dana, 241
Walton, Frederick, 159
washing glasses and silverware, 160
Webster, Daniel, 122
Wells, Richard, 165
White, Blanche, 81–82
White, Charles Stanley, 112
White, Jasper, 72, 76
White, Stanford, 16
White House Cookbook, The (Gillette), 63, 88
Wholesome Fare (Delamere and Delamere), 84
Wilde, Oscar, 83
wine, 18, 221–23
    served at Fannie Farmer Dinner, 223
Winthrop, John, 87
witches, 109–10
women, jobs for, 162–63
Women's Education Association, 23–24
Women's Home Companion, 241
wood cookstoves, 103–6, 111, 129, 231
World's Columbian Exposition, 180

yeast, 193–94
Young, William, 164